THE DEAD SEA SCROLLS
FOR A NEW MILLENNIUM

The Dead Sea Scrolls
for a New Millennium

PHILLIP R. CALLAWAY

CASCADE *Books* · Eugene, Oregon

Cascade Books
An Imprint of Wipf and Stock Publishers
199 W. 8th Ave., Suite 3
Eugene, OR 97401
www.wipfandstock.com

ISBN 13: 978-1-60899-660-5

Cataloging-in-Publication data:

Callaway, Phillip R.

The Dead Sea scrolls for a new millennium / Phillip R. Callaway.

xii + 226 p. ; 23 cm—Includes bibliographical references and index.

ISBN 13: 978-1-60899-660-5

1. Dead Sea scrolls. 2. Dead Sea scrolls—History. 3. Qumran community—History. I. Title.

BM487 C3 2011

Manufactured in the U.S.A.

Scriptural quotations are from the Oxford Annotated Bible/Revised Standard Version © 1962.

Pitts Theology Library, Emory University for use of images from their Digital Image Archives © 2011

Paleography of the Scrolls, Treasure Locations of the Copper Scroll, and Temple Scroll's Courts are from Philip R. Davies, George J. Brooke, and Phillip R. Callaway, *The Complete World of the Dead Sea Scrolls*. London: Thames & Hudson ©2002

Map of Israel in New Testament Times is from http://www.bible.history.com/maps/palestine_nt_times.html © 2011

To Azusa

Contents

Maps, Illustrations, and Tables

Illustrations

Tables

Preface

STUDYING THE DEAD SEA Scrolls is a fascinating way to spend one's life. Along the way you are permitted to share what you have learned with others who care about the Scrolls. You are constantly asking yourself what they meant in the past and what they might mean for the future. My fortune has been to have been introduced to the Scrolls by John H. Hayes in his class on the Apocrypha and Pseudepigrapha at Emory University in Atlanta, Georgia. It was amazing to discover that so much ancient Jewish literature had not been part of the canon I knew. Hayes also introduced me to Josephus' *Antiquities, War,* and *Life.* With Hartmut Stegemann at the Qumranforschungsstelle in Marburg and Göttingen, Germany I first read Yadin's Hebrew transcription of the *Temple Scroll,* the Aramaic fragments of Enoch, got a taste of *Some of the Works of the Law,* and realized that reconstructing history is a very human enterprise just as is the reconstruction of partial scrolls. In Philip R. Davies, a stimulating conversationalist, I found a scholar of similar curiosity and a willingness to question the status quo in Dead Sea Scrolls studies.

When I study the series Discoveries in the Judaean Desert (DJD), I understand how much I have learned from and admire the editors of each volume in that incredible scholarly series. No doubt, I have also profited from all the preliminary editions that I have read in the journals and several editions of scrolls outside DJD. No doubt, I have also been influenced by numerous authors who have written on the Scrolls.

Above all, studying the Dead Sea Scrolls has shown me that I, too, am one of those clearing a path in wilderness, which is mentioned in Isaiah and the *Rule of the Community* (1QS). I too have spent a goodly

portion of my life reading and re-reading the ancient manuscripts trying to get to know their authors, editors, and scribes, attempting to
understand why they would think such a thing and decide to write it
down. The first part of my personal journey with the Scrolls focused
on the 364-day calendar as a central reason for the emergence of the
Qumran community. In the next stage of my adventure I asked quite
seriously whether one can reconstruct a history of the Qumran community based on the language of the so-called historical Scrolls. I did
this because I wanted to study history and not theology. The Dead Sea
Scrolls are certainly historical, but preserve little material for writing a
history of the Qumran community within the broader context of Second
Temple Judaism. In the last twenty years I began to feel that the Scrolls
represent the library or personal collections of people like Ben Sira and
his grandfather. In short, I realized that the Scrolls are not the vestiges
of an insignificant hyper-orthodox group that rejected everything about
their traditions. In fact, just the opposite seems to be the case. The Dead
Sea Scrolls represent the largest collection of Jewish literature in Hebrew,
Aramaic, and Greek that existed in the Second Temple period and, for
that matter, in the First Temple period. It is a very traditional collection
compared with the historical writings of Josephus and the philosophical
tomes of Philo. Nevertheless, it has its own emphases and surprises.

As supplemental or comparative reading to *The Dead Sea Scrolls for a
New Millennium*, I would also like to recommend James C. VanderKam's
The Dead Sea Scrolls Today (2010), Lawrence H. Schiffman's *Reclaiming
the Dead Sea Scrolls* (1994), Hartmut Stegemann's *The Library of Qumran*
(1998), Martin Abegg, Jr., Peter Flint, and Eugene Ulrich's, *The Dead Sea
Scrolls Bible* (1999), and Geza Vermes', *The Complete Dead Sea Scrolls in
English* (1997).

English quotations from the Jewish Bible come from my copy of the
Oxford Annotated Bible/Revised Standard Version (1962). English quotations of the non-biblical Scrolls derive from Geza Vermes' translation,
The Complete Dead Sea Scrolls in English (1997). English quotations of
readings from the biblical manuscripts depend greatly on the translation
of Abegg, Flint, and Ulrich, *The Dead Sea Scrolls Bible* (1999).

Abbreviations

Ant.	Josephus, *Antiquities of the Judeans*
b.	Babylonian Talmud (*Babli*)
BA	*Biblical Archaeologist*
BAR	*Biblical Archaeology Review*
BASOR	*Bulletin of the American Schools of Oriental Research*
Bib	*Biblica*
BR	*Bible Review*
col.	column
DSD	*Dead Sea Discoveries*
frag.	fragment
IEJ	*Israel Exploration Journal*
JBLSup	Journal of Biblical Literature Supplement
JJS	*Journal of Jewish Studies*
JSOTSup	Journal for the Study of the Old Testament Supplements
l.	line
LXX	Septuagint
m.	Mishnah
MT	Masoretic text
NTS	*New Testament Studies*
PJBR	*The Polish Journal for Biblical Research*
QC	*The Qumran Chronicle*
RB	*Revue Biblique*
RQ	*Revue de Qumran*
Sam	Samaritan Pentateuch
STDJ	Studies on the Texts of the Desert of Judah
VTSup	Vetus Testamentum Supplement
War	Josephus, *Judean War*

Temple Scroll Courts

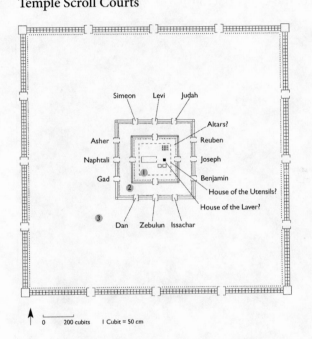

(Left) A diagram of the square Temple precinct as depicted in the Temple Scroll, with 12 gates, one for each tribe, and three courts.

Simeon Levi Judah

Altars?

Asher

Reuben

Naphtali

Joseph

Gad

Benjamin

House of the Utensils?

House of the Laver?

Dan Zebulun Issachar

1 Inner court (priests)
2 Middle court (males)
3 Outer court (Israelites)

0 200 cubits 1 Cubit = 50 cm

Treasure Locations of the Copper Scroll

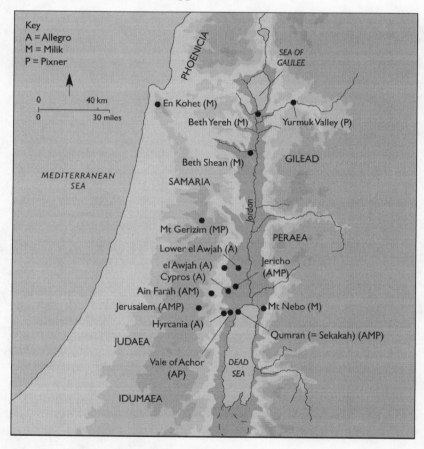

Key
A = Allegro
M = Milik
P = Pixner

0 ___ 40 km
0 ___ 30 miles

PHOENICIA

SEA OF GALILEE

● En Kohet (M)

Beth Yereh (M)

Yurmuk Valley (P)

GILEAD

Beth Shean (M)

MEDITERRANEAN SEA

SAMARIA

Jordan

Mt Gerizim (MP)

PERAEA

Lower el Awjah (A)

el Awjah (A)
Cypros (A)

Jericho (AMP)

Ain Farah (AM)

Jerusalem (AMP)

Mt Nebo (M)

Hyrcania (A)

Qumran (= Sekakah) (AMP)

JUDAEA

Vale of Achor (AP)

DEAD SEA

IDUMAEA

✥ONE✥

Introduction

THE DISCOVERY OF THE Dead Sea Scrolls, the search for other scrolls, the attempts to sell and acquire the scrolls, and the ensuing fireworks among scholars about proprietorship could be transformed into a script for an exhilarating action movie. Numerous times the exotic, mysterious, and controversial scrolls from the Qumran caves have been featured in cable television documentaries. Even at the grocery store, the front page of a gossip magazine prints a headline saying that a Dead Sea Scroll predicted the birth of the messiah or the end of the world.

At some time in 1946–47 three young bedouin were herding their flocks of goats or sheep near the eastern shore of the Dead Sea, known in the area as the "Salt Sea" along the cliffs in the Judaean wilderness. According to one story, a boy named Muhammed ed-Dib ('the Wolf') cast a stone into a cave and heard something break. He entered finding several large jars. He left, but he returned with a friend or two. They looked into the ten jars discovering in one of them three bundles, two of which were wrapped in linen. Back in the camp they opened one of the linen bundles and unraveled leather inscribed in a language they did not know. Eventually, they brought their bundles to an antiquities dealer called Kando (Khalil Iskander Shahin) in Bethlehem. A middle man named George Isaiah transported the written materials to a Syrian monastery called St. Mark's in Jerusalem. Furtive trips to the cave resulted in the discovery of a total of seven scrolls. It seems likely that the Syrian Metropolitan Yeshua Samuel himself was involved in this treasure hunt. The Metropolitan paid £24 (about $100 at the time) for four of the scrolls—later identified as an *Isaiah Scroll* (1QIsaᵃ), a *Manual of Discipline* (here the *Rule of the Community*, 1QS), a *Commentary on Habakkuk* (1QpHab), and a *Commentary on Genesis*, now known as the *Genesis Apocryphon* (1QGenApoc). This is, of course, a simplified version of what happened and the people involved.

When Professor Eleazar Sukenik of the Hebrew University was contacted, he traveled to Bethlehem in November 1947 where he saw and purchased the other three scrolls—a scroll of *Thanksgiving Hymns* (1QH), a *War Scroll* (here the *Rule of War*, 1QM), and an *Isaiah Scroll* (1QIsaᵇ). He recognized the writing as Hebrew and had some appreciation for their antiquity and value from his study of first century tomb inscriptions.

The Metropolitan also contacted the famous American Schools of Oriental Research (ASOR) located in what was then Jordanian Jerusalem. A researcher named John Trever photographed the scrolls and turning to his own paleographical charts realized that these scrolls were undoubtedly ancient. They shared their opinions with William F. Albright, a renowned archaeologist and epigrapher in Baltimore, Maryland. Albright placed them in the time of Judas Maccabeus and wrote: ". . . the greatest MS [manuscript] discovery of modern times!"[1] On April 12, 1948 *The Times* (London) announced this discovery of ancient scrolls which, according to the press release from ASOR, had belonged to a monastic order like the ancient Essenes. Two weeks later the *New York Times* reported on Sukenik's scrolls.

Albright wrote that these scrolls would "revolutionize intertestamental studies, and . . . soon antiquate all present handbooks on the background of the New Testament and on the textual criticism and interpretation of the Old Testament."[2] What a claim to make based on two scrolls of Isaiah and five other scrolls, one of which reminded Millar Burrows at Yale University of the "Discipline" of the Methodist Church, two commentaries on biblical books, a hymnal, and a sort of war manual. In 1954 the Metropolitan Samuel took his four scrolls to the United States where he advertized them in the *Wall Street Journal*. The State of Israel purchased them for $250,000 dollars, becoming the sole proprietors of the seven scrolls from Cave 1.

As scholars began archaeological work at the site Khirbet Qumran, about 1 km southeast of Cave 1, another ten caves were found. During the next decade the remains of about 850 manuscripts written in Hebrew, Aramaic, and Greek were discovered. In fact, Cave 4 proved to hold the mother lode, nearly 10,000 fragments from 500 ancient manuscripts. Albright was correct in dubbing the first seven manuscripts as revolutionary, but Caves 4 and 11 revealed that those seven were only a portion of the nearly one thousand manuscripts from all the caves. The Dead Sea Scrolls have become the literary basis or the prism through which we now try to understand ancient Judaism, the parent of rabbinic Judaism, Christianity, and other sectors of ancient Judaism of which we knew little to nothing before the discovery of the Scrolls.

OTHER EARLY SCROLLS DISCOVERIES

In search of the original text of the Bible the Christian scholar Origen (185–284 CE) collected and studied Hebrew and Greek manuscripts known during his time.[3] Around 230–238 CE the Christian scholar Origen began a project he hoped would encourage dialogue between Christians and Jews. He decided to collect and present known Hebrew and Greek texts of the Jewish Bible. From left to right he included the Hebrew text current during his day, a translation of the same text into Greek characters, followed by the Greek versions of Aquila, Symmachus, the LXX, and Theodotion for some works of the Bible. Origen also used incomplete versions of the Quinta, the Sexta, and the Septima. His synoptic Bible seems to have existed in several different versions. He used a system of symbols to indicate additions and omissions in the Hebrew and Greek text when compared with the standard texts of his day.

In his Hexapla, a work in six parts, Origen reproduced the most important of those manuscripts. The sixth version of the Psalms in his Hexapla reportedly came from a jar found near Jericho, a city 12 km (7.5 miles) north of the Qumran caves.

Although Origen believed that the original LXX text was closest to the Hebrew text he knew (similar to the Masoretic Text), many of its readings were felt to be even older. Evidence from the biblical manuscripts at Qumran make clear that many Hebrew and Greek readings that may have been older continued to circulate even after the destruction of the Jerusalem and its temple in 70 CE.

It is estimated that Origen's Hexapla ran at least to five hundred pages in fifteen volumes. The most valuable manuscripts of his Hexapla are Codex Sarravanius (G), Coislianus (M), which includes the Pentateuch and some of the historical books, and the Chi'zi manuscripts 86 and 88, which preserve the prophets.

Origen's collection of ancient manuscripts and his textual notations about comparative readings was actually a harbinger of what one would eventual discover among the Dead Sea Scrolls. These scrolls leave no room for anyone to doubt that hundreds, if not thousands, of ancient readings in biblical works had their own intrinsic value for posterity. The scrolls even go beyond that in showing that the production of many other writings, some of which might easily have been viewed as scriptural, were customarily copied, read, and studied in the Hasmonean and Herodian periods.

The Christian church historian, Eusebius, also mentioned the Psalms text from Jericho that had been discovered during the reign of the Roman emperor Caracalla (211–217 CE). At some time before 805 CE, Timotheus I (727–819), the Nestorian patriarch of Seleucia, told the Mar or Metropolitan Sergius that trustworthy Jewish converts to Christianity reported that Jews from Jerusalem had discovered (and most likely retrieved) manuscripts of the Hebrew Bible and other texts in a chamber in the rocks. According to this story, more than two hundred psalms of David were among those manuscripts.

Almost exactly a half a century before the Dead Sea Scrolls were discovered, Solomon Schechter of Cambridge University uncovered a huge collection of medieval manuscripts in a synagogue in Cairo, Egypt. There is a famous photograph in which Professor Schechter is immortalized sitting hunched over a table covered with leaves of manuscripts reading.[4] Around him are scattered crates full of the loose leaves of medieval Jewish writings. The one most relevant to the Dead Sea Scrolls Schechter originally dubbed *Fragments of a Zadokite Work*. Later it was called the *Damascus Document* (CD). Numerous fragments of this work were found in some of Qumran's Caves 4–6, indicating that the heritage of this medieval work clearly lay in the distant Jewish past. Schechter discerned a manuscript A and a manuscript B. Part of the work constitutes a sermon explaining what God had done and still plans to do with his people. It speaks of a "new covenant in the land of Damascus." Experts have long argued whether the reference to Damascus should be taken literally. There has been no doubt, however, that the reference to the "new covenant" suggests that the "old covenant" had not been successful and needed improvement or replacement.

The other part of this work is a legal codex of sorts preserving laws apparently for those who lived the traditional married life with a spouse and children and other laws for those who seem to have lived in single-gendered groups, presumably men. The *Damascus Document* comes from a group that advocated a most rigorous interpretation of the Law of Moses. The individual laws mentioned include swearing oaths (compare Matt 5:37); vows and free-will offerings; leprosy and other contagions; sexual intercourse; the Gentiles; the Sabbath; and monthly support for orphans, widows, and victims of war. In several places words like "the Priests," "the Levites," and "the Zadokites" are given special interpretations. "Serpents" are identified as kings of the peoples, and Greece is referred to in particular, indicating that this ancient writing belonged originally to a Hellenistic context. A "teacher," a "liar," and the future messiah of Aaron and Israel, and a book of jubilees and weeks are also mentioned. Most scholars take this to mean the famous *Book of Jubilees*, an important pseudepigraphical work from intertestamental times. Most readers today would be struck by the rather extensive Sabbath laws. The *Damascus Document* and related fragments from the Qumran caves will be discussed later.

SOME PERSPECTIVE

The Dead Sea Scrolls constitute the oldest and most expansive collection of ancient Jewish literature found to date. Palaeographers, physicists, and archaeologists have dated the Scrolls roughly from 300 BCE to 70 CE. It has been estimated that about 850 manuscripts survived, although in damaged form, in the Qumran caves. In addition to the 200 or so biblical manuscripts that have been easily identified before they were known from later codices, about 650 other manuscripts came from non-biblical works. Because of the Scrolls' discoveries, scholars now know much more about the broad array of Jewish religious thinking in the pre-Christian era than ever before. These Scrolls are causing everyone to rethink what we knew about Judaism before the fall of the temple in 70 CE.

Scholars usually speak of manuscripts even when they are referring to one or more fragments that look like they were penned in the same style by a single individual writing about the same topic. Sometimes it may not be clear to the modern reader that scholars have had to reassemble fragments in order to make complete sense of an ancient manuscript. Often such a fragment may consist of a few words, verses, or partial verses. Excluding the great *Isaiah Scroll* (1QIsa[a]), the rest of the Jewish Bible from the Qumran caves is highly fragmentary. One hardly ever finds more than contiguous portions of two partial columns. The *Temple Scroll* is a rare example of a non-biblical scroll that is very close to being complete. If one compares the surviving incomplete portions of Genesis through Malachi, roughly 300 (27%) of the Bible's 1,100 chapters did not survive in the Qumran caves. On the positive side, nearer 75% did.

If one compares the literary remains from the sites Masada, Naḥal Ḥever/Seiyal, and Murabbaʿat with the Dead Sea Scrolls, one gains an illustrative perspective from antiquity.[5] At Masada archaeologists found portions of Genesis, Leviticus, Deuteronomy, Psalms, Ezekiel, *Jubilees*, Ben Sira, an apocryphal Joshua, *Songs of the Sabbath Sacrifice*, and a text presumed to have been of Samaritan origin. The few texts from Masada look like the Qumran collection, but on a much more limited scale. Naḥal Ḥever/Seiyal yield parts of Jonah, Micah, Nahum, Habakkuk, Zephaniah, Haggai, and Zechariah, all of which belong to the Minor Prophets. At Murabbaʿat parts of Genesis, Exodus, Numbers, Deuteronomy, Isaiah, and phylacteries were found. Even when taken together, these sites contribute only portions of 23 literary works compared with the 850 or so manuscripts from the Qumran caves. The Qumran collection differs chiefly by including literally hundreds of non-biblical and community-oriented texts of which no one had heard before the first discoveries in 1947. The surviving scrolls have now been published. Most of the professional controversies among scholars have been laid to rest, even if every interpretive problem about the Scrolls has not been resolved. In the new millennium one will value the Scrolls from newer and fresher perspectives.

OBSERVATIONS ON THE SCROLLS

Now that the Dead Sea Scrolls are fully published it is possible to make both general and specific observations about the entire collection.

1. Parts of all the writings of the traditional Hebrew Bible are represented.
2. The Bible manuscripts reflect different degrees of conformity to the Masoretic Hebrew text, the Samaritan text, and the Hebrew that apparently underlay the Greek translation.

3. Some of these manuscripts are tightly connected with the known books of the Jewish Bible, but their specific details seem to be rather independent.

4. Greek manuscripts of the Pentateuch were also found, indicating that its owners used Greek scriptures.

5. Writings that previously had only been known in later Christian canonical lists now seem to be Jewish in origin.

6. Many other new pseudepigrapha by or about scriptural personalities show that hagiography had become an accepted component of Second Temple religious literature.

7. Many new liturgical pieces, prayers, and hymns appear, often having some connection to daily worship.

8. Many phylacteries and *mezuzot* reflect both traditional and flexible attitudes toward prayer texts.

9. Affiliated with these texts, several writings were discovered that advocate or assume the liturgical use of a 364-day divine year opposed to a 354-day calendar.

10. Some works underscore the division of world time into jubilees and weeks.

11. A handful of writings is concerned with astronomy, astrology, and meteorology.

12. Numerous writings reveal an enhanced interest in the role of angels both in heaven and on earth.

13. Many writings reflect ancient contemporary interpretation of words and phrases in the Jewish Bible. Sometimes legal texts are read together or against each other. At other times a biblical narrative has been embellished to emphasize the piety of the ancients, to prove that even they were able to obey God's law, or to show that a certain historical event occurred on specific dates in a 364-day year. In other works, such as the thematic and running commentaries, the words of a text are viewed as prophetic but additionally as having a special eschatological meaning for the near future.

14. A few fragments refer by name to known people and events of the first century BCE and perhaps the first century CE.

15. One major work is a long list of treasures hidden especially to the east and north of Jerusalem.

16. Some manuscripts were penned in paleo-Hebrew, therefore giving the impression of antiquity and credibility to these works.

17. A few works were composed in a Hebrew closer to the language of the Mishnah than to the language of the late books of the Jewish Bible.

18. Several writings reflect the communal and theological interests of at least two ancient Jewish groups that were somehow related and their memberships.

The Scrolls reveal what Second Temple Judaism had become after the time of Ezra and Nehemiah. Many of the same interests are there, but to a greater degree. Interpretations of divine law and prophetic pronouncements were taken seriously. Private religious associations were formed that in some cases demanded devotion to the study of the classics. These groups must have maintained allegiance to the Jerusalem temple to varying degrees, but they also emphasized that study of the ancients and prayer with the proper intention held as much value as a bloody sacrifice at the temple. Such private associations led inevitably to innovations and reforms. The Scrolls provide a broader literary backdrop against which one can better understand the concerns of late Second Temple Judaism.

Chronology of Jewish History from Antiochus III to Simon Bar Kokhba

198 BCE	Antiochus III, Seleucid ruler in Syria, captures Palestine from the Ptolemies
175 BCE	Assassination of Onias III during struggles for high priesthood (2 Macc 4:1–34)
168–167 BCE	Antiochus IV prohibits Jewish practices and erects altar to Zeus in the Jerusalem temple (Dan 11:30–35)
164 BCE	Judas Maccabeus rededicates Jerusalem temple (2 Macc 10:1–8)
160 BCE	Judas Maccabeus is killed
152 BCE	Jonathan Maccabeus rules Judaea and becomes the high priest
143/142 BCE	Jonathan is murdered, and his brother Simon succeeds him
134 BCE	Simon is murdered and is succeeded by his son, John Hyrcanus

107 BCE	Hyrcanus destroys the Samaritan temple on Mt. Gerizim
104 BCE	Aristobulus I succeeds Hyrcanus
103 BCE	Alexander Jannaeus succeeds his brother, Aristobulus I
76 BCE	Shelamzion (Salome) Alexandra succeeds her husband, Alexander Jannaeus
68–67 BCE	Salome's sons, Hyrcanus II and Aristobulus II, are at war with each other
63 BCE	Roman general M. Aemilius Scaurus governs Syria (see 4Q333); Pompey enters Jerusalem
40 BCE	Romans crown Herod King of Judaea
19 BCE	Herod the Great starts rebuilding the Jerusalem temple
4 BCE	Herod the Great dies, and his kingdom is divided between Archelaus, Antipas, and Philip
26–36 CE	Pontius Pilate governs Judaea (see Matt 27:2)
41 CE	Agrippa I becomes king of Judaea and Samaria
44 CE	Judaea returns to Roman rule (see Acts 25–26), and Agrippa II succeeds his father as king of the Jews
66 CE	First Jewish Revolt against Roman rule breaks out
70 CE	Fall of Jerusalem to Romans and destruction of the temple
73/74 CE	Masada falls
132–135 CE	Hadrian reconstructs and renames Jerusalem Aelia Capitolina, Second Jewish Revolt against Roman rule led by Simon Bar Kokhba

Map of Israel in New Testament Times

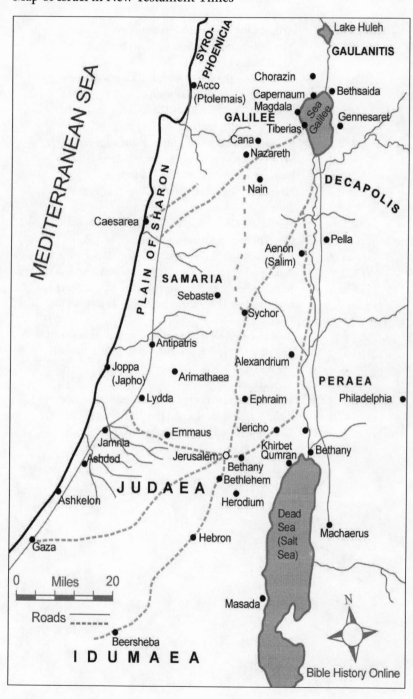

Scholars and Scribes

❧TWO❧

Editing the Scrolls

THE HISTORY

THE FIRST DEAD SEA Scrolls from Cave 1 were published rather quickly. E. L. Sukenik published the *Rule of War* (1QM) and the *Thanksgiving Hymns* (1QH) in Hebrew from 1948–1950.[1] ASOR published transcriptions and photographs of the Great *Isaiah Scroll* (1QIsa^a), the *Rule of the Community* (1QS), and the *Commentary on Habakkuk* (1QpHab) in 1950–1951. Sukenik's work on Isaiah B (1QIsa^b), the *Rule of War* (1QM), and the *Thanksgiving Hymns* (1QH) was published posthumously in 1955. The first volume in the series Discoveries in the Judaean Desert (DJD) appeared the same year. The next year Yigael Yadin, son of E. L. Sukenik, and Nahman Avigad published the *Genesis Apocryphon* (1QGenApoc).

In 1952 bedouin turned up with thousands of fragments from Cave 4. At this point it was obvious that a team was needed. In 1953–1954 Roland de Vaux recruited J. T. Milik, Frank M. Cross Jr., John M. Allegro, Jean Starcky, Patrick W. Skehan, John Strugnell, and Claus-Huno Hunzinger (who was soon replaced by Maurice Baillet). Each scholar was simply asked to edit and present for publication his batch of manuscripts. It is doubtful, since this was a new enterprise including several young scholars, to what extent working procedures, methodologies, and recording of evidence was discussed. From photographs we know that many of these scholars smoked cigarettes while inspecting fragments and used tape to connect them. Funding came from various sources: the National Center for Scientific Research in Paris, Ecole Biblique in Jerusalem, John D. Rockefeller, the Deutsche Forschungsgemeinschaft, and the British Trust.

In 1956 Cave 11 was discovered. ASOR and the Royal Academy of Sciences in the Netherlands purchased the rights to certain scrolls. James Sanders edited the beautiful *Psalms Scroll* (11QPs^a). J. van der Ploeg and A. S. van de Woude published the *Job Targum*. By 1958, the remaining Cave 4 fragments had been bought from the bedouin. In 1960, when the Rockefeller funding ended, about 511 manuscripts had been separated out and preserved under 620 museum plates.

In 1976 Milik's long-awaited work on the Enoch fragments from Cave 4 appeared. One year later, in 1977, Yigael Yadin, published his Hebrew commentary on the *Temple Scroll* (11QT^a). His English commentary appeared in 1983. In the same year Geza Vermes, known primarily for his series of translations of the Scrolls, characterized the failure to publish many biblical and non-biblical manuscripts as an academic scandal. Other scholars agreed, sensing that they might have already completed the editing process for certain materials, if they had been given the opportunity. These scholars decried the isolated working conditions of the initial editorial team and urged more cooperation. David N. Freedman completed his edition of Leviticus from Cave 11 (11QpaleoLev) after a decade in 1985. Skehan, who was responsible for the paleo-Hebrew texts, died in 1980. His manuscripts went to Eugene Ulrich, who retained some for himself and distributed others to graduate students. In 1987 the editor, Father Benoit, died. He was succeeded as editor-in-chief by John Strugnell, who had been granted the largest batch of manuscripts. Strugnell worked on *The Angelic Liturgy*, but it was his student Carol Newsom who published it as *The Songs of the Sabbath Sacrifice* (4QShirShab, 11QShirShab). Another of his students, Eileen Schuller, was entrusted with editing numerous non-biblical psalms.

By 1987 scholars who were not permitted to see the unpublished manuscripts were demanding that the editor-in-chief, John Strugnell, establish projected completion dates. In 1989, scholars at a Scrolls conference in Poland, organized by Z. J. Kapera, editor of *The Qumran Chronicle*, *The Polish Journal of Biblical Research*, and various *Mogilany*

Papers, released the so-called Mogilany Resolution that demanded the release of all plates of the scrolls' fragments immediately. In 1991 Ben Zion Wacholder and his student Martin Abegg used new computer software to reconstruct a series of texts. Scrolls photos had been transferred to the Huntington Library, violating traditionally accepted protocol and agreements. The Huntington Library in California announced it would open access to the Scrolls to all qualified scholars. Robert Eisenman and Michael O. Wise produced a volume of fifty previously unpublished texts along with translations and commentary.

Around this time, Kapera published a fold-out text of the underground copy of the work today known as *Some of the Works of the Law* (4QMMT), whose publication had been delayed for decades. Under threat of legal suit, Kapera simply stopped publishing the work. Hershel Shanks, editor of the *Biblical Archaeology Review*, was sued by one of the editors of *Some of the Works of the Law*, Elisha Qimron. In 1994, one decade after Qimron gave a presentation of its fragments in Jerusalem, he and Strugnell published their edition of this 120-line text and commentary.

Soon the editorial team was expanded and reorganized under the leadership of Emanuel Tov. Suddenly, many volumes of Cave 4 texts began to roll off the Clarendon Press in Oxford, England. Now practically all the Dead Sea Scrolls have been published. Enlarging the team to 100 or so ambitious and often younger editors paid off quite well.[2]

SCHOLARLY LANGUAGE AND ABBREVIATIONS FOR SCROLLS AND FRAGMENTS

Nothing like the discovery of the Dead Sea Scrolls had prepared the editorial team for creating an inventory of the scrolls and fragments. In fact, the task might have been simple if Cave 4 had not been found. The editors simply began to name and number the manuscripts. The first cave was registered as 1Q. A major scroll revealed in 1Q was a relatively complete scroll of the prophet Isaiah. It was logical to designate it as 1QIsa[a], but it turned out to be just one of two Isaiah scrolls. Thus one was called 1QIsa[a] and the other 1QIsa[b]. Knowing the list of books in the Jewish Bible, the Apocrypha, and the Pseudepigrapha helps with deducing which work has been mentioned. Works from Cave 2 would appear as 2Q plus an identifier, then 3Q, 4Q, and so forth. Very often, however, the editors were faced with how to inventory a manuscript whose content did not match books in the Bible, Apocrypha, and Pseudepigrapha. In that case, the editors gave the manuscript a content and/or genre name.

In the table of contents of his translations of the Dead Sea Scrolls, Geza Vermes, former director of the Oxford Forum for Qumran Research at the Oxford Centre for Hebrew and Jewish Studies, used the accepted content titles followed in parentheses by the scholarly shorthand.[3] This seemed to work out quite well. Still, one wonders how one should decipher 1QS? What is the "S"? It stands for the Hebrew word *serek,* which has often been translated as "order" or "rule." The work itself has been titled *The Community Rule.* Here it is called *The Rule of the Community.* In parenthesis, one reads 1QS, 4Q255–64, 4Q280, 286–87, 4Q502, 5Q11, 13. This is scholarly notation for one "*serek*" manuscript from Cave 1, thirteen "*serek*" manuscripts from Cave 4, and two from Cave 5. One also finds 1QSa. The "a" refers to an addendum to 1QS. 1QSb is the second addendum to 1QS. It is called *The Blessings.* In one case, one reads "CD" or "D," which refers to the "Covenant of Damascus" or the *Damascus Document.* Another manuscript that has been central to discussions about the history of the Dead Sea Scroll community is 1QpHab, which is code for Cave 1 at Qumran, a *pesher* commentary on the book of Habakkuk. *Pesher* refers basically to a contemporizing or futuristic interpretation (see chapter 7 below). Also represented among the scrolls retrieved from Cave 1 is 1QM, the M meaning *milḥamah* (Hebrew for "war"). The Cave 4 manuscripts run to about 580, which would be represented as 4Q580.

Occasionally the reader needs a few tips on understanding the English titles, because they were created by scholars who study Hebrew and Aramaic texts. "MMT" is an English abbreviation for the Hebrew title of "Some of the Works of the Law." Another text is called *tohorot* or "purities." *Otot* means "signs." *Berakhot* stands for "blessings." *Targum* means "Aramaic translation." *Netinim* were "temple servants." Readers should now understand how scholars talk to each other about the scrolls. When it is necessary, further clarifications will be offered.

DISCOVERIES IN THE JUDAEAN DESERT

While scholars write and read literature written in modern languages on the Scrolls, if they want to know what the Hebrew, Aramaic, or Greek text actually said, they turn to the series Discoveries in the Judaean Desert (DJD).[4] These volumes contain introductions, commentaries,

transliterations, translations, and photographic plates. A simple catego-
rization according to the volume number, names of editors, and title
helps one to know where to find different types of text in this series.

Type	Volume Number	Editors	Content
Biblical	9	P. W. Skehan et al.	Paleo-Hebrew and Greek Biblical Manuscripts
Biblical	12	E. Ulrich et al.	Genesis to Numbers
Biblical	14	E. Ulrich et al.	Deuteronomy, Joshua, Judges, Kings
Biblical	15	E. Ulrich et al.	Prophets
Biblical	16	E. Ulrich et al.	Psalms to Chronicles
Biblical	17	F. M. Cross et al.	1–2 Samuel
Biblical	32	P. W. Flint et al.	Isaiah
Biblical	39	E. Tov	Texts from Judaean Desert
Biblical	8	E. Tov et al.	Greek Minor Prophets from Nahal Hever
Biblical (?)	6	de Vaux et al.	Phylacteries, mezuzot, targums
Parabiblical	13	H. Attridge et al.	Variety
Parabiblical	19	M. Broshi et al.	Variety
Parabiblical	22	G. J. Brooke et al.	Variety
Parabiblical	30	D. Dimant	Variety
Poetic, Liturgical	11	E. Eshel et al.	Variety
Poetic, Liturgical	29	E. Chazon et al.	Variety
Wisdom	20	T. Elgvin	Variety
Wisdom	34	J. Strugnell et al.	Variety
Law	10	E. Qimron et al.	*Some Works of the Law*
Law, Narrative	18	J. M. Baumgarten	*Damascus Document*
Law	35	J. M. Baumgarten	Variety
Other	21	S. Talmon et al.	Calendar Texts
Other	26	P. Alexander	*Rule of Community* and Related Texts
Other	36	S. Pfann	Cryptic Texts

Type	Volume Number	Editors	Content
Other	40	C. Newsom et al.	*Thanksgiving Hymns*
Other	7	M. Baillet	4Q482–520
Other	25	E. Puech	4Q521–28, 576–79
Other	23	F. García Martínez et al.	11Q2–18, 20–31
Other	37	E. Puech	Aramaic texts, 4Q550–75, 580–82
Other	38	J. Charlesworth et al.	Miscellaneous
Other	24	M. J. Leith	Seal Impressions from Wadi Daliyeh
Other	27	H.M. Cotton et al.	Documentary Texts from Nahal Hever
Other	38	D. Gropp	Samaria Papyri from Wadi Daliyeh

The volumes in this series provide abundant information on various aspects of the manuscripts presented. Above all, one is able to compare photographs of the manuscripts with modern transcriptions and other texts. Volumes 8, 24, 27, 28, 38 and 39 include manuscripts from the Judaean desert in the broadest sense, but these are not strictly speaking Dead Sea Scrolls from the Qumran caves.

RECONSTRUCTING A SCROLL

After the discovery of the thousands of fragments in Cave 4 it became obvious to members of the small editorial team that it would be necessary to reconstitute, as far as it was possible, the original scrolls. They began to sort the manuscripts according to whether they were made of parchment or papyrus. At the same time the thickness or color of the material was important. If the manuscript represented a known biblical work, this made reconstruction easier. The assumption was that all biblical manuscripts from antiquity looked very much like the later exemplars used by scholars. The final edition of the manuscripts would include a transcription, a translation, paleographical and textual analysis.

In 1963 a German student at the University of Heidelberg, Hartmut Stegemann, presented a doctoral dissertation in which he reconstructed the hymn fragments of the *Thanksgiving Hymns* (4QH). Just as previous editors had done, Stegemann collected all the fragments deemed to belong to a single manuscript, compared material, scripts, and contents. Then he looked for structural clues to guide his reconstruction. As in assembling a jigsaw puzzle, he sought the top, bottom, and side margins of each column, transitions between columns, and even uninscribed lines or spaces. This permitted him to draw conclusions about the height and width of column. If a fragment did not provide a structural clue, it belonged inside the frame.

Stegemann's approach borrowed an idea from E. L. Sukenik, who had observed damage patterns in the *Thanksgiving Hymns* (1QH). Many of the scrolls were greatly damaged by moisture seeping through one layer after another. Stegemann realized that similarly shaped fragments should be placed on a horizontal axis, and then the challenge was to decide which fragments preceded a certain known point and which followed that point. He also noticed that one had to experiment with the idea that a scroll might have been rolled up from the first column or from the last. The most external column would absorb the most deterioration. Stegemann also measured distances between damage patterns and compensated for rolling and unrolling. Although this approach is attributed to Stegemann, he was reluctant to take credit for it.[5]

In the 1980s the editorial team began to grow. A major change occurred when John Strugnell of Harvard began to distribute his assigned manuscripts to graduate students. Strugnell had written about a fascinating work that he called *The Angelic Liturgy*. He passed the fragments on to Carol Newsom, now of Emory University, who worked with Stegemann to produce a reconstruction. She renamed the work *The Songs of the Sabbath Sacrifice* (4QShirShab, 11QShirShab). Using Stegemann's procedure and advice, about 100 fragments from the manuscript called 4Q405 were assembled to form fourteen reconstructed columns. Besides the most obvious external physical clues, internal structural clues were addressed. They noticed that numbering language in the fragments permitted one to establish a textual sequence. Several of the songs are dated to specific Sabbaths within the first quarter of a 364-day calendar. Additionally, they discovered sequential references to princes and tongues of fire. This reconstruction of a major work from Qumran has always been considered quite successful.[6]

Strugnell gave another of his students, Eileen Schuller, a batch of non-canonical psalms. Schuller used Stegemann's ideas with some success, but questioned his placement of seventy-nine fragments used to reconstruct a sequence of six columns of non-canonical psalms.[7]

Stegemann also reconstructed the *Songs of the Sage* (4Q511) using introductory and concluding formulas. His idea was straightforward: if ordering elements are presented, such as dates, dates of the week, sequential chronological notes, continuous quotation of a known text, and even a traditional story line, one could possibly reconstruct at least a partial scroll.[8]

Despite Stegemann's optimism certain pitfalls have emerged in reconstruction work. Multiple scribes are sometimes responsible for copying parts of a single work so that misattribution of fragments is still possible. Physical misalignment of fragments may occur, if one does not carefully measure distances between lines, letter heights, and sometimes the tendency toward cursive writing.

The reconstruction of the fragments titled *Some of the Works of the Law* (4QMMT) provides an illustrative example. With the help of Stegemann, Strugnell, and later his co-editor, Elisha Qimron, reconstructed this work, which has no recognizable beginning point. Analysis of the scripts shows that certain fragments do not seem to belong to a single manuscript. Among the fragments spelling sometimes differs. Certain fragments are clearly misaligned. Only the last two columns form the conclusion to the work, but even the two witnesses to this are not identical in all details. Fortunately, if one reads carefully, the editors themselves offer their own doubts about parts of their reconstruction.[9]

Scrolls reconstruction received an impetus from a different direction starting in the 1950s and 1960s. Several editorial assistants, Joseph A. Fitzmyer, Raymond E. Brown, William Oxtoby, and J. Teixidor were involved in creating an alphabetical list of vocabulary cards and textual location. (Stegemann was involved in the same kind of project led by Kuhn at the University of Heidelberg in the Qumranforschungsstelle in the 1960s.) The project ended when funding dried up. In the 1980s these cards were arranged in order and a small number of copies was sent to libraries around the world.[10]

At roughly the same time Ben Zion Wacholder, a well-known scholar of Judaism in the Hellenistic period, and his student Martin Abegg used a computer and the recently distributed concordance to reconstruct Cave 4 texts. Because the vocabulary cards had been numbered consecutively in the bottom left-hand corner, it was possible to reconstitute a textual sequence. By the early 1990s Wacholder and Abegg's new imaging software helped them to reconstruct the Damascus Document, the priestly rota (*mishmerot*), wisdom, visions, thanksgiving hymns, and other texts. Technology had improved textual reconstruction immensely. Although Wacholder and Abegg were criticized for using a bootleg or renegade version of the texts, Wacholder said, "Now I am an old man. . . . It is a painful thing to have been so close to something so rare. But I realized that if I waited, I would long be dead."[11] Photographic and computer image enhancement have facilitated the combination and study of previously separate or illegible fragments.

Most recently Torleif Elgvin described very precisely how, using the methods of Hartmut Stegemann mentioned above, he had reconstructed *4QParaphrase of Genesis and Exodus* to recreate a small scroll.[12] Initially, he accepted Qimron's placement of five Exodus fragments to form the upper part of a column 15 cm in width with visible margins on the left and right sides. Elgvin noticed that fragments 1–3 were similar in size and that fragment 1 preserved a paraphrase of Gen 2:1. He discovered that fragments 2–3 dealt with the flood in Gen 6–9 and fragment 10a–e represented the plagues in Exodus 7–12. Various fragments fit in the margins or the top part of the manuscript. Other fragments would then have to be inserted within supposed columns. Elgvin took a millimeter ruler and measured between fragments, trying to determine distances between columns. Eventually, he realized he was dealing with a short paraphrase or sermon on major episodes in Genesis and Exodus. In terms of this scroll's content, Elgvin noticed parallels with the language of Ben Sira, *Jubilees*, *Words of the Luminaries*, and *4QTime of Righteousness*.

The reconstruction of "original" scrolls from scattered fragments is both a technique and an art. Its contributions to the field of manuscript restoration are incalculable. No doubt, the public and private efforts of Hartmut Stegemann to reconstitute two thousand-year manuscripts from disparate pieces of Hebrew text have made modern biblical research aware of the importance of studying ancient manuscripts carefully. Today digital imaging will aid the physical placement of fragments on vertical and horizontal axes in order to rediscover the shape of ancient texts. Certainly, other techniques will emerge that will help in still unsuspected ways.

Paleography of the Scrolls

Palaeography is the study of ancient scripts. In the case of the Qumran scrolls, palaeography is used to classify the various kinds of handwriting styles, though it can also determine manuscripts written by the same scribe.

From his study of the scrolls and other texts from the Second Temple period (6th century BCE–1st century CE), Frank M. Cross has developed a typology of Qumran Hebrew scripts which is followed by many if not most Qumran editors:

Archaic *c.* 250–150 BCE
(mostly biblical texts)
Hasmonaean *c.* 150–50 BCE
Herodian *c.* 50 BCE–70 CE
(This period far exceeds the reign of Herod the Great, but covers his dynasty, down to Agrippa II)

Because letter forms constantly evolve, it is possible to be more precise, for example in assigning texts to the early or late Hasmonaean or Herodian, or even to a transitional Hasmonaean-Herodian. Within the Hasmonaean and Herodian scripts one can also distinguish between formal, semiformal and cursive.

But the major problem with Cross's system is already evident in these names, because he believes that typological differences can be precisely converted into dates – so precisely that he and his followers believe they can assign any manuscript, on the basis of its script, to within 25 years. This view implies that a scribe, over a 30- or 40-year career, would change his own script uniformly. It also assumes that all scribes belonged to the same school (at Qumran) and were taught to write the same way.

While Cross's typology is excellent, it does not automatically yield chronology. The margin in dating needs to be at least 25 years *in each direction* (the lifetime of a scribe). Recent Carbon-14 (AMS) datings, claimed to support Cross's datings, actually do not support the precision he claims, though this method of dating is not sufficiently close to determine the matter.

How does the palaeographer examine scripts? The analysis is largely based on the shape of individual letters. The features of these letters include 'arms', 'roofs', downstrokes, 'legs', angles, curves, the number of strokes, base strokes, location of a crossbar, serifs, and ligatures. These features can be convex, concave, long, short, rounded, curved, hooked, open, closed, and triangular. Ada Yardeni, perhaps the leading Israeli palaeographer, notes that scribes regularly used differing executions of a single letter within a single manuscript.

1	2	3	4	
ⴕ	א	א	א	aleph
ⅎ	ꓘ	ב	ב	bet
٦	ʌ	ג	ג	gimmel
△	ⴞ	ד	ד	dalet
ⴄ	ⴉ	ה	ה	he
ⵝ	٦	ו	ו	waw
ⵤ	ı	ז	ז	zayin
ⴓ	ⴕ	ח	ח	het
⊕	๖	ט	ט	tet
ⵀ	٦	י	י	yod
ⵍ	ⴅ	כ	כ	kaph
	ⵙ	ⴽ	ך	final kaph
ⵏ	٦	ⴙ	ⴷ	lamed
ⵖ	ⵙ	ⴽ	מ	mem
	ⴽ	ⴽ	ם	final mem
ⵢ	ノ	ⴵ	ⴵ	nun
	ⵑ	ⴼ	ⵑ	final nun
ⵅ	ⵗ	ⴴ	ⴴ	samech
ⴰ	ⵘ	ⵢ	ⵥ	ayin
ⵎ	ⴽ	ⴽ	ⴼ	peh
	ⵦ	ⴽ	ⴽ	final peh (feh)
ⵎ	ⵣ	ⵣ	ⵥ	zade
	ⵤ	ⵧ	ⵥ	final zade
ⴽ	ⵔ	ⴵ	ⵧ	qof
ⵊ	ⴼ	ⴽ	ⴽ	resh
ⵡ	ⵍ	ⵯ	ⵯ	shin
×	ⴽ	ⴽ	ⴽ	tav

Ezra in Prayer

❖THREE❖

The World of the Scrolls

FROM THE BABYLONIAN EXILE TO BAR KOKHBAH

THE STORY OF THE Jewish exile to Babylon and the return is recounted in some of the later historical books of the Bible.[1] It is supplemented by the Books of Maccabees, Josephus, and other works. Second Kings, Chronicles, and Jeremiah all view the exile as divine punishment particularly for the wicked deeds of King Manasseh. Nebuchadrezzar transported the royal household, its treasures along with those of the Jerusalem temple, soldiers, 10,000 captives, craftsmen, and smiths to Babylon (2 Kings 24). Ten years later Nebuchadrezzar again attacked Jerusalem and captured King Zedekiah fleeing in the plain of Jericho (Jer 39:5–7). Not long after that, Nebuzaraddan the captain of Nebuchadrezzar's personal bodyguard, burned the Jerusalem temple and the royal quarters and demolished the city's walls. He removed vessels from the temple. In the city of Riblah he executed priests and military leaders. Nebuzaraddan then set up Gedaliah as governor. In the thirty-seventh year of the exile, which was around 560 BCE, the Babylonian ruler, Evil-merodach, freed Johoiachin, the Judaean king, from prison and granted him a regular ration at the royal table.

Second Chronicles 36 narrates the wicked deeds of Kings Jehoiachim, Jehoiachin, and finally Zedekiah, who would not humble himself before

God's messenger Jeremiah. These leaders and their people repeatedly disregarded God's warnings and wrath for a period of seventy years until the rise of the Persian leader Cyrus, which fulfilled the words of Jeremiah (Jer 25:12–14). Interestingly, Cyrus claimed that the God of the Jews had charged him with rebuilding the Jerusalem temple (2 Chron 36:23). Soon Jewish leaders living in Babylon traveled to reconstitute the holy city. Among those who arrived were Ezra and Nehemiah. Ezra, the scribe, also credited Cyrus with sending the earliest missions to Jerusalem (Ezra 1–2). A certain Sheshbazzar, a Judaean prince, brought with him a variety of temple vessels and other Jews. Thousands of exiles, priests, Levites, temple personnel, royal servants, and others accompanied Zerubbabel to Jerusalem. It must have been a huge shock to the city's and the land's inhabitants when, as Ezra reports, over 50,000 people arrived.

According to the narrative, although the foundation of the temple had not been laid, the altar was restored after seven months and the feast of booths was celebrated (Ezra 3:2–6). In the next year the temple personnel celebrated the laying of the foundations (3:8–11). Many from the countryside were harshly rebuffed when they offered to help with the rebuilding and wrote the Persian administrators for help (Ezra 4:11–16). The recent returnees who had been working on the temple were forced to halt this work until the second year of Darius. As the prophets Haggai and Zechariah prophesied, work on the temple continued. The returnees requested that the Persian authorities find and send them a copy of Cyrus's permission to rebuild the temple. According to Ezra the temple was completed in the sixth year of Darius and dedicated just in time to celebrate Passover and the Feast of Unleavened Bread (6:14–22).

Ezra 7 reports that Ezra, a teacher of the Law, came to Jerusalem during the reign of Artaxerxes. At the Ahava River, Ezra and his companions prayed and fasted and then proceeded to Jerusalem (Ezra 8). Upon arrival Ezra was outraged that so many of the returnees had not already disassociated themselves from the surrounding peoples (Ezra 9). He demanded that the priests and the Levites abandon all foreign practices. He scheduled a sort of national assembly to be held in three days on the 20th of the ninth month (Ezra 10:9–44). Mincing no words Ezra ordered that those present reaffirm their Jewish identity by renouncing their foreign wives and their foreign practices. If this account is to be believed, few opposed Ezra's harsh mandate.

Nehemiah's account also tells of lamentations, weeping, fasting, and prayer. Like his counterpart Ezra, Nehemiah applied to Artaxerxes to rebuild Jerusalem and Judaea. Among those concerned about Nehemiah's ambitions were Sanballat, the governor of Samaria, the Ammonite leader Tobiah, and an Arab named Geshem (Neh 2:19–20). Nehemiah suspected the intent of his enemies and inspected the city walls by night. While construction rang out, guards were posted. Even the high priest and other temple personnel are listed among those who were involved in rebuilding the walls of Jerusalem. Over forty personal names are listed in Ezra, including the cities of Jericho, Tekoa, Mizpah, Jerusalem, Zanoah, Beth Hakkerem, Beth Zur, Keilah, priests (men of the plain), magistrates, goldsmiths, and perfumers (Nehemiah 3). Many workers worried about their supplies and defenses. Many worried about mortgaging their homes to get grain. Still others had borrowed money to repay royal taxes on their fields and vineyards. Some forced their children into slavery. Nehemiah counseled against all of these measures and demanded that no interest should be charged within the community. For a dozen years those who were rebuilding the city refused to consume the governor's provisions. The Samaritan Sanballat and the Arab Geshem spread the rumor that Nehemiah had engaged his own prophets to preach on his behalf (Nehemiah 6).

The book of Nehemiah speaks of Ezra as the man of God's word (Nehemiah 8). On the first day of the seventh month, Ezra stood in an open assembly and read from the Law while the Levites explained it to the people. The following day, priests, Levites, and the heads of families arrived to learn the Law and know how to celebrate the Feast of Booths. This sounds like a reenactment of the Golden Age under Joshua. A collective confession was made followed by a reading from the Law and a vow to separate from the foreigners. After concluding the prayer eighty-four people signed off on the new covenant (Neh 10:1–28). Then the curse and oath were pronounced. Those in agreement promised not to marry their daughters to the people of the land, nor to purchase anything from them on Sabbaths and festival days, nor to farm during a Sabbath year nor collect debts, to pay a 1/3 shekel annual tax to the temple, to bring wood offerings and first-fruits, and to permit the Levites to collect tithes. Jerusalem was repopulated (Neh 10:29–39). When the walls were dedicated, the law barring foreigners from entering the assembly of God was read (Neh 13:1).

As soon as Nehemiah returned to Babylon, it was discovered that the priest Eliashib had prepared a chamber for Tobiah the Ammonite in the temple (Neh 13:4–9). Nehemiah installed treasurers over the storehouses. He stopped Jewish and Syrian business in Jerusalem on the Sabbath. If children were discovered who could not speak Hebrew, they were beaten, their hair was pulled, and they were forced to swear an oath of allegiance (Neh 13:10–31). Ezra and Nehemiah were always faced with re-teaching the law and taking punitive measures. Certainly, resentment escalated. Those who were in power enjoyed the popularity of the rebuilding the temple, the walls, and repopulating the city, but this recentralization most likely threatened the many regional interests that had been developing for the seventy years since the exile.

From the late fourth to the late third century little is reported about Israel and Judaea. Of course, Josephus reports that Alexander the Great paid a visit to the Samaritan temple (*Ant.* 11:322–324). During the third century BCE Jerusalem's leaders and the surrounding regions remained loyal to the Ptolemies, but the pendulum moved in the opposite direction when the Seleucids won the Battle of Panion in 200 BCE. Many of those who had been Ptolemaic puppets departed for Egypt. Others simply accepted the new Seleucid hegemony.

Many Jews were certainly patriotic and nationalistic as the Maccabees seem to have been (1–2 Maccabees). After the death of their father, the Maccabean sons Mattathias, Judas, Jonathan, and Simon successively dominated Judaean foreign and domestic politics for about thirty years (mid-160s to mid-130s). Jonathan[2] and Simon had been high priests ca. 152 and 140 BCE. Josephus claims this post for Judas as well. During the years of Maccabean ascendance, Antiochus IV was rebuffed, the temple was rededicated, taxation was reduced, and the Seleucid-Syrian control was disrupted.[3] Antiochus IV was famous primarily for prohibiting the practice of worship in the Jerusalem temple and the possession of books of the Law. Simon was perhaps the most powerful of the brothers. He became high priest, military commander, and governor in perpetuity according to 1 Macc 14:41–49.[4]

A brief battle against the Seleucids ensued when John Hyrcanus came to power (*Ant.* 13.236–299; *War* 1.68–69).[5] Hyrcanus ruthlessly expanded Jewish boundaries to the north, south, and east. He destroyed the Samaritan temple on Mount Gerizim and converted Idumeans to Judaism by circumcision. He annexed the population east of the Jordan

Valley. No doubt, many hated Hyrcanus. He had neglected the religious, had plundered the tomb of King David, and had hired a massive army of foreigners. Some Pharisees even questioned whether he was Jewish since his mother may have been a prisoner of Antiochus. When Hyrcanus died in 104 BCE, his son Judas or Aristobulus continued his father's policy of territorial expansion (*Ant.* 13.301–318). He forced those who lived in Galilee to become Jews. Many of them were in fact Greek or Syrian. As he had his brother murdered and permitted his mother to starve, he proclaimed himself "King of the Jews."

One might think that the worst was over after Hyrcanus; but his widow, Salome Alexandra,[6] released her dead husband's brother—Jonathan (a.k.a. Alexander Jannaeus)—from prison, married him, and had him proclaimed high priest and king.[7] The most pious Jews must have been shocked by his assumption of both offices. The marriage itself as well as Salome's political power certain incensed many. For about thirty years (107–76 BCE) Jannaeus conquered territory in the Transjordanian highlands and along the Mediterranean coast (*Ant.* 13.334–421). He was disliked by many. Once at the Feast of Booths those assembled threw citrons at him saying he was unfit for the high priesthood since his mother had been a war captive. Josephus reports that Jannaeus killed more than 6,000 Jews during a six-year civil war. When Jannaeus's opponents begged the Seleucids to aid them in fighting against Jannaeus, the latter had some 800 of them crucified.[8] For a decade after his death, Jannaeus's wife Salome remained queen (76–67 BCE). During a relatively peaceful seven-year respite from civil war, her son Hyrcanus II was high priest (*Ant.* 14.4–33; *War* 1.120–130).[9] Aristobulus II, his brother, led a coalition of Sadducees and military forces (67–63 BCE). Encouraged by the Idumeans, Hyrcanus attempted to overthrow his brother without success.

During this period the Roman general Pompey arrived in Damascus (63 BCE). Immediately, the three main groups in Jerusalem appealed to him for help (*Ant.* 14.41–76; *War* 1.145–151). There was a Hyrcanus contingent, an Aristobulus faction, and another one that claimed to represent all Jews. All Jewish military authority was abolished, and Judaea became a state with a high priest at its head. Aristobulus and 12,000 men were massacred on the temple mount. Pompey entered the temple's holy of holies on the sacred Day of Atonement. The Romans were there to stay, and most likely many pious groups felt that God was repaying them for rampant territorial acquisition and internecine feuds and killings.

The Roman tributary Judaea included Judaea, part of Idumaea, east Jordanian Peraea, and Galilee. The Roman governor resided in Jerusalem and forced the Jews to repay an indemnity of ten thousand talents. The Romans, not the Jews, appointed Hyrcanus to be high priest (*Ant.* 14.73–74; *War* 1.153–154). When Julius Caesar succeeded Pompey, Hyrcanus became the ethnarch and Antipater the governor of the people. Antipater then appointed his son Phasael governor of Jerusalem and his other son Herod governor of Galilee. At a certain point Aristobulus's son Antigonus and the Parthians invaded and recaptured Jerusalem (*Ant.* 14.47–53; *War* 1.133–137). Hyrcanus was disqualified from the high priesthood by mutilation (Lev 21:16–23), and Antigonus became both high priest and king (*Ant.* 14.327–380; *War* 1.248–281).

If that were not confusing enough, Herod whose star had ascended in Rome was named "King of Judaea" in 40 BCE by Antony, Octavius, and the Roman Senate (*Ant.* 14.370–380; *War* 1.274–281). Three years later Herod sat upon his throne and enjoyed thirty-four years of power and success (*Antiquities* 15–17). Roman land grants expanded his influence to the north and east of the Sea of Galilee (modern-day northern Jordan and the Golan Heights). Herod became famous for rebuilding or creating Hellenistic cities. Not only did he have the harbor at Caesarea built, he reconstructed the Jerusalem temple and constructed fortresses and residences at Masada, Herodium, and at Machaereus across the Jordan. He married the Hasmonean Mariamne, whose mother was Alexandra and whose brother was Aristobulus (*Ant.* 15.23–24). He was loved, hated, and feared. He was not really a Jew, but acted out a drama balancing the interests of his local constituency, his in-laws, and his far-reaching Roman patrons.

For ten years from 4 BCE to 6 CE Herod's son, Archaeleus ruled as ethnarch of Judaea, Samaria, and Idumea (*Ant.* 17.199–344; *War* 1.673—2.111). In 4 BCE violent armed conflict broke out between Roman soldiers and Jewish pilgrims who were celebrating the Feast of Weeks. Another son, Philip, was tetrarch of the territory to the north and east of the Sea of Galilee until 34 CE. Herod Antipas, a third brother, ruled over Galilee and Peraea until 39 CE. He is best known for marrying the wife of his half-brother and having John the Baptist executed (*Ant.* 18.110–112). In Galilee there arose a man named Judas and a Pharisee named Zadok who headed a revolt against the Syrians who had just initiated a census for taxation purposes (*Ant.* 18.2–25; *War* 2.118). Josephus says that the Romans crucified more than 2000 of these Galilean rebels. In 6 CE Joazar, a pro-Roman high priest, urged his people to comply with the census.

After Archaeleus was deposed Roman procurators ruled until 41 CE (*Ant.* 18.181–256; *War* 2.117–177). They chiefly appointed high priests and taxed the people. The best known of these was Pontius Pilate who served for 10 years from 26–36 CE. Besides washing his hands of the crucifixion of Jesus, he permitted Roman images in the temple, confiscated temple funds to construct a city aqueduct, and massacred many Samaritans. From 37–44 CE Agrippa I ruled over nearly the same territory as his grandfather Herod the Great had (*Ant.* 18.147—19.352). In 39 CE, as an act of vengeance, Gaius Caligula erected a statue of himself or Zeus in the Jerusalem temple. Several years later in 45 CE (Acts 5:36) the Romans executed hundreds of people who followed a prophet named Theudas at the Jordan (*Ant.* 20.97–99; Acts 5:36–37). Not long after that two sons of Judas the Galilean were crucified. Josephus reports that between 20,000 and 30,000 Jews were killed (*Ant.* 20.105–12; *War* 2.224–27) under the procuratorship of Comanus (48–52 CE). The dangerous dagger-wielding Sicarii were also about killing anyone who supported the Romans (*Ant.* 20.137–166; *War* 2.247–268).

Officially, the first revolt against the Romans began in 66 CE (*War* 2.408—7.406). Its effects were felt from Caesarea on the coast to the treasury of the Jerusalem temple. Eleazar, the high priest's son, ordered that the daily sacrifice on behalf of the Roman emperor and people stop. Jewish Zealots overran the Roman garrison at Masada. Another son of Judas the Galilean, Menahem first found success at Masada but was killed when he returned to Jerusalem. The Romans dispatched the Twelfth Roman Legion to Jerusalem, but found the task of taking Jerusalem more difficult than they had anticipated. The Jewish rebels controlled the city, struck their own coins, and established militia districts. In due time conflict among the Jews and their leader caused them to lose focus and their advantage. In late August 70 CE the temple was captured, plundered, and burned (*War* 5.258—6.408). From this time on the war moved southward. Three years later atop Masada, Eleazar ben Jair and hundreds of other defenders took their own lives before the Romans could claim victory at Masada (*War* 7.252–406).

For those Jews whose existence depended on Jerusalem, the temple, and the commercial and cultural advantage of city everything changed dramatically. Not only were they occupied by a foreign force, the Jews had to admit defeat and certainly interpreted their fate as divine punishment. Roman coins inscribed with the words *Judea Capta* and the renaming of Jerusalem as Aelia Capitolina were daily reminders of this bitter loss. However, acceptance of this harsh reality forced the Jews to emphasize the more private aspects of their cultural and religious life. This included the creation of communities around synagogues, prayer, study of religious texts, and the application of purity laws originally intended for the temple to their lives in community and privately. This was of course nothing new in Israel and Judaea. Outside of Israel and Judaea resentment grew as well. There were Jewish revolts in Cyrenaica in 115 CE and in Egypt, Cyprus, and Mesopotamia in 116–117 CE.[11] No doubt, sparks from these areas rekindled fires in the homeland.

In the 130s CE some Jews regrouped, retook Jerusalem for a while, and minted their own coins. Some scholars say that the prophetic seventy years had passed, and this inspired the Jews in the land to rebel. The most famous of these warriors was Shimon ben Kosiba (a.k.a. Bar Kokhba). South of Khirbet Qumran in a cave at Murabba'at the correspondence between Shimon ben Kosiba and others was discovered.[12] In one letter, signed by Shimon ben Kosiba himself, the self-acclaimed president of Israel, wrote to Joshua ben Galgula and the people of Ha-Baruk telling them if they mistreated the Galileans he would put their feet in iron as he had done to a certain Ben 'Aphul. In another letter Shimon said that he was sending people to Joshua ben Galgulah with five kors of wheat. He told Joshua to let these people stay there until after the Sabbath when they would leave. In a more urgent tone Shimon wrote to Jonathan and to Masabala ordering that they send all the Tekoans or any other men to him lest they be punished. In still another missive to Eleazar ben Hitta in 'En Gedi he ordered that the wheat and fruits be confiscated. Should anyone oppose this order, they would be punished. In another he demanded that four donkey-loads of salt be sent. Ben Kosiba appears in a different light requesting a *lulav*, an *ertrog*, a *hadas*, and an *arava*. These are all naturalia associated with the Feast of Booths—the palm leaf, the citron, the myrtle, and the popular. Romans are said to be close by, and on another occasion Shimon said he will deal with the Romans. This correspondence presents Shimon ben Kosiba as a stern leader, one concerned with the lack of supplies and active support, and as a practicing Jew concerned that his people not travel on the Sabbath and that he get what is required for the Feast of Booths.

Reviewing almost seven centuries from the exile to Babylon to the uprising of Bar Kokhba (587 BCE—135 CE), a variety of topics recur regularly—the role of foreigners in executing God's punishment of the Jews, the prohibition of marriage with foreigners and acceptance of foreign customs, the importance of the temple and its festivals, and who could and could not help to rebuild the temple. By the time of Bar Kokhba even this leader had come to worry about daily subsistence and solidarity among his people while trying to observe the Sabbath and the festivals in a state of war.

RELIGIOUS LIFE

Throughout the centuries Jews have focused on the holy city of Jerusalem, even if there were other places where they conveniently practiced their faith from day to day. During the post-exilic period Jews were concerned to rebuild the Jerusalem temple and continue to worship God in a reformed and refined fashion still based on scriptural instructions. The temple was more than a centralized location for worship.[13] It was a center of priestly power, wealth, influence, and commerce. Numerous businesses, such as masons, carpenters, suppliers of wood, animals, and clothing did well when the temple was flourishing. Representatives of priestly families served twice a year. Pilgrims flocked to Jerusalem to experience festivals at the Jerusalem temple. Jews were expected to bring first fruits and pay the annual temple tax. The temple was also a center where Jews could discuss and even argue about whether current practices had divine sanction. It was quite political in that sense.

In addition to worshipping at the temple, Jews were reared hearing and reading sacred scriptures and implementing its requirements in their daily lives. They were concerned to fulfill the letter of law and often paid great attention to the meaning of the sacred texts. Besides laws telling them to go to the temple with their offerings at certain times of the year, Jews competed to practice the purities laws exactly. Some Jews applied laws meant for priests within the temple to themselves wherever they lived. In addition to the Jewish Scripture as known today, the Dead Sea Scrolls show that a thriving literary industry existed whose chief purpose was to enhance the body of edifying religious literature. By the

Persian and Hellenistic periods the Jews had their own collections of classical literature, which were being translated into Greek for the benefit of non-Hebrew-speaking Jews.

Ezra's reading of the Law and the Levites' interpretation of it reveal sacred Law as the center of the agenda of a national assembly. In other group settings the Jews studied, discussed, and lived according to the will of God as express in Scriptures and ultimately also found ways to experience divine revelation. The Dead Sea Scrolls prove that while Scripture had to a great extent been standardized, God still spoke to special individuals who made God's announcement to a contemporaneous audience. If two such spokespersons conflicted in revealing God's will, this led obviously to friction, conflict, and perhaps even physical aggression. Against this context scholars have often and still see the beginnings of the Qumran community. A typical interpretation says that arguments over the high priesthood in Jerusalem led the eventual leader of the Dead Sea Community to abandon Jerusalem and set up his headquarters at Khirbet Qumran on the shores of the Dead Sea.

Private religious practice was usually connected with the temple or the Scriptures. Prayer and the celebration of holy days were oriented toward the temple.[14] Compliance with circumcision, diet, and Sabbath laws were parts of Jewish life that could be regulated outside of the temple, but based on Scripture. The practice of the Jewish way of life depended on how groups and individuals understood the scriptures that had been handed down to them over the centuries and even over a millennium. Proper interpretation was learned in the context not only of the family, but in organizations and places designed to intensify the study and practice of Judaism. This required learned instructors who not only knew Scripture by heart, but even masters who were familiar with its subtleties and who knew how to apply ancient stories and laws to a modern situation.

Deuteronomy 6:4–8 tells the Israelites to place the laws in their heart, to bind them on their hands, to attach them between their eyes, and to write them upon the doorposts of their houses. Certain scriptural passages were indeed copied in tiny scripts, folded, placed in containers called phylacteries or *tefillin*. These were worn on the arms and forehead during prayer. If inscribed on the door of a house, this was called a *mezuzah*. Numerous phylacteries and *mezuzot* were discovered in the Qumran and Murabba'at caves.[15]

Private religious practice also involved imagining oneself as an angel in the heavenly temple or reciting prayers for certain times of the day and special occasions.[16] It included a desire to be protected from evil spirits,[17] and this led to the creation and use of amulets. Songs and spells were composed to ward off all forms of wickedness that might attack one in moments of weakness. People specialized in predicting national history based on meteorological conditions and composed horoscopes based on birth dates and physical characteristics.[18] Ancient specialists in studying Jewish history in the context of world history focused on issues regarding the calendar. Probably the same people were concerned to synchronize the activities of priests at the temple and believing Jews with the divine services in heaven and God's plan for the final days.[19]

RELIGIOUS AND POLITICAL AFFILIATIONS

The Essenes

Two thousand years ago the Alexandrian Jew, Philo, the Roman, Pliny the Elder, and the Jewish Pharisee, Josephus ben Mattathius wrote about a Jewish group they called the Essenes. Two of the narratives were penned in Rome and one in Alexandria. Each report is distinctive. Occasionally one detail or another is found in more than one source. Sometimes the reports seem contradictory. In general, modern scholars have tried to understand each report as supplementing the others in some way.

Philo, who lived roughly seventy-five years (30 BCE—45 CE), provides two valuable notes on the Essenes. In *Every Man is Free* 75–91, he claims that there were 4,000 virtuous persons known as Essenes. He derives their name from the Greek word for 'holiness.' For the Essene, holiness of the mind was of singular importance. Philo says that the Essenes fled the ungodly cities and dwelled in villages, contenting themselves with farm work and crafts. They had nothing to do with business nor did they hold slaves (as other Jews apparently did). They did not hoard silver, gold, or land. Since none of them had his own house, they lived in common, sharing meals, clothing, and a single communal fund. They were responsible for their self-imposed seclusion, because they felt that reversals of fate had forced them to do so. Unlike other Jews, they did not offer animal sacrifice.

Contrasting the Essenes with Hellenistic philosophers, Philo emphasized that the Essenes preferred ethics to theoretical talk. Toward that end they studied their ancestral laws especially in their synagogues on the Sabbath day. Teaching in symbols, their lessons concerned God's love, virtue, and humanity. They cared for the sick, aged, and weak and clearly rejected the idea that God caused evil and suffering in the world. In his *Apology for the Jews*, Philo added that the Essenes were farmers, shepherds, beekeepers, and craftsmen, thus extending his statement on professions. He noted that they banned marriage, ordered continence, and had no children, adolescents, or young men in the community.

The Roman historian, Pliny the Elder, lived ca. 23/24–79 CE. In his *Natural History* (5.17.4 [73]) he locates the Essenes somewhere above 'En Gedi on the northwestern shore of the Dead Sea. Like Philo, he also says that the Essenes had neither money nor women in their community. Similar to the Alexandrian, Pliny, he wrote that throngs of new members come to this community precisely because "the fluctuations of fortune" had wearied them.

Most scholars have put the Jewish historian Josephus at the center of their descriptions of the Essenes, in part because Josephus claimed to have joined the Essenes for a time. He was a slightly younger contemporary of Pliny the Elder (38–93 CE). Although he never writes about a specific Essene headquarters, he does provide the richest and most varied accounts. He preserves brief anecdotes about individual Essenes. In one case, he recounts the prophecy of a certain Judas, who had predicted the death of Antigonus, also a certain Simon, who had prophesied the trial of Archaeleus, and a man named John who served as general in charge of the toparchy of Tamna, Lydda, Joppa, and Ammaus during the late-first-century revolt against Roman rule in Israel-Judaea. This general John is surrounded by other individuals such as Josephus ben Simon, Niger the Peraean, and Silas the Babylonian. Josephus also recounts how Menahem, another Essene prophet, had foretold Herod's hegemony that would last for twenty or thirty years. Besides studying with the Essenes, Josephus says that he spent time with other Jewish denominations of his time, finally choosing to become a Pharisee.

Consistent with Philo and Pliny, Josephus notes that the Essenes renounced pleasure and followed a path of continence. Nevertheless, he contradicts Philo by saying that they adopted the children of others. They did not prohibit marriage per se (some Essenes married), but were concerned about the licentiousness of women. He says that they despised riches, dressed in white, avoided oaths and using oil, lived an egalitarian lifestyle, carried arms only when traveling, offered prayers at sunrise, assembled at the fifth hour of the day for prayer and to study the written works of the ancients. Beyond all this, he calls them masters of healing with roots and stones. Within the Essene communities there were four levels of purity, those with seniority being envied by others at the lower levels.

In the context of the Jewish revolt against the Romans, Josephus inserts an unusually extensive statement on the Essenes as martyrs. He claims that they believed in the immortality of souls that reside beyond the Ocean. Again he emphasizes that they studied their ancient scriptures, followed their own purification rituals, and were well-known as prophets.

Of the three ancient writers, Josephus is the only one who offered an account of the initiation process upon joining the Essene community. In most respects his account confirms information in 1QS 6:13–24. For one year the prospective member would be tested. After that, if he were found to be acceptable to the community's discipline, his property and earnings would be deposited with the community's bursar. In the following year this initiate would be permitted to partake of the pure meal of the community. If he passed muster during the second year, his wealth would be merged with communal funds, and he was invited to enjoy the pure drink of the community.

Josephus records that an Essene could be banished from the community, if he revealed any secrets of the group or even the names of the angels or questioned the authority of the community's leadership (*War* 2.141–144). Precisely these matters are paralleled in parts of 1QS and CD. Josephus presents other details that are corroborated in other Dead Sea Scrolls. Some scholars point out the Josephus is often providing information that could apply to other Second Temple Jews and even early Christians—shared views on purificatory baths, spitting in assemblies, Sabbath worship, toilet rules, avoidance of oil, and angelology. Nevertheless, most scholars still identify the people of Khirbet Qumran with the Essenes of the ancient reports. Many admit that the Essene communities were not restricted to the Dead Sea area, but resided throughout Palestinian Syria. The Essenes formed a community of shared beliefs and rules for living, but certainly the Essenes must have been as individual in makeup as members of any other group of the time.

Josephus's chief distinction between the Essenes, the Pharisees, and the Sadducees lies in their views on fate, human will, and the afterlife, philosophical issues that would have charmed his Roman audience. He was not at all concerned to emphasize subtle differences in their understanding and practice of purity laws, liturgical calendars, and exegesis, although as a former adherent he would have been expert on such debates and conflicts. In general, however, the three main religious denominations of the time probably agreed more on how to conduct a righteous and holy life before God than we can imagine. Faced with a common national enemy and hopes that God would intervene on their side, the Essenes and other Jewish groups joined ranks to oppose the Romans and defend their common heritage.

The Pharisees and the Sadducees

Josephus reported in the late first century CE that the Pharisees, the group with which he affiliated himself when he was nineteen, believes that fate played a role in some aspects of life but that the direction of one's fate was something that individuals could decide (*Ant.* 13.171). Elsewhere in the *Antiquities* he emphasizes the role of human will in attaining certain results in this life. Josephus said that the Pharisees believed that souls survived the death of the body and based on the balance of virtue and vice in their lives they would be rewarded or punished (18.13–14). In his *War*, Josephus says that humans are in charge of how they behave, but fate and God also participate in these decisions (2.162–163). In the same passage the souls of the wicked suffer eternal damnation while virtuous souls pass into another body. In terms of the laws, Josephus notes that they passed on certain laws handed down by previous generations that were not recorded in the Law of Moses (*Ant.* 13.297).

In contrast to the views of the Pharisees, Josephus's Sadducees believed that the soul perished with the body. Accordingly, there was no reward or punishment after death (*Ant.* 18.16). The Sadducees left no room for belief in fate saying that humans were given the free choice to decide for good or evil. In particular, Josephus distances God from the commission of evil and the sight of evil (*War* 2.164–165). In terms of laws, Josephus said that the Sadducees rejected the Pharisees because of the non-Mosaic laws that they taught and practiced, which were not authoritative. The two groups conflicted on such matters (*Ant.* 13.297–298).

The Samaritans

According to the narrative in 2 Kings 17, the Samaritans were foreigners whom the Assyrians had settled in Samaria in the late seventh century BCE. Genesis 34, *Jubilees* 30, and Judith 9 have similar traditions. The books of Ezra and Nehemiah depict the Samaritans in opposition to the rebuilding of the Jerusalem temple and the city walls. No one knows exactly when this antagonism to the Samaritans began or why. The Samaritans are said to have only the five books of Moses as their scripture, but distinguished themselves from the Jews of Jerusalem by erecting their own temple on Mt. Gerizim. When Alexander the Great destroyed Samaria and garrisoned his troops there, many Samaritans fled to Shechem and elsewhere. Two centuries later, when John Hyrcanus rose to power in Jerusalem, he too destroyed the Samaritan temple and annexed the region of Samaria. Herod the Great built the city Sebaste there. Some Samaritans were involved in anti-Roman uprisings, and the Roman general Vespasian (later the emperor) slaughtered 10,000 Samaritans at Mt. Gerizim.

Among the biblical manuscripts at Qumran, several have "Samaritan" textual features. This is prominent in a manuscript of 4QExod^m penned in a paleo-Hebrew script. Possibly, the so-called *Rewritten Pentateuch* (RP) may reflect Samaritan scribal tendencies in part. It has been suggested that the *Temple Scroll* (11QT^a) and *Jubilees* give prominence to Jacob and the north. John 4:9 says that the Jews had no dealing with the Samaritans. Although this sounds like an exaggeration, it certainly reflects a centuries-long dislike of certain northerners. Historical records reveal nothing about the interactions, agreements, and disagreements among Samaritans and Jews.

The Zealots

Josephus writes about a group that arose during the rebellions that came in the wake of the death of Herod the Great. For Josephus these Zealots were essentially Pharisees who exhibited a greater desire to free themselves from Roman rule. Although originally the term "zealot" referred to those who followed a Galilean named Judas who was affiliated with a Pharisee Zadok, Josephus's Zealot party instigated the First Jewish Revolt against Rome. A descendent of Judas, led the Zealots atop Masada when it fell to the Romans in 74 CE.

Although the Scrolls do not speak of the Zealots, it is possible that a religious nationalism is represented in the Scrolls. 11QT^a, *Some Works of the Law* (4QMMT), and the *Rule of War* (1QM) reflect a heightened concern with the presence of foreigners in the Holy Land. In fact, certain passages in the Scrolls reveal a desire to see God bring foreign domination of Jerusalem and the Holy Land to an end. 1QM, no matter how one might describe it, reads like a play to be orchestrated by the priests to carry out a long war against and eradicate the foreigners.

Early Christians

The New Testament book Acts presents the earliest Christians as followers of the Jew Jesus. For these Jews the messiah had arrived in Jesus. People would now be liberated from sin and death. James, the brother of Jesus, led a faction of followers in Jerusalem that adhered to Jewish law. Like those who wrote the so-called community scrolls connected with the Qumran community, Jesus and his followers saw Scripture fulfilled in their lives and expected soon to experience salvation through God's spirit. Most likely the earliest followers of Jesus and James worshiped at the Jerusalem temple. Although it would be an exaggeration to say that the Qumran community and the Jesus community were identical in many respects, there are important similarities. The Teacher of Righteousness of the Scrolls and Jesus were treated as messianic figures. Both are victims of a contemporary. Some scrolls refer to the "children of light" and the "children of darkness," a motif familiar from the New Testament. Reverence for the angel Melchizedek is found in both groups. Apparently, according to interpretations of some of the Scrolls, the Qumran community lived in an antagonistic relationship with the Pharisees, as Jesus seemed to have done also. Possibly militant individuals like the Zealots could be found in both groups. In brief, while there are some significant parallels, probably the stringent practice of the Law, as found in major works among the Dead Sea Scrolls, was a centrally defining distinction between the two groups. Pauline Christianity, a missionary movement, distanced itself from the legal concerns of the leaders in Jerusalem and the legalists of the Scrolls. Devotion to the Law and the traditions of the elders was passed on to the rabbis, while the early Christian movement expanded throughout the Mediterranean sharing the message of a savior who could change one's life and bring peace and salvation.

Creation of Adam and Eve

⚜FOUR⚜

The Caves, the Scrolls, and
the Site Khirbet Qumran

A TOTAL OF ELEVEN caves in the limestone cliffs and the marl terrace near the Dead Sea preserved the remains of thousands of fragments and some nearly complete manuscripts of what are now called the Dead Sea Scrolls. According to the famous story, two or three Ta'amireh bedouin found a cave, threw a rock inside, hitting something solid, which prickled the curiosity of one of the bedouin. He entered the cave, discovered two large clay pots and the remains of eight others. From one of these pots he retrieved three parchment manuscripts. In time, the bedouin admitted that they had found four other writings. Although the bedouin had no idea what they had stumbled upon, it did not take long for them to learn that they would be valuable on the antiquities market. From then on bedouin and archaeologists seemed to compete in searching out the cliffs and the terrace near the site of Khirbet Qumran. A second cave was also discovered by the bedouin. Archaeologists found the third one. The Bedouin found a large fourth cave near the ruins of Khirbet Qumran. The archaeologists are credited with discovering Caves 5–10. Finally, the bedouin turned up the eleventh cave. Between 1947 and 1956 they had discovered three of the caves containing the majority of the scrolls and fragments—Caves 1, 4, and 11. The archaeologists found Cave 3, which held a tantalizing treasure of its own. This ongoing search for written treasures along the Dead Sea brought to life the most extensive Jewish literary collection from antiquity.[1]

CAVE 1

The bedouin stumbled onto Cave 1 in the fall of 1946 or the winter of 1947. By early 1948 several of the best-preserved scrolls had been photographed. Archaeologists had no idea of the whereabouts of this cave until a year later when a detachment of British and Jordanian troops found it in the cliffs. The cave lies about 1½km north-northwest of Khirbet Qumran west of the Dead Sea. The bedouin reported that the cave contained ten jars. Some were about two feet tall. 1QIsa[a] had been found in such a jar. It has been estimated there may have been over fifty jars that originally held 80-90 large and medium-sized scrolls, 1QS, 1QSa, and 1QSb, the 1QH, 1QM, 1QpHab, 1QGenApoc, and portions of several biblical works—Genesis, Exodus, Leviticus, Deuteronomy, Judges, Samuel, Ezekiel, Psalms, and Daniel. Other works included *Jubilees*, a book of Noah, a *Lamech Apocalypse*, a *Testament of Levi*, *Words of Moses*, a work about an ideal city like Jerusalem, a book of *Mysteries*, commentaries on Micah, Zephaniah, the Psalms, liturgies, and hymns. Much of what was discovered was highly fragmentary. When the archaeologists arrived, they discovered pottery, which they connected with some pieces at Khirbet Qumran, olive stones, date stones, desiccated dates, scraps of cloth, palm fibers, and even a leather phylactery case. Despite the poor state of many of the manuscripts, Cave 1 was indeed a major find because of the variety of writings—biblical, non-biblical, and communal—and other remains of human life.

CAVE 2

Roughly 150 m due south of the first cave the bedouin found Cave 2. The archaeologists who came later described this cave as having an uneven floor that had several small cavities on the two levels. Although the bedouin discovered and sold the few fragments that they took from this cave, the archaeologists only found the vestiges of several 'scroll' jars, like the ones in Cave 1, a lid, and three bowls. Cave 2 preserved the remains of the books of Genesis through Deuteronomy, Jeremiah, the Psalms, Job, Ruth, Ben Sira, *Jubilees*, Moses and David aprocrypha, a work about an ideal city (later called the *New Jerusalem* text), and others. Cave 2 was discovered and excavated in 1952.

CAVE 3

Located about 600m north of Cave 1, this cave is the most northerly of all the scrolls caves. The archaeologists, theologians, and historians discovered the sherds presumably of 35 jars that may have held between 70 and 140 small to medium-sized scrolls. Portions of Ezekiel, Psalms, Lamentations, a commentary on Isaiah, and few other fragments were salvaged among the other hides and papyrus strewn about. Propped up against the wall of the cave were two oxidized scrolls of copper. It turned out to be an inventory of hidden and buried treasures stretching from the Qumran area to Jericho, Jerusalem, and perhaps farther afield. These scrolls, which constituted two parts of a single work, came to be called the *Copper Scroll* (3Q15). Cave 3 was found in 1952.

CAVE 4

The proverbial mother lode was just a few hundred feet west from Khirbet Qumran across the ravine the bedouin found Cave 4. In short order they began to flood the antiquities market with about 15,000 fragments from this cave. Then came the archaeologists and scholars. This cave located in the marl terrace was in fact an artificially hewn chamber opening into two small chambers. In the walls there were holes dug rather deeply, as the archaeologists suggested, probably for inserting wooden planks that would support the great number of manuscripts stored there. The archaeologists salvaged about 100 different manuscripts. Another several hundred were bought by the Jordanian government, since this area no longer belonged to the British Mandate, and by several academic and religious institutions. Among the domestic pottery discovered were jars, jugs, a pot, a juglet, and a lamp. It has been claimed that the bedouin mixed fragments from the two separate chambers during their clandestine searches.

The discovery of Cave 4 gave impetus to the creation of an editorial team in 1956 that would study and publish the manuscripts and other artifacts from the cave. Roughly half a dozen scholars were lined up to do this work. One editor turned out a volume of twenty-nine non-biblical or quasi-biblical texts from Cave 4 in 1968. Two others published the *tefillin*, the *mezuzot*, and *targumim* in 1977. Another finished his thirty-nine manuscripts in 1982. Still, another editor, instead of publishing his lots of fragments, gave them to his graduate students in 1985–1986. Other editors were added to the team. In the year 1994 these editors published many of the manuscripts from Cave 4—a so-called legal letter between two high priests, a volume of parabiblical texts (an expression replacing the other term 'bible-like'), manuscripts of Deuteronomy through Kings, a work now known as the *Damascus Document* (CD), prophets, wisdom, and even documentary texts, twenty of which supposedly came from Cave 4.

The diversity of the texts, whether biblical, parabiblical, nonbiblical, or sectarian, is similar to what was found in the other caves. Of course, Cave 4 produced numerous works that had no counterparts in the other caves. Scholars have often claimed that this cave represented the library of the community that had lived at Khirbet Qumran 2,000 years ago. That being the case, one wonders whether some of the manuscripts found in the other caves had once been stored in Cave 4. No doubt, history has not been kind enough to help us answer such questions with any certainty.

CAVES 5-10

All of these caves were located in the marl terrace in the years 1952-1955. Caves 5 and 6 lie to west of the ruins. Besides the rotted fragments from approximately 25–50 scrolls, including Deuteronomy, Kings, Isaiah, Amos, Psalms, Lamentations, CD, copies of 1QS, manuscripts of the *New Jerusalem* text, and some curses, scholars think that the cave also served as human shelter at some point. Cave 6 held fragments from Genesis and Exodus in paleo-Hebrew, Deuteronomy, Kings, Psalms, the Song of Songs, Daniel, the *Book of Giants*, CD, some blessings, unknown apocrypha, and calendar materials. Cave 7 presumably had four jars and portions of 17 scrolls, including Exodus and Jeremiah in Greek. Cave 8 preserves fragments of Genesis, Psalms, a phylactery, and a *mezuzah*. Cave 9 yielded a single unidentifiable fragment. Cave 10, which may also have been used for shelter or protection, preserved an ostracon bearing ten letters of the Hebrew alphabet. Although these caves, along with Caves 2 and 3, are often considered minor caves, they are by no means insignificant. Most of them preserve some biblical works, manuscripts of communal literature, and relics of religious practice—the phylacteries and the *mezuzot*.

CAVE 11

In 1956, after discovering Caves 1 and 4, the bedouin stumbled upon Cave 11 about 2km north of Khirbet Qumran but less than 1km north of Cave 1 and about ½km south of Cave 3. Cave 11 preserved twenty-one manuscripts. Some of them were surprisingly intact compared with the thousands of fragments from Cave 4. Perhaps one of the biggest prizes was a large *Psalms Scroll* (11QPs^a) now known for its unexpected arrangement of traditional psalms and other previously unknown psalms. There was also a *targum* on the book of Leviticus. Other manuscripts from the cave include Leviticus, Deuteronomy, Psalms, *Jubilees*, some blessings, and hymns. Although the magnificent *Temple Scroll* (11QT^a) was acquired from the home of an antiquities dealer, it too presumably derived from Cave 11. A work named the *Songs of the Sabbath Sacrifice* (11QShirShab), of which there are fragments in Cave 4 (4QShirSab) and at Masada, was also discovered.

THE CAVES, THE SCROLLS, AND THE SETTLEMENT AT KHIRBET QUMRAN

The Jewish Bible, the books of Maccabees, and Josephus depict the caves along the Jordan River and the Dead Sea as places of temporary refuge in times of political and religious crises. The Bar Kokhba letters show that this was the case during the Second Jewish War against the Rome. But already in the year 69 CE or a little later, the Romans seem to have destroyed the settlement at Khirbet Qumran.

In the years after the Cave 1 manuscripts were made public and archaeologists had studied the cave, scholars began to think that the many caves in the limestone cliffs and the marl terrace were perhaps storage, living, and workshop areas. Except for Cave 5, the other caves were used to store or hide scrolls and partial manuscripts.

Caves 3 and 10, in particular, were thought to have served as living quarters because of their size and layouts. Perhaps Cave 4 also housed a few people at some time. Those who have entered Cave 4 say it is the only cave where one could endure the extreme heat of the Dead Sea area. Scholars think that Caves 7–9 functioned as workshops. Cave 8 was presumably a place for making tabs for binding up scrolls. Scraps of phylactery cases found in Caves 1, 4, 7, and 8 suggest that these caves served in some capacity as shelter.

The 1952 survey in the wilderness of Judaea located about three hundred caves, many of which had been at least temporary homes for some individuals. Perhaps their occupants were goatherds, shepherds, travelers, desperados, or perhaps even leaders of the Jewish society. Most likely, the people settled at Khirbet Qumran were connected to those who placed the scrolls in the caves. Of the nearly three hundred caves viewed, only 10 of the 11 Dead Sea Scrolls caves preserved inscribed texts. In Cave 10, there was a single ostracon.

Although one might naturally connect the ruins at Khirbet Qumran with the caves based on proximity, especially Cave 4, just what are the material connections that have been discovered? In both Cave 1 and at Khirbet Qumran the so-called scroll jars were found. This linch pin seemed to be enough to permit both the site and the scrolls in the caves to be designated as Essene, an ancient group given attention in the writings of Josephus, Philo, and Pliny.

KHIRBET QUMRAN

The ruins of Khirbet Qumran are located about 20km east of Jerusalem, 15km south of Jericho, 32km north of 'En Gedi, and walking distance from the Dead Sea. In 1861 the F. de Saulcy believed he had stumbled upon the biblical city Gomorrah. F.-M. Abel took a look at the cemetery and said it was an Arabic or pre-Mohammedan graveyard. In the early twentieth century Gustav Dalman identified the ruins as a Roman fortress.[2] This is precisely what Roland de Vaux, Khirbet Qumran's chief archaeologist, thought before reading the scrolls changed his mind. Scholars have also drawn attention to "the City of Salt" mentioned in Josh 15:62, suggesting the antiquity of the site. Qumran's *lamelek* ("for the king") stamps show that it probably was connected with the Judaean monarchy in the Iron age.

Once the material culture, primarily the ceramic types, was connected between the caves and Khirbet Qumran, then archaeologists spent several years working on the site and developing a chronology. Most of what has been written and said about Khirbet Qumran comes from Roland de Vaux's *Archaeology and the Dead Sea Scrolls*, a series of popular lectures presumably based on his journals and field notes.[3] Even in the Iron Age this site had been inhabited, but after that it seems to have been abandoned until the second century BCE at least. Roland de Vaux, head of the archaeological work at Khirbet Qumran, used pottery and coins to date the levels of settlement in the Hellenistic period. Although he spoke of a Period Ia at Qumran, he admitted regularly that this occupation level usually could not be separated from the later Period Ib. E.-M. Laperrousaz and Philip Davies had demonstrated that the site had not been settled in the second century BCE.[4] Recently the archaeologist Jodi Magness decided to eliminate Period Ia altogether and start her analysis with Period Ib.[5]

	DE VAUX	MAGNESS
Period Ia	ca. 130–100 BCE	not distinguishable
Period Ib	ca. 100–31 BCE	ca. 100–9/8 or 4 BCE
Period II	4–1 BCE to 68 CE	4–1 BCE to 68 CE
Period III	68–73/74 CE	68–73/74 CE

During Period Ib de Vaux has surmised that an earthquake caused the site to be abandoned for about thirty years. Magness as well as others before and after her propose that the earthquake caused much disruption of life at Qumran. They believe that more or less the same community of people stayed at Qumran roughly from 100 BCE or some decades thereafter until the Romans destroyed the site in 68 CE and was maintained by the Romans for a few years.

De Vaux characterized Period Ib as Qumran's definitive phase, because it was expanded in many respects. Water channels were constructed as were two rectangular cisterns. Covered buildings, rooms, and kilns were added. Next to the northern entrance had been a two-story tower. Workshops were installed. There was an assembly room, apparently with benches for sitting. A paved rectangular room with fireplaces may have been a kitchen. A rather large stepped cistern was constructed in the southern part of the building, for water supply was a central concern of this period. A room where more than 1,000 fragmentary vessels had been stacked up has been designated as a crockery. There were also courtyards. According to published plans de Vaux's Period Ia, which was rectangular in shape, it would have measured roughly 40m by 30m. Periods Ib and II were built upon the older rectangular structure but was extended on the northwestern, the western, the southwestern, and southeastern sides, which makes the settlement look rather rhomboidal (but approximately 602m^2).

Most peculiar, but perhaps directly pertinent to the function of the settlement are the cemeteries 50m east of the settlement. Already in 1873 some of the graves were dug up and the remains of skeletons lying supine were discovered. De Vaux identified an orderly central cemetery for males and secondary ones for females and children. Of the 43 graves opened, 30 have been identified as male, 7 as female, and 4 as graves for children. Now it is even doubted that one can make gender identifications based on the remains. Similar burials have since been discovered south of Qumran at Ain el Ghuweir, north of Qumran at Jericho, to the west in Jerusalem, and to the east in Transjordan. Therefore, although the orientation of the corpse may indicate something different about the community that settled Qumran and or was buried there, no longer can one say that these people were isolated.

De Vaux, Magness, and others define periods Ib, II, and the III, the brief Roman phase by the architectural structures, the pottery types, and the coins. Because of the burned layer above level II, arrowheads, and coins that date to 68 CE, the second year of the first Jewish War against Rome, it is believed that a Roman attack on Khirbet Qumran ended its century to century-and-a-half communal existence. Still, even if the people of Khirbet Qumran and the caves were one and the same, who were they?

THE NATURE AND FUNCTION OF KHIRBET QUMRAN

Most scholars of Khirbet Qumran believe that the Dead Sea Scrolls belonged to and were written and cared for by the inhabitants of the site. Others insist that many scrolls were brought to the settlement from outside. Both views can be right. Unfortunately, not a single scroll was found on the site. A single controversial inscribed ostracon was discovered in the 1990s and was interpreted by some to refer to an individual's deeding property upon admission to the Qumran community.[6] This view has come under attack because the word in question—supposedly *yahad*—is illegible. Unlike the biblical and non-biblical manuscripts discovered atop Masada as well as the lots, Khirbet Qumran itself yielded no literary or religious texts.

The experienced scholar, Eliezar Sukenik, already connected the community of these scrolls with Josephus's Essenes shortly after he acquired them. A little later, the younger scholar, Frank M. Cross Jr., placed the burden of disproving the Essene identification on anyone who doubted this view. Jodi Magness does the same in a slightly different way by posing an either or question: Should Khirbet Qumran be interpreted as a sectarian settlement although no scrolls turned up there, or should one assume that the scrolls came from the settlement? She first says that one ought not treat the site as a sectarian settlement nor as a villa, manor, commercial headquarters, or fortress. She adds that the site is unparalleled because of the combination of the cemetery, the ritual baths, and the deposits of animal bones. Like de Vaux and others before her, Magness opts to use the scrolls to elucidate the dead stones of Khirbet Qumran and interpret the site as a communal center of the Essenes.

Magness argues that the potters at Qumran fabricated their own pots because of their heightened concern with ritual purity. Connected with the issue of importing impurities, she emphasizes the absence of several ceramic types found at many other contemporary sites. These include Western Terra Sigillata, amphoras, Roman mold-made oil lamps, Eastern Sigillata A, and Pseudo-Nabatean fine ware. On the other hand, Magness interprets Qumran's cylindrical and ovoid jars as serving to preserve purity and religious rules. The wide mouths prevented spillage. Instead of having been sealed with a stopper of some sort, these jars were probably covered with bowl shaped lids so that the injunction against breaking seals on the Sabbath would not be violated. She connects this observation directly to such a law in CD 11:9. Magness also believes that cylindrical and ovoid jars could have been used in conjunction with funnels and dippers to avoid the creation of an impure stream of liquid: "and also regarding the pouring, we say that it contains no purity. And similarly the pouring does not separate the impure (from the pure) for the poured liquid and what is in the receptacle are alike, a single liquid" (4QMMT B55–58). In short, dry and liquid foods stored in these containers were believed to be ritually pure.

Magness also connects the *miqva'ot* or immersion pools with the intensified purity concerns of the community. These pools would have served to purify one before meals, after visiting the cemetery, after toilet, after leaving a workshop, and in many other instances. Ronnie Reich has counted sixteen pools at Khirbet Qumran and designated ten of them as *miqva'ot*.[7] In fact, numerous *miqva'ot* in and around Jerusalem are similar in style and function. The mere number of immersion pools and cisterns suggests a major preoccupation with the need for water, and perhaps especially to carry out ritual immersions. Since several scrolls emphasize the topic, it is obvious that the *miqva'ot* at Qumran may have served people of several ranks and genders—priests, levites, Israelites, first-year initiates, second-year members, full members, men, women, and children. Magness draws many parallels to the purity concerns expressed in the 11QT[a]. One cannot pretend to know exactly how this community used the *miqva'ot* except to say that it would have been similar to how they were used in Jerusalem, Jericho, and other places. Recent regional studies show that numerous immersion pools exist at sites used by agricultural workers, people in transit, and worshipers. The phenomenon of *miqva'ot* does not prove an especially heightened attention to ritual purity.

Starting with de Vaux numerous discoveries of broken animals bones have been interpreted as evidence of communal meals that were understood as analogous to the sacrificial meals of priests at the Jerusalem temple. This seems, however, to be reading too much into bones, which were buried around the perimeter of the dining areas and in one instance inside the complex. Evidence for an indoor toilet also complicates matters, because Josephus said that the Essenes dug holes in open areas such as a field carefully covering their excrement, and because 11QT^a legislates for covered toilet buildings at a distance from cities and the temple. Perhaps one should not try to force a very detailed theory of sacred space on the settlement at Khirbet Qumran, but rather one should be satisfied with having recognized its excessive concern with purity and simplicity, two features that at once represent a challenge to Hellenistic and Roman culture in Judaea. In light of this, Magness says, the inhabitants of Qumran were not Jerusalem's upperclass Sadducees. What seems clear is that the inhabitants of Khirbet Qumran disliked ostentation and chose to emphasize purity in some or all aspects of their daily life. The immersion pools do require explanation, but do not point us unambiguously in the direction of one or another Jewish group in antiquity.

THE SCRIPTORIUM

Roland de Vaux initially thought that Khirbet Qumran had served as a fortress. After he began to study the scrolls from Cave 1 his interpretation changed. He believed strongly that a second-storey room had served as a scriptorium for the scoring and copying of manuscripts, and here he was of course alluding to the Dead Sea Scrolls. His chief body of evidence was plaster that was reconstructed to represent a writing table measuring 15m in length and two or three inkwells.[8] In more recent years Robert Donceel and Pauline Donceel-Voute questioned the function of the plastered objects and interpreted the "tables" as reclining benches for a dining area.[9] Nowadays both views are treated as suspect.

OTHER IDEAS ABOUT THE SETTLEMENT

Not only Roland de Vaux, but even explorers from the previous century thought Khirbet Qumran had served as a fort or outpost. This was certainly true in the Iron Age, and the remains of its tower suggest this was at least one of its functions. Nevertheless, neither the tower nor the walls of the settlement would have held off attackers very long. Based on their reinterpretation of the plastered pieces that had fallen from the second storey, Donceel and Donceel-Voute suggested that these pieces had served as reclining benches in a dining room.[10] They also mentioned the pieces of columns and vestiges of glass in her argument that Qumran not be described as a haven of "monastic simplicity."[11] Contradicting other analysts Donceel-Voute emphasizes the existence of molded ceramics, imports, bottles with decoration, lids for amphorae, colored stone slabs for pavements, key-fibula, bone ivory, and even a fluted urn.[12]

Yitzhar Hirschfeld, who believes that Khirbet Qumran was occupied in Period Ia, posits that the site served different purposes at distinct times. He views Khirbet Qumran in a broader, more regional context as a fortified component of an estate that extended from Qumran to 'Ain Feshka. In the Hasmonean period it may have served as a fort. In the Herodian period this complex was involved in the perfume industry.[13] J. Patrich discovered a single jug containing a balsamic substance that perhaps had been used in perfumes.[14] Pliny the Elder (23–79 CE), in his *Natural History* 12.54 [112–118] describes Jericho and the Dead Sea areas as quite fertile.

Still not satisfactorily explained is the connection between the huge graveyard, the immersion pools at the settlement, and the scrolls deposited in the caves.[15] Was it a place where local workers were laid to rest? Could it have been a place to which lepers came to die? Was it a communal headquarters of a hyper-orthodox religious group and the place where its members were carefully buried? Apparently, some of the dead had been transported there from elsewhere.

If you visit Khirbet Qumran today you will see rocks and structures and modern signs explaining the function of various areas. The simplicity remains. The architectural and ceramic variety was removed long ago. The aridity of the area is impressive. How does one make the supposed simplistic of the site fit with the ownership of scrolls, not to mention a fully operational scribal industry lasting for nearly two centuries? The scrolls were obviously not the products of an uneducated working class, but rather the concerns of many pious and studious individuals, perhaps schools, and synagogues.

Most scholars admit that many scrolls found in the caves were imported from elsewhere. It would seem that the scrolls were somehow connected both with the settlement at Khirbet Qumran and the Jerusalem temple. Anyone who would deny the connection of the owners of the scrolls to the Jerusalem and those who participated in the temple need to explain how roughly 850 manuscripts, of which over half are biblical or quasi-biblical in nature, were composed, copied, used at Khirbet Qumran and stored in caves at various distances from the site. One should also not forget that perhaps many manuscripts perished in the caves or were salvaged by those departing the area at the time of the First Jewish Revolt and even centuries later.

The interpretation of the ruins of Khirbet Qumran depends in every case on the human imagination. The first excavator certainly used his eyes when he interpreted the settlement at Khirbet Qumran in light of a few passages in the scrolls and sketched out the occupational history of Khirbet Qumran. No doubt, the site takes on an added aspect when one learns that it had once held more impressive architecture and ceramic pieces of a patrician nature than those that have been published to date. This would fall more in line with the abundance and variety of scroll fragments from Cave 4 and the more distant caves. To be honest, it is true that we are still guessing about the identity of the people who lived at Khirbet Qumran, the functions of components of the site, and the identity of those who wrote, copied, and treasured the Dead Sea Scrolls.

POTTERY INSCRIPTIONS AND KHIRBET QUMRAN

The world of Dead Sea Scrolls studies was shocked by the report of an archaeological discovery at the settlement of Qumran that demonstrated how community members deeded their properties to the community. There were three ostraca from two different texts found in an unstratified context at the base of the site's eastern wall. The first ostracon was read as legally transferring lands and a slave to the Qumran community.[16] The second and third ostracon still preserved several names and locations.[17]

Despite its illegibility, its editors optimistically deciphered the first ostracon as a legally binding instrument proving the communal procedure for accepting a member into the inner circle of the sectarian community at Qumran.

In year two of . . . in Jericho, Honi son of . . . gave to 'El'azar son of
Nahamani . . . Hisday from Holon . . . from this day to perpetui[ty
and the boundaries of the house and . . . the fig trees, the ol[ive
trees, and] when he completes. . . .

This text has 15–16 partly illegible lines. For the first time, if the
editors are correct, the word *yaḥad*, the community, is used outside
1QS. The controversial line reads: "when he fulfills (his oath) to the
community" (l. 8). Some scholars agree with their reading. Others have
expressed skepticism based on the difficulty of deciphering faded or
missing letters. Scholars are also in disagreement about the date of the
ostracon. The original editors date it between 50 and 69 CE. Another
paleographer believed it could be a century older. Quite possibly the
ostracon came from the period after the First Jewish Revolt against the
Romans (post-70 CE).

The other broken ostraca have been all but ignored, primarily
because one must completely conjure up a historical context for it. It
mentions the names Jehoseph son of Nathan and sons from 'En Gedi.
Taken together with the so-called *yaḥad* ostracon, they preserve four
names of individuals who lived at Khirbet Qumran or traveled there in
the Roman period and had connections to Jericho, Holon, and 'En Gedi.
No one knows in what way any of these named individuals may have
been connected to the community settled at Khirbet Qumran.

WRITING EXERCISE C

For several decades scholars interpreted this square-shaped writing
as the travelogue of an itinerate doctor on his rounds.[18] John Allegro
described it as a mixture of translated Greek, Aramaic, and grammati-
cally irregular Hebrew. He compared it with the script of the average
physician. The calligraphy is quite attractive, but the text seemed to be
a listing of the names Caiphus, Mephibosheth, Hyrcanus Yani, Etros
Yose, Aquila, Zakariel, Eli, and Omriel. In Allegro's translation Hyrcanus
Yanni was receiving treatment for an ulcer. Someone else was diagnosed
as colicky. A certain Eli was the witness, and Omriel dictated the text.

A second interpretation came from Joseph Naveh who viewed the
writing as an exercise, a sort of warm-up abecedary.[19] He cited comparable practice alphabets from Murabba'at, Masada, and other places. The
key to the work, in his view, is to see it as a list of names in alphabetical
order. Quite possibly the scribe was not merely following the order of

the letters of the alphabet, because he was not consistent in this. One sees the alphabetic model in line 1, but in lines 4–5 the words start with the Hebrew *mem*. In lines 6–9 one sees again the alphabet. It seems that something else was influencing the scribe.[20]

The letter combination *shrh* in line 2 makes no sense by itself, but if the writer is learning to distinguish similar sounding letters, practicing with *samek* and *taw* could be helpful. The combinations *shrh* and *tyr* share three similar sounds—the *s/t*, the *resh*, and the *h/q*. It is probably no accident that both words include a *samek*, one at the beginning and one at the end. The Greek-sounding "*os*" or "*is*" pops up frequently as well as the Hebrew *shin*. If one pronounces the first word in line 4, it repeats the sounds practiced in lines 2–3. In lines 4–5 one reads the combinations *mgns*, *mlkyh*, *mnys*. In lines 7 one finds *hlkos* and *hrqnos*, two combinations which have the confusing letters "l" and "r" in them.

Naveh is correct about the alphabet, but beyond that the writer is playing with words. He is essentially practicing phonics, making combinations, especially combinations that may be difficult for someone. Perhaps the scribe was a foreigner trying to distinguish in writing the letter sounds that he heard dictated. Whether the scribe was simply warming up his pen or even making an effort to separate sounds that are not easy for him, one wonders whether *Writing Exercise* C might have further ramifications. Perhaps it does.

Much of the full orthography that characterizes scrolls written in the "Qumran" style was an aid to pronunciation. The practicing of sound combinations recalls the 4Q266 frg. 5 II: "Whoever speaks too fast or with a staccato voice and does not split his words to make heard, no one from among these shall read the Book of [the] La[w] that he may not misguide someone in a capital manner . . ."[21] This rule applies to Aaronite priests whose inability to inscribe properly was due to their tendency not to hear the language well. Priests who demonstrated such a weakness would be disqualified. One might imagine Jews from abroad and converts to Judaism trying to pass some sort of literacy requirement.[22] This is of course speculative, but still within the realm of the possible.

A PROPHETIC TEXT ON STONE FROM
THE FIRST CENTURY BCE/CE

In 2003 Ada Yardeni, a well-known palaeographer of the Scrolls, received photographs of a stone slab almost 1m tall and 1/3m wide. She dated its script to the late first century BCE or the early first century CE.[23] This work was penned with ink very much like the Dead Sea Scrolls and in fact it was carefully written. The first and last penned lines are illegible. Fewer than 300 words have been preserved. Because the unwritten side of the work is smooth, Yardeni thinks it may have hung on a wall or on a floor.

The text on the slab sounds like a biblical prophecy. It refers to "my (?) house, Israel" (this formulation or a variation of it), "Jerusalem" (seven times), "in three days" (twice), "in a little while" (once), "prophets" (twice), "messenger or angel" (four times), and "Michael" (once), "Gabriel" (three times), "David" (twice). The text emphasizes the greatness of Jerusalem despite its many enemies, the prophets, the Hasidim, and the glory of God. The prophecy emphasizes that God will shake the heavens and the earth in three days or a little while. The text mentions "prophets that I have sent to my people, three" (column B line 70) and later "three shepherds" (column B line 75). In spite of an imperfect text, the author seems to want to announce that God, by means of his angels, will save and restore Jerusalem.

A key feature of the text is the repetitious mention of God in several forms.

> l. 10 *kn 'mr 'lhym tsv'wt*
> l. 13 *[kn] 'mr yhwh 'lhy 'sr'l*
> l. 18 *ky 'mr yhwh tsv'wt 'lhy ysr'l*
> ll. 19–20 *ky 'mr yhwh 'lhym tv'wt*
> ll. 25–26 *kvod yhwh 'lhym tsv'wt 'lhy ysr'l*
> l. 29 *kn 'mr yhwh 'lhym tsv'wt 'lhy ysr'l*
> ll. 39–40 *y'mr yhwh tsv'wt*
> ll. 57–59 *ky 'mr yhwh tsv'wt 'lhy ysr'l*
> l. 68 *yhwh tsv'ot 'l[h]y ysr'l*
> l. 69 *kh 'mr yhwh tssv't*
> l. 84 *yhwh tsv't*

These divine epithets serve to open individual prophetic sayings within the larger context.

Obviously, this prophecy written on stone concerns the house of Israel, the Israelites, God's sending of prophets and messengers such as Michael and Gabriel. Around l. 10 one reads "Thus said Elohim Tsevaot: I will tell you about the great things concerning Jerusalem." This is followed immediately by "Thus said Yahweh Elohe Israel: Behold, all the foreigners [will come up] against Jerusalem." However, there will be

Hasidim and of course there was David, God's servant, who preserved faithfulness in the land. In lines 19–22 one reads: "For Yahweh Elohim Tsevaot Elohe Israel . . . the evil will be broken before the righteous." In lines 23–25 one reads of God's vengeance: "Blessed is the glory of Yahweh Elohim from his dwelling . . . In a little while I will rattle the heavens and the earth." Another link in the prophecy seems to start right there in lines 25: "Behold, the glory of Yahweh Elohim Tsevaot Elohe Israel: These are the chariots at the gate of Jerusalem, at the gates of Judah." Much later in the text one reads clearly: "Sealed is the blood of the sacrifices of Jerusalem, for Yahweh Tseva[ot] Elohe Israel . . . Thus said Yahweh Tsevaot Elohe Israel" (57–59). "Thus said Yahweh Tsevaot Elohe Israel: I send prophets to my people" (lines 69–70). And David, the servant, is mentioned again (line 72). One reads again of the shaking of the heavens and the earth (line 73; cf. lines 24–25). As the prophecy comes to its conclusion, one reads of Yahweh Tseva[o]t: "Then you will stand forever" (lines 84–87). Yardeni and others understand the text as messianic. David is mentioned as the model of faithful servant, but there seems to be no reference to any messianic figure. It is a simple multi-part prophecy of destruction and hope.

A comparison of the stone's text with the Dead Sea Scrolls reveals no really obvious similarities in language, theology, key topics, and history. Even though the handwriting appears to be very old, there is nothing at all "Qumranic" about it. Nor does the stone's inscription reflect the careful literary hands of the Dead Sea Scrolls. Even the formulation of the prophecy or prophecies bears no resemblance to the eschatological texts among the Dead Sea Scrolls.

The jury is still out on the provenance of this so-called Vision of Gabriel. The controversial line 80 is intriguing. Does the text actually read "in three days, live! I, Gabriel, com[mand] you!"? It has been suggested, probably with merit, that the text originally had the Hebrew word 'ot, which refers to a heavenly sign.[24] No one has yet demonstrated the connection between this inscribed stone, the Dead Sea Scrolls, and Khirbet Qumran.

PREPARING SCROLLS FOR INSCRIPTION

Several comments in the Hebrew Bible indicate that important texts were written and copied on scrolls (Jer 36:2; Ezek 2:9–10, 31–33; Zech 5:1; and Ps 40:8). The discovery of the Scrolls in the Qumran caves provides ample evidence of the picture presented in the Bible.[25] The Scriptures do not offer instructions on the preparation of a scroll, on its length, and other physical features. The length of a scroll varied depending on the extent of a particular written work. 1QIsa[a], which has 66 chapters, measures some 7.5 meters. 11QT[a] measures about 9 meters. Some scholars have speculated that the 4Q394–395 may have run to 30 meters in length, although that seems unlikely based on physical and literary considerations.[26] These are all parchment scrolls. The famous Papyrus Harris in the British Museum, which contains the Egyptian *Book of the Dead*, is 40 meters long.

There is evidence among the biblical scrolls that Genesis and Exodus, Exodus and Leviticus, as well as Leviticus and Numbers were sometimes combined in a single scroll. This is not true for Deuteronomy, but the Scroll of the Minor Prophets shows that numerous shorter works could be combined.

The majority of the Scrolls were made of prepared animal skins. A very small number of works was written on papyrus. Sometimes the same literary work has been found on both parchment and papyrus. Jeremiah 8:8 and Ps 45:2 refer to the scribe's pen, and Jer 36:18 mentions ink. Among the ruins only two or three inkwells were found. The inks used in the Scrolls were either carbonic or vegetable.

The production of the Scrolls found in the caves involved a variety of skills, tools, and materials. One first needed animals, such as sheep, goats, calves, or kids, whose hides required treatment before any inscription could take place. For a long time scholars thought that Khirbet Qumran had its own tanning workshop and a scriptorium for the scribes. The skins were first washed, soaked, and cleansed of all flesh and hair. Some of the scroll fragments still preserve bristles today. Then the skins were soaked in soft cold or warm rain water. The duration of the process always depended on the size of the animal skin. In the tanning process, the hides would be treated with some type of vegetable or organic matter or dressed with alum and dusted with sifted chalk. Then the hide would be beaten in order to induce pliability.

Once the treatment process had been completed, the parchment was cut into sheets and sewn together to form a scroll. Either based on experience or request, this person decided the length, width, and height of the scroll. 11QT[a] was copied on nineteen sheets, each containing three to four columns in accord with a later rabbinic scribal convention mentioned in *Masseketh Soferim* 2.10: "No sheet should have less than three columns or more than eight." 1QIsa^a adheres to this norm until the final two sheets which have two columns each. The extant portions of the 1QM had nineteen or twenty columns. These were spread out rather evenly over five sheets. Sheet 1 had four columns; sheet 2, six; sheet 3, five; sheet 4, three, and sheet 5 has one or two columns.

The availability of parchment, the size of the parchment, probably dictated specific features of a scroll such as the number of scored columns to a sheet, the number of lines to a column, and the width of the margins. It is not clear whether the person who cut the parchment was also responsible for scoring it. Scoring involved using a pointed tool to horizontally line the columns and set the margins vertically. Nor does one know whether the person who sewed the sheets together was the same one who cut the parchment into pieces. Occasionally a used or damaged scroll needed a patch or an entirely new sheet. Several columns at the beginning of the 11QT^a were restored by a later scribe. The *targum* of Job has a round patch which shows the ancient needle holes and the Hebrew writing.

The preparation of a papyrus scroll involved cross-layering strips of papyrus at right angles, beating or pressing the strips together, and polishing the dried sheets with pumice, and cutting them to a standard size. All of this work would have required many of the tools used in working with parchment. A paste would have been made and applied. Nothing short of a highly skilled cottage industry supported the production and preparation before inscription. Once the parchment was ready for inscription, the scribe has to consider how much space he needed to copy his text. Often one sees that he first wrote moderately large, then realized that his space was becoming scarce, and he adjusted the size of his lettering. Sometimes the writing became much smaller and cramped.

PALEOGRAPHY OF THE SCROLLS

Historians and theologians who study the Dead Sea Scrolls depend on the dating of numerous types of ancient Hebrew and Aramaic handwritings, because its experts have not only described the intricacies of each script but have also created a relative chronology of scripts. Without this hypothesized chronology, one is left to wonder when roughly a certain manuscript was written or copied. The study of Hebrew and Aramaic scripts was relatively new when Cave 1 was discovered. Eliezer Sukenik, the first editor of the 1QH, immediately noted the Qumran scripts were similar to first century CE funeral inscriptions from Jerusalem. Soon after the discovery of the thousands of fragments in Cave 4, Frank M. Cross Jr., like John Trever before him, pointed out the similarities to the Nash Papyrus, which his teacher, William F. Albright, had dated to the time of the Maccabees. Even without any basis in scientific fact, since the comparative material was either older or younger in most cases, scholars had already decided that the scripts belonged chiefly between the second century BCE and the first century CE.

Qumran paleographers established their upper limit with the Aramaic papyri from Elephantine in Egypt, which was described as a cursive hand dating to the fifth century BCE. The Edfu papyri came from the third century BCE. At the chronologically lower end belong the Masada and Wadi Murabba'at writings. Absolute datings are provided on this end by a contract from Murabba'at from the second year of Nero (55/56 CE) and a Bar Kokhba letter dated internally to 134 CE. The inscribed materials found at Masada would naturally predate its destruction in 73/74 CE. In practice, the paleographers placed the Qumran scrolls within a broad timeframe and then developed a typology of scripts matching historical periods within that framework—Archaic or pre-Maccabean, Maccabean-Hasmonean, and Herodian. In 1959 Frank M. Cross's typology and periodization was published and revolutionized ancient Hebrew and Aramaic paleography.[27]

Paleographers deal in images on ancient surfaces. Most of the Qumran scrolls were inscribed on parchment, but some papyri were preserved. The paleographer's first duty is to observe and record information about the script. Numerous characteristics of a single script were then compared with other scripts with the goal of categorizing them in relation to each other. Handwriting analysts carefully study: (a) the size or stance of the letters, (b) their angularity or roundness, (c) the length of pen strokes, (d) the length of the letters' legs, (e) how letters are oriented toward a visibly scored line, (f) ligatures between letters, and (g) ornamental features such as ticks. At this stage paleographers are helped by manuscripts that are dated internally or by some connection with another text. Dates are gradually assigned, and then the paleographers begin to talk about the evolution of letters of the alphabet and subsequently of scripts.

Cross designated the formal hand as Archaic (250–150 BCE), Hasmonean (150–30 BCE), or Herodian (30 BCE–70 CE). The year 70 CE is used at the final date, because traditionally scholars say that the Romans destroyed the settlement at Khirbet Qumran about that time. Within these broad periods Cross and other paleographers discern evolved letter forms which are described as early or late Hasmonean, Hasmonean transitional to Herodian. Hasmonean and Herodian writing styles include formal, semi-formal, and cursive. Cross characterizes the Archaic script as broad with squat letters of varying size, and little if any distinction in the use of medial and final forms of certain letters. This script would look more like the Elephantine and Edfu scripts than the later scripts from Qumran. Cross dates a Samuel manuscript (4QSam[b]) to the late third century BCE and a Jeremiah manuscript (4QJer[a]) a little later. An Exodus manuscript (4QEx[f]) is dated to the late third or early second century BCE. Several manuscripts date to the second quarter of the second century BCE—Ecclesiastes (4QQoh[a]), *Prayers* (1Q34bis, 4Q507-509), and Deuteronomy (4QDeut[a]). Following Albright, Cross dates the Nash Papyrus to 150 BCE and treats this datum as a chronological peg. However, he only dates a few biblical manuscripts to this period. No non-biblical manuscript has been assigned paleographically to Cross's Archaic period. The majority of manuscripts were copied in the Hasmonean and Herodian periods.

For the scripts designated Hasmonean, Cross discerns a tendency toward uniformity in size yet an idiosyncracy in shading. The oldest manuscript of 1QS dates to the middle or the late Hasmonean period as do fragments of CD (although most manuscripts of the latter work are Herodian). By the Herodian period the letters have become rather uniform, and there is a feeling for the base line. Ligatures and serifs (ornamentation) are in style. Cross is most comfortable when describing scripts from this time. The earliest Herodian form hand is, according to his analysis, that of 1QM, which can be compared with a Numbers manuscript (4QNum[b]). Among the latest Herodian hands are 4QDeut[j], 4QDan[b], and 4QPsalms, which Cross compared with the biblical manuscripts discovered at Murabba'at. The commentaries, known as *pesharim*, on prophets and psalms, come from the Herodian period. One manuscript of 4QShirShab/11QShirShab, a work that also turned up at Masada, is categorized as Late Herodian. Some of the last writings copied among the Qumran collections were books of the Bible—4QDeut[j], 4QDan[b], 4QPss, and 11QPs[a]. Several manuscripts of CD and 1QS come from the Herodian period, even if versions existed much earlier. The majority of the surviving manuscripts derive from this last period.

Several manuscripts among the Scrolls were written in an archaizing paleo-Hebrew script. Just as this script was used on coins to appeal to nostalgia, it was also employed in certain manuscripts to give them a feel of age and authority, if not a certain mystique: 1-2paleoLeviticus, 4QpaleoGenesis-Exodus[l], 4QpaleoGenesis[m], 4QpaleoExodus[m], 4Qpaleo-Deut[r,s], 4QpaleoJoshua, 4QpaleoJob, 6QpaleoGenesis, 6QpaleoExodus, 11QpaleoLeviticus, and *Horoscopes* in part (4Q186). In some texts the divine names Yahweh and El were inserted written in paleo-Hebrew into the body of the text written in a square script (11QPs[a], 4QCD, 4Qpseu-doDaniel[a]ar). It is difficult to date the paleo-Hebrew scripts.

Cave 4 also yielded Greek manuscripts of Leviticus, Numbers, and Deuteronomy, which demonstrate that probably among the owners and users of these scrolls were Greek-speaking Jews. P. J. Parson dates these manuscripts to the late first century BCE and not later than the early years of the first century CE.[28]

Until roughly the last decade scholars followed Cross's typology of scripts and his chronological assessments rather slavishly. Increasingly, researchers speak with less confidence of his precise datings of letter forms and hands to 25-, 30-, 40-, and 50-year ranges. Also rather recently carbon-14 analyses have been deployed to support both Cross's claims and his overall periodization. The results are, however, rather difficult to interpret and, above all, it should be remembered that this form of physical analysis has broader ranges depending upon the level of statistical probability one accepts. Even Ada Yardeni, an Israeli paleographer, examined several manuscripts not studied by Cross. Among these are the important communal copies of the CD from Cave 4. She classifies 4Q271 as "early Herodian or Late Herodian," while she says 4Q266 is contemporary with 4Q271 and other manuscripts that are simply called Herodian. Thus, even Yardeni's terminology is not entirely consistent when typologizing various scripts for the same document. 4Q268 is called "calligraphic Herodian," by which she obviously means to say that the script is beautiful.[29] Certainly, all scripts are relatively speaking attractive or not. Some were penned by a more skilled hand than others. Some certainly derive from distinct handwriting traditions. Two scribes of the same generation and sharing similar scribal traditions may have indeed used different scripts.

Similarly, two palaeographers such as Cross and Yardeni can dis-agree on reading the same text and placing it within a chronological framework. The best example is that of an ostracon discovered at Khirbet Qumran in the late 1990s. Cross treated its chaotic script with its multiple executions of the same letter forms as late Herodian and said he could read the word *yaḥad*, community. Yardeni also attributed the script to the Herodian period, but admitted it could be older and she read "types of trees,"[30] where Cross saw *yaḥad*.

Hebrew and Aramaic paleography—that is, script typology—is rigorous in its description and well-meaning in its intentions, but it just cannot be precise about dating the hands in the Scrolls. It remains help-ful to use its broader periodization, even if only to establish the antiquity of the Scrolls and provide a backdrop against which to read many of the documents.

Scholars date most of the Scrolls to the Hasmonean and Herodian periods. That means roughly that they belong the late second century BCE to the first century CE.[31] Some biblical manuscripts are older and some documentary texts appear to be younger. The *Copper Scroll*'s text was inscribed on metal. It has been considered Herodian or later. The same seems to be true for the *Yahad Ostracon*.[32] Numerous manuscripts were written in a paleo-Hebrew or in a cryptic script that is not easy to date or place within a certain period.

Damascus Document	Hasmonean, Herodian
Rule of the Commmunity, Rule of the Congregation, and Blessings	Hasmonean, Herodian
Rule of War	Hasmonean, Herodian
Thanksgiving Hymns	Hasmonean, Herodian
The Running Commentaries (*pesharim*)	Herodian
Genesis Apocryphon	Herodian
The Book of Jubilees	Hasmonean, Herodian
The New Jerusalem	Hasmonean, Herodian
The Copper Scroll	Herodian, post-Herodian
The Commentaries on Genesis	Hasmonean
Targums Leviticus and Job	Hasmonean, Late Herodian
Rewritten Pentateuch	Hasmonean,Herodian
The Apocryphon of Joshua	Herodian

Tobit	Hasmonean, Herodian
The Books of Enoch	Hasmonean, Herodian
Florilegium	Herodian
Testimonia	Hasmonean
Ordinances	Hasmonean
The Calendar Texts	Hasmonean, Herodian
Some Works of the Law	Hasmonean, Herodian
Wisdom Texts	Herodian
The Angelic Songs of the Sabbath Sacrifice	Hasmonean, Herodian
Documentary Texts	Herodian, post-Herodian
The Temple Scroll	Herodian
The Psalms Scroll (11QPs^a)	Herodian
Melchizedek	Hasmonean
The Yahad Ostracon	Herodian, post-Herodian
4QSam^b (1-2 Samuel)	Pre-Hasmonean
4QJer^a (Jeremiah)	PreHasmonean
4QExod^f (Exodus)	Pre-Hasmonean
4QQoh^a (Ecclesiastes)	Pre-Hasmonean
4QDeut^j	Herodian
4QDan^b	Herodian
4QPss(?)	Herodian

MODERN CARBON-14 DATING

In late 1950, barely three years after the discovery of carbon-14 dating process, G. Lankaster Harding, Director of the Jordanian Department of Antiquities, gave W. F. Libby of the University of Chicago a piece of the linen wrapping from Cave 1. Two months later Libby concluded that the linen dated roughly 33 CE +/- 200 years (167 BCE–233 CE). This established the antiquity of the scrolls. Later a burned palm log from Qumran locus 6 was dated to 66 CE +/- 85 years (19 BC–151 CE).

With the refinement of carbon-14 methods in conjunction with Accelerator Mass Spectrometry (AMS), only a milligram sample was necessary to obtain reliable results, which are expressed according to two levels of probability.[33] The 1σ probability provides a chronological range with a reported 68% confidence. The 2σ probability has a wider range with 95% confidence. The purpose of the AMS is to confirm to general reliability of the chronological results of previous paleographical analysis. Scholars often accept this presumed confirmation, although the actual results are much more complicated. In general, AMS shows that the scrolls are ancient and belong to the last centuries BCE and the first couple of centuries CE. Closer inspection shows that the paleographical datings, which of course have no intrinsic probability, demonstrate rather specific ranges. The 1σ and 2σ ranges are always much broader, sometimes overlapping with the palaeographical ranges and sometimes fall outside those ranges.

OTHER SCIENCES, TECHNOLOGY, AND THE SCROLLS

Besides the fascinating, but controversial, dating of scrolls by AMS, in recent years numerous scientific and technological advances are helping us to know more about the texts of the scrolls and the world from which the scrolls came. Using aDNA, that is, ancient DNA analysis, it is possible to determine whether two fragments came from the same animal hide. It may also suggest the original locations of herds and flocks before they were slaughtered and became part of the lives of the Dead Sea Scrolls. Already, we know that most scrolls were inscribed on goat and sheep skins. Some were written on calf skin. One can even talk about the texture of the sheep's wool. It is possible that the skins of gazelle, ibex, or deer we used. The application of aDNA as a genetic fingerprint is still in its infancy.[34]

In the 1950s and early 1960s Cave 4 fragments were photographed and given a designation. For example, one might speak of PAM 43.989–992, which are photographs of 11QShirShab. In the 1980s and 1990s Bruce and Kenneth Zuckerman used new experimental techniques in black-and-white, color, and infrared formats and used computer enhancement of digital images.[35] Gregory Bearman of the Jet Propulsion Laboratory in California and the Zuckermans combined forces and were able to provide better images of parts of 1QGenApoc.[36]

The official editions of the Dead Sea Scrolls, *Discoveries in the Judaean Desert* (DJD), benefited from enhanced photographic digitization in the 1990s and the 2000s. Now there is an electronic library of the Scrolls, and the Scrolls can be studied on the Internet.[37]

❊FIVE❊

The Bible and the Dead Sea Scrolls

AN EMERGING CANON

TRADITIONALLY, ONE SPEAKS OF the Jewish Bible having been essentially complete by the time of the Babylonian exile in 597 BCE. Some writers believe that editors continued to improve the biblical text for several more centuries. It has become increasingly difficult to talk comfortably about "the Bible," "the Scriptures," and "the canon" when referring to Jewish religious literature. Evidence from the Dead Sea Scrolls seems to make the conversation even more complicated, requiring us regularly to qualify our statements about the Jewish Bible. Although the terms "canon" or "doctrinal stipulation" are not used in ancient writings to establish the boundaries of the Jewish Bible, several writings from Second Temple times refer to an established body of venerated and sacred literature.

In the second century BCE, the author of Ben Sira (Ecclesiasticus) presents his grandfather's own wisdom instruction as a contribution to the writings read in the Jewish community: "Since many things and great have been delivered unto us through the Law and Prophets and the others who followed after them . . ." (the prologue). Under the rubrics "Law" and "Prophets" one usually imagines collections like the traditional books of Moses, Genesis through Deuteronomy, and the various prophetic works from Joshua on. But Ben Sira does not detail the parameters of his Scriptures. The category "the other books of our fathers" may have referred to known writings or even a more open set of acknowledged works of wisdom. Ben Sira's list of famous ancestors in chapters 44–49 starts with Enoch and continues down through Nehemiah. It seems that Ben Sira's list of authoritative writings looked very traditional.

Roughly contemporary with the composition of Ben Sira, 2 Maccabees recounts that Judas Maccabeus collected a number of writings: "These things [including a story about King Solomon] were also narrated in the archives or memoirs of Nehemiah; as well as how he founded a library and collected the books about the kings and the prophets and the books of David and letters of kings about sacred gifts" (1:13–15). One expects that the books about kings referred to collections like 1–2 Samuel, 1–2 Kings, and 1–2 Chronicles, while the books of David were psalms, and kings' letters about gifts may have alluded to books like Ezra and Nehemiah. But this is a conservative interpretation.

Writing about a Jewish group that he calls the Therapeutae, Philo Judaeus of Alexandria mentions their use of "laws and oracles delivered through the mouth of the prophets and psalms and other books by which knowledge and piety may be increased and perfected" (*On the Contemplative Life* 25).

The New Testament preserves a few statements shedding light on the issue of Jewish Scriptures. In Matt 22:34–40, Jesus, while being interrogated by the Pharisees, reduces the Law and the Prophets to the love of God and the neighbor. This does not deny the existence of a much larger body of religious literature, but merely summarizes their essence according to Jesus or the New Testament writer. As the interchange between Jesus and the Pharisees continued, the Psalms are cited as authoritative. Luke 24:27 mentions Moses probably as shorthand for "the books of Moses" and all the prophets. A few verses later, in Luke 24:44, the writer speaks of the Law of Moses, the Prophets, and the Psalms. Thus, it seems that well into the first century CE the list of Jewish Scriptures had concretized into three chief categories. However, "the other books" continued to exist and be used as well.

Near the end of the first century CE, Josephus, the Jewish general and historian wrote: "we do not possess myriads of inconsistent books, conflicting with each other. Our books, those which are justly accredited, are but two and twenty, and [these] contain the record of all time" (*Contra Apion* 1.37–39). This is a clear reference to a list very similar to that accepted by the rabbis and even until today. However, addressing a foreign audience, Josephus is trying to dispel the notion that the people of Judaea used a collection of religious literature that might contradict itself. He wanted to emphasize that his Scriptures contain a consistently truthful presentation of God and his people's activities throughout history. A perusal of Josephus's *Antiquities* shows that he was keenly aware of other Jewish writings from the Persian to the Roman periods.

The least ambiguous account of the list of acceptable Jewish religious writings appeared in 2 Esdras, a Greek work of the early second century CE. In chapter 14, Ezra engages five skilled scribes to record his dictation. At the end of forty days these five scribes had finished copying ninety-four scrolls. Then God, known as the Most High God, told Ezra: "Make public the twenty-four books that you wrote first and let the worthy and the unworthy read them, but keep the seventy that were written last, in order to give them to the wise among your people, for in them is the spring of understanding, the fountain of wisdom, and the river of knowledge" (14:44–48).

On the surface what these witnesses to Jewish Scriptures say seems confusing, but one can draw a few interesting conclusions.

1. Individual writers had different ways of talking about which writings should be used for religious edification.

2. None of these writers speaks of the specific contents of the collections to which they referred.

3. A nebulous concept of "other writings" existed, a notion which permitted the creation and publication of other wisdom works considered revelatory, inspired, and worthy of study.

4. Early on one could speak of the Law as a known body of sacred Scripture.

5. Over a period of time an accepted collection of prophets was added thus creating the expression "the Law and the Prophets."

6. In the first century CE, writers could speak about the Law of Moses, the Prophets, and the Psalms.

7. A traditional list of works, whose number was twenty-two or twenty-four, for public or communal consumption had more or less been established.

8. In addition to this public list, one learns that almost four times that many writings had some sort of divine or prophetic approval by the second century CE.

The biblical works among the Dead Sea Scrolls were copied within the extensive period that ran from the late Persian or early Hellenistic era until the period of Roman occupation of Israel in the first century CE. In a broader sense the collections known as the Dead Sea Scrolls reflect an extensive list of ancient Jewish writings that one could very well understand as public writings for general edification and other writings for the learned. Some of these scrolls make comments very much like those adduced from other writings in late antiquity.

Among the scrolls and fragments recovered in the Dead Sea caves scholars found portions of all the books of the known Jewish Bible except for Esther. Apparently these manuscripts did not preserve a definitive statement on the canon, but did offer recommendations for reading. They seem to assume that the Law, the Prophets, and the Psalms were authoritative. Among the books of Moses, Deuteronomy is the most represented legal work. Isaiah was the most frequently copied prophetic work, and numerous manuscripts of the Psalms survived two millennia.

It seems, however, that the book of *Jubilees* and perhaps the book of *Enoch* served the theological and needs of their original owners. CD cites the book of *Jubilees* as an authority on chronology. 11QT^a, which has been characterized as a sixth book of the Law, depends both on the known Pentateuch and expands that collection by including a variety of legal traditions that had not been known previously. For someone and some group this majestic work represented the word of God just as much as the received Law of Moses. In the exhortation section of the 4QMMT, the writer, who identifies himself and his group as separatists, tells his audience: "we [have written] to you that you should understand [the Book of Moses] and the Book[s of the Pr]ophets and Davi[d and all the events] of every age . . ." His authoritative collections seem to be the Law, the Prophets, Psalms, and some other work that explains history. Again, he mentions the book of Moses and the books of the prophets in connection with the fulfillment of blessings and curses. Some scholars believe this correspondence was intended for a reigning monarch.

One statement in 11QPs^a scroll shows that some ancient Jews literally believed that King David composed numerous poetic pieces that had not been included in the received books of the Psalms.

> David son of Jesse was wise and brilliant like the light of the sun,
> a scribe, intelligent and perfect in all his ways before God and
> men. Yahweh gave him an intelligent and brilliant spirit, and he

wrote 3,600 psalms and 364 songs to sing before the altar for the daily perpetual sacrifice, for all the days of the year, and fifty-two songs for the Sabbath offerings, and thirty songs for the new moons, for feast-days and for the Day of Atonement. In all, the songs which he [David] uttered were 446 and four songs to make music on behalf of those stricken. In all, they were 4,050. All of these he uttered through prophecy which was given him from the presence of the Most High [God].

This passage shows clearly that prophecy had not really ended during the time that this piece was written. It also demonstrates that it is best to attribute new or unknown compositions to a famous figure like David. With respect to the numbers of pieces written by David, 364 songs for each day of the year and the 52 songs for each week fit nicely with the calendar theme found in a few other manuscripts. While Chronicles states that David was master of the temple liturgy, the statement in 11QPs[a] about David makes it clear just how prolific he was thought to have been.

Even the entertaining little booklet about Tobit and his search for a bride survived in Cave 4.

Debate continues among scholars about the nature of the canon advocated or represented among the Dead Sea Scrolls. It seems doubtful that one can demonstrate that the writers of the Scrolls advocated a limited canon per se. They probably had and used favorite works. At the same time, many scribes seem to be involved in creating further scripture, authoritative, and entertaining works. These new compositions build upon older works but make no apologies as later spin-offs. Without proof to the contrary, many works seem to be simply extending the concept of scripture somewhat like the definition given in 2 Esdras.

QUMRAN CAVES AND BIBLICAL MANUSCRIPTS

The following chart shows how many manuscripts of each book were retrieved from the Qumran caves.[1] These manuscripts are almost always fragmentary, and in some cases reflect a handful of fragments or even fewer. It is not surprising that Genesis—Leviticus, Deuteronomy, Isaiah, and the Psalms are all in double digits. These were highly esteemed and often used works. It seems that *Jubilees* and *Enoch* were also significant for the owners of the Scrolls. One should perhaps not generalize too much about writings for which there are few exemplars, but it is noteworthy that the historical books are greatly underrepresented.

Name of Scroll	Number of Qumran Manuscripts
Genesis	19/20
Exodus	17/18
Leviticus	13/14
Numbers	7/8
Deuteronomy	30/33
Joshua	2
Judges	3
Samuel	4
Kings	3
Isaiah	21
Jeremiah	6
Ezekiel	6
Minor Prophets	8
Psalms	36/37
Proverbs	2
Job	4
Song of Songs	4
Ruth	4
Lamentations	4
Ecclesiastes	2
Esther	0
Daniel	8
Ezra	1
Nehemiah	1
Chronicles	1
Letter of Jeremiah*	1
Tobit*	5
Ben Sira*	3
*Jubilees**	15
*Enoch**	20

* These works likely were considered to be Scripture. The high number of manuscripts of *Jubilees* and *Enoch* suggests that these writings were extremely popular and influential for the people who owned the Dead Sea Scrolls.

SELECTED READINGS IN THE BIBLE MANUSCRIPTS
FROM QUMRAN

The biblical manuscripts from Qumran were copied two thousand years ago. There was apparently no standard text for all the books, nor was there a canonical list of acceptable writings. Many scholars are now careful not to use the word "biblical" because no clear boundaries had been established at least for the owners of the Dead Sea Scrolls. The term "scripture" is sufficiently descriptive and vague enough to capture the great variety of religious literary works among the scrolls, but "biblical" may be used to refer to the traditional listing of works in the oldest canon of the Jewish and Christian Bibles.

The most basic question is not about a limited canon of writings, but about how many and which literary works were treated as scripture but never found their way into the biblical canon. The book of Ben Sira is known at Qumran, Masada, and in numerous Greek manuscripts of the Bible. Some scholars believe *Jubilees*, which was discovered at Masada, *Enoch*, and some non-canonical psalms were also considered scriptural in antiquity.[2] At least one can say that the literary works from the Qumran caves constitute the largest collection of Jewish religious writings that existed before the destruction of Jerusalem in 70 CE.

Since the codex had not been invented yet, there was no bound copy of two dozen sacred works selected by traditional. Physical evidence shows that individual works usually appeared on a single scroll, but sometimes two books of the Pentateuch were combined on one scroll (4QpaleoGen-Exod[l] and 4QGen-Exod[a], 4QExod-Lev[f], 1paleoLev-Numb[a], and 4QLev-Num[a]). From Deuteronomy on there is no evidence for this, except perhaps in the case of 1–2 Samuel and the Twelve Minor Prophets. All of the known works of the Jewish Bible except Esther were found in the Qumran caves.

When scholars talk about the ancient texts of the biblical books, they speak of the Masoretic text (MT), the Septuaguint (LXX), and Samaritan (Sam) texts. For Genesis through Deuteronomy the label Samaritan has its usefulness. The MT refers broadly speaking to a group of Hebrew texts that has been accepted as standard in scholarship. The LXX is the Greek text of a longer list of writings included in the Christian Bible. The Sam is a Hebrew text traced back to the religious community settled in and around Shechem. Textual scholarship normally compares the biblical texts with the manuscripts of these three families. At times a text agrees more with the MT or the LXX. Several manuscripts from Qumran exhibit strong agreements with the Sam. Very often a manuscript reflects an independent text. With this is mind, it is instructive to look at some interesting readings in Qumran's biblical manuscripts.[3]

GENESIS THROUGH DEUTERONOMY

Genesis

About twenty fragmentary manuscripts of this book were found at Qumran. The guard page of 4QGen[h]-title preserves the book's title. In Genesis three variants are noteworthy. 4QGen[h] 1 1:9 reads: "Let the waters . . . be gathered together in one gathering." The MT has "Let the waters . . . be gathered together in one place." In 41:16 of 4QGen[j]: "[Apart from Go]d, the welfare of Phar[aoh] will not be answered." This agrees with Sam and the LXX. It has been suggested that the most ancient version may have read: "Apart from me, [Joseph], God will give no answer concerning Pharaoh's." Such a reading would emphasize Joseph's powers and not those of God. The MT is more humble: "It is not in me. God will give Pharaoh a suitable answer." In 48:7 4QGen[f] says, "[Rac]hel died to my sorrow in the land of Canaan on the way, when there was still some distance to come to Ephrath, that is, Bethlehem." The MT, LXX, and Sam read: "Ephrath. And I buried her there on the way to Ephrath."

Exodus

Qumran's seventeen manuscripts of Exodus fall broadly into Samaritan and other categories. The longest witness is the Samaritan-like 4Qpaleo-Exod[m]. Already 4QExod[b] 1:5, like the LXX and Acts 7:14, reads: "[All the people that c]ame from the loins of J[acob were]-five and seventy." The MT and Sam speak of "seventy people, and Joseph was in Egypt already." In 12:40 4QExod[c], although quite fragmentary, says that the Israelites lived in Egypt for 430 years. The Sam and LXX apply the 430 years to the stays in Egypt and Canaan. For ancient chronographers this discrepancy would have provided fuel for discussion.

The manuscript 4QExod[d] seems to preserve the introduction to the "Song of the Sea" in 13:16b: "[Then M]oses and the children of Israel sang . . . The horse and his rider [. . .]," whereas the MT, LXX, and Sam have it later in 15:1. Perhaps the location of these words in 13:16b served to anticipate the song which appears later. Otherwise, it is now unclear what the advantage would have been.

4QExod-Lev^f 39:21 has the phrase "just as the Lord commanded Moses." This happens in Sam, but not in the MT and LXX. The same manuscript adds a chronological phrase, "after they came out of Egypt" in 40:17.

Perhaps the most distinctive manuscript of Exodus is 4QpaleoExod^m, which shares numerous textual features with Sam. Sometimes the text of this manuscript repeats God's words a second time, not directed to Moses and Aaron, but to the Egyptian pharaoh or his official. This occurs in the story of the plague when 7:16–18a is recapitulated in 7:18b, 8:1–4a recurs in 8:4b, 8:20c–23a is expanded in 8:23, when 9:3–5a is extended in 9:5b, and when 9:13–19a is added to 9:19b. The same type of phenomenon appears in 10:2, which serves as an introduction to Moses and Aaron addressing the pharaoh in 10:3.

In two cases 4QpaleoExod^m inserts passages from Deuteronomy. In 18:25, a text concerning the elders is simply replaced by Deut 1:9–18. Similarly, the Israelites' brief response to Moses' reading of the Ten Commandments in Exod 20:19 is supplemented by Deut 5:24–27.

The Sam and 4QpaleoExod^m place the description of the altar of incense after 26:35, contrasting starkly with the MT and LXX where it appears in 30:1–10. This was an editorial decision that seemed more logical to the ancient scribe.

Although 4QpaleoExod^m is expansive in certain parts, it lacks 29:21.

> And you shall take some of the blood that is on the altar, and some of the anointing oil, and sprinkle it on Aaron, and on his garments, and on his sons, and on the garments of his sons with him. And he shall be sanctified, and his garments, and his sons, and his sons' garments with him.

Perhaps this was a scribal oversight like the deletion of the end of 31:13 and the beginning of 31:14, a feature shared by the MT, Sam, and LXX:

> It is a sign between me and you throughout your generations that you may know that I am the Lord who sanctifies you. You shall keep the Sabbath, for it is holy for you."

Leviticus

This book is represented by sixteen manuscripts. Some of its variant readings are pithy and explanatory, reflecting none of the expansive tendencies of 4QpaleoExod^m. In 2:1 4QExod-Lev^f agrees with Sam and

LXX by adding the phrase, "[. . . it is] a grain offering." The manuscript pap4QLXXLev^b 3:11, like LXX, has the descriptive phrase, "[for a pleasing od]or," which is not found in MT and Sam. In this manuscript other such parenthetical expressions appear in 4:6, 23, 5:6, 9:24, 10:1, and 14:36. 4QLev-Num^a lacks 14:40: "and the priest shall take the lamb of the guilt offering and the log of oil, and the priest shall wave them for a wave offering," which the MT, Sam, and LXX have. In 1QpaleoLev one finds Num1:48–50 and 36:7–8 inserted between Leviticus 23 and 27 (perhaps combined excerpts).

Numbers

The eight partial manuscripts of Numbers contain some interesting readings. On occasion 4QNum^b agrees with the Sam. The MT and LXX refer to "going up" and "spying out," but 4QNum^b adds "entering" the land. Both this manuscript and the LXX use the past tense to express having already been chosen by God (16:5). The MT and the Sam put this choice in the future (Num 20:13a). As in Sam and 4QpaleoExod^m, the writer adds Moses' response from Deut 3:24–25, 26b–28, and 2:2–6. For striking the rock, Moses and Aaron were prohibited from entering the Promised Land, but in the additions Moses pleads for a concession, and God permits him to ascend to the top of Pisgah to see the land in every direction. In the blessing of Joshua, 4QNum^b 27:23 says that Moses placed his hands upon Joshua. What follows apparently came from Deut 3:21–22. In 4QNum^b 36:4, the language of verses 1–2 is repeated to emphasize a response to an earlier command. This is reminiscent of the repetitions in 4QpaleoExod^m.

Deuteronomy

The most copied book of the Mosaic Torah was Deuteronomy. This is proven by the thirty fragmentary manuscripts found in the Qumran caves. Sometimes a manuscript has a singular pronoun; sometimes, a plural. In 4QDeut^h 2:3 one reads: "You [singular] have circled this mountain long enough." The MT, Sam, and LXX have "you" plural. The singular emphasizes Moses, and the plural focuses on the people. In 34:6 4QDeut^l, some manuscripts of Sam, and LXX have "they" buried Moses, but the MT, Sam, and a manuscript of Deuteronomy from Masada say that "he," that is, God interred him. Specific numbers are also fragile and subject to modification within a text. 4QDeut16:8 has: "[For s]even days unleavened bread you shall eat . . . ," which conforms with 16:3–4. The MT, LXX, and Sam speak of "six days."

Sometimes a reading seems to be explanatory. 4QDeut^c 4:14 speaks of "[the land] wh[ere you are crossing over the] Jordan. . . ." The MT, Sam, and LXX lack the river's name. In 5QDeut 7:15 one sees the scribe at work. He copied ". . . none of the evil diseases of Egypt which you have seen," but then added above the line "which you know." This created "which you have seen and which you know," a reading found in the LXX. It is not clear whether the scribe was adapting his text to such a reading or whether he was correcting a mistake. The traditional witnesses to Deut 8:6 refer to "fearing" God, but 4QDeut^n says "by loving him." In 4QDeut^j 11:21 one finds an addition that is very similar to Exod 12:43–44: "And [the Lord] s[aid to Moses and Aaron. This is the ordinance of the Passover] n[o] forei[gner shall eat of it. But every man's servant who is bought for money when you have circumcised him], then he shall e[at of it]." This longer text looks like combinations found in other manuscripts. 4QDeut^h 31:9 and LXX emphasize that Moses wrote the Law in a book and delivered it to the priests, the sons of Levi. The MT and Sam merely say it was written.

For decades scholars have known about an exciting reading in 4QDeut^j 32:8 that agrees with the LXX: "According to the number of the children of God." The MT and Sam refer to the "children of Israel."[4] At first glance one might think these are simply synonyms for the Israelites, but if read in the larger context, including v. 43, the expression "the children of God" can be understood as divine beings that God established to protect boundaries. Deuteronomy 32:43 also mentions the heavenly realm in 4QDeut^q: "Rejoice, O heavens, together with him, and bow down to him all you divine beings, for he will avenge the blood of his sons, and will render vengeance to his enemies, and will recompense those who hate him, and will atone for the land of his people." In the MT and Sam, the nations are addressed. The long phrase "and will recompense those who hate him, and will atone for the land of his people" is found in the LXX. In contrast to 4QDeut^q, the atonement occurred in the past in the MT and Sam.

JOSHUA THROUGH KINGS

Joshua

Joshua is represented by only two partial scrolls from Cave 4. In 3:15 4QJosh[b] and LXX refer to crossing the Jordan at the time of the harvest. The scribe added the word "wheat" above the line for clarification. This does not occur in the MT. In 3:17 the name Joshua is mentioned but absent in the MT and the LXX (also in 4:35, 6:7).

Just before 4QJosh 5 the text concludes with the erection of an altar.[5] This is found at the end of chapter 8 in the MT and after 9:2 in the LXX. Josephus's Greek text is very much like 4QJosh 5:16–20.

Judges

Only three partial manuscripts of Judges survived. 4QJudg lacks the deuteronomic-sounding section in 6:7–10. Not much else is surprising in the Qumran manuscripts of Judges.

Samuel

The surviving manuscripts of 1–2 Samuel preserve some of the most interesting textual variants and also scribal mistakes.[6] The most celebrated text is a paragraph found before 4QSam[a] 11:1. It reads:

> [Na]hash, king of the Ammonites, oppressed the Gadites and the Reubenites viciously. He put out the right [ey]e of a[ll] of them and brought fe[ar and trembling] on [Is]rael. Not one of the Israelites in the region be[yond the Jordan] remained [whose] right eye Naha[sh king of] the Ammonites did n[ot pu]t out, except seven thousand men [who escaped from the Ammonites and went to [Ja]besh-Gilead.

This paragraph is confirmed in Josephus whose Greek text has the same account (*Ant* 6.68–71). This is a case of an ancient manuscript preserving an entire section that makes the shortened biblical account more comprehensible.

Another fascinating feature of 4QSam[a] 2 Sam 10:6 is its textual similarity to parts of 1 Chron 19:6–7 in the MT and LXX.

> [Hanun and the Ammonites sent] a thousand silver talents [to hire] chariots and horsemen [from Aram-naharaim, Ara-maa] cah [and Zobah. They hired thir]ty-[two] thousand chari[ots, the king of Maacah, and the me]n of Tob. [When they came and

encamped near Medeba,] the Ammon[ites] mustered from [their cities. . . .]

Second Samuel 10:6–7 in the MT has a much different text.

> . . . the Ammonites sent and hired twenty thousand foot soldiers from the Arameans of Beth-rehob and Zobah, the king of Maacah with a thousand men, and twelve thousand men from the men of Tob.

Any later readers comparing 2 Samuel and 1 Chronicles would immediately see that the latter emphasizes payment, details about the number of chariots, and Medeba as the place of battle. Second Samuel has none of these details. One has the impression that the text from Chronicles has been inserted into 2 Samuel 10. This scribal intervention is quite familiar from some other Qumran manuscripts of the Pentateuch.

In 4QSam[a] 2 Sam 24 (between vv. 16 and 17) one finds a text like 1 Chron 21:16 in the MT. It also presents a paragraph that is lacking in the MT and LXX of 2 Samuel 24: "David raised his eyes and saw the angel of the Lord standing between earth and heaven. His drawn sword was in his hand stretched out toward Jerusalem. David and the elders, covered in sackcloth, fell down on their faces." In this passage one sees the leaders of Israel in repentance mode in view of the impending destruction of Jerusalem.

The story of Goliath, certainly a favorite in antiquity and perhaps especially for the owners of the Scrolls because of their interest in the offspring of the fallen angels, encourages speculation about Goliath's height. In the MT and some Greek manuscripts he is six cubits tall. Some other Greek manuscripts say he was five cubits tall. According to 4QSam[a] Goliath was four cubits and a span tall (thought to be about six feet plus or close to two meters).

The Samuel manuscripts from Qumran reveal many of the scribal features one finds in other manuscripts—mistakes in copying, preservation of lengthy passages known from the Greek or independently, differences in the number of persons represented by pronouns, differences in verb tenses (present or past), and disagreement about specific numeric data.

Kings

Compared with the Samuel manuscripts from Qumran, little remains of the books of Kings. Despite preserving a fragmentary text, 4QKings 1 Kgs 8:16 preserves a reading not found in the MT of this book, but which is preserved rather completely in 2 Chron 6:5b–6: "[. . . nor did I choose anyone] to be a leader over [my] people [Israel, but I chose Jerusalem for my name to be there. . . .]" The LXX preserves part of this passage.

THE MAJOR PROPHETS

Isaiah

Twenty-one manuscripts of the book of Isaiah were found in the caves, making Isaiah the most popular of the prophets The Great *Isaiah Scroll* (1QIsaᵃ) belonged to the first batch of scrolls found in Cave 1. Because of its completeness, a rarity among the Scrolls, scholars have given it the most attention and have commented especially on its full spelling (the use of written vowels), other physical features, and its readings. In this manuscript one is privileged to witness not only a generally beautiful script, but even the stains made by human hands. It is exhilarating to see that scribes added letters and words above other words and lines. Even longer phrases and passages that had been omitted during the initial copying were later squeezed into the margins and between lines. A series of dots is sometimes used to indicate a deletion. Marginal notations suggest that the ancient readers found something especially enlightening about the marked passages.

In textual studies poetic parallelism sometimes helps to decide which is the better or best reading. In 1:15, 1QIsaᵃ offers a parallelism found neither in the MT nor in 4QIsaᶠ. After the words "Your hands are filled with blood," 1QIsaᵃ adds "your fingers with iniquity." In 3:24 one again sees that the scribe inserted a parallelism that may have been absent in the text he was copying. In a series of six clauses that say "instead of x, y," the final parallel lacks the second component. 1QIsaᵃ reads "instead of beauty, shame." This seems to be an improvement over the MT. It is not clear whether it also should be treated as parallelism, but 4:2 has both "remnant of Israel and Judah." The MT fails to mention Judah. Isaiah 30:20 presents a text that completes a parallelism. It says "when the forest comes down, and the wood will be completely laid low."

The MT has "the city," which is based on a misplacement/miscopying of one Hebrew letter. A similar phenomenon occurred in 1QIsaᵃ and the MT which read "from the west" or "the sea," while 4QIsaᶜ has "from the day." The latter reading, which is based on a confusion of the Hebrew *yod* and *waw*, does not fit the context.

Omissions are also possible when copying from one manuscript to another and certainly probable if the scribe is tired, distracted, or recording a passage from memory. For example, the scribe's eye jumped from the first occurrence of "by day" in 4:5 to the second occurrence in v. 6 losing the words "and smoke, and the brilliance of a flaming fire by night. Over the glorious whole there will be a canopy and shelter, a shade by day from the heat." The same thing happened in 4QIsaᵃ 23:15, when the scribe lost the intervening words between two references to Tyre. What remained was "to Tyre as in the song of the prostitute." A much more lengthy text is found in 4QIsaᶜ, the MT, and the LXX, and it may be original : "that Tyre will be forgotten for seventy years, the span of a king's life, but at the end of seventy years it will happen to Tyre as in the song of the prostitute." It is also puzzling that 1QIsaᵃ 34 initially lacked two and one-half verses in the MT and the LXX at the end of chapter 34 and the beginning of chapter 35.

> Forever they will possess it. From generation to generation will they dwell in it. The wilderness and the dry land will rejoice. The desert will celebrate and blossom like the crocus. It will blossom luxuriantly and rejoice greatly with joy and song. The glory of Lebanon will be given to it, the splendor of Carmel and Sharon. They will see the glory of the Lord, the splendor of our God.

A later scribal hand inserted these missing words to reconstitute what he considered as the correct text.

One also encounters numerous corrections. In 1QIsaᵃ 2:4 the scribe wrote the first letters of the word "judgment" in Hebrew and at the beginning of the next line he wrote the entire word again. In 3:15 the words "my Lord" were added above the line. In 19:12, the scribe discovered a mistake and inserted "of hosts" above the line. In 38:20–22 one finds two scribal interventions. The first scribe stopped after v. 20: "O Lord, save me!" Another scribe continued: "The living, the living will praise you, as I do this day. Parents will make your loyalty known to their children. O Lord, save! And we will make music with stringed instruments all the days of our lives in the house of the Lord."

In 21:16 the versions disagree on when the end of the nation Kedar would come. 1QIsa^a predicts "within three years." The MT and the LXX say "within one year." It is quite possible that ancient scholars argued about this numeric discrepancy. Absent from the MT, but present in 1QIsa^a, 1QIsa^b, 4QIsa^d, and the LXX is the sentence: "Out of the suffering of his soul he will see light."

Certainly, hundreds of other oddities in 1QIsa^a could have been mentioned, because its text bears the signs of scribal activity throughout. The fact that 1QIsa^a is a complete manuscript that includes lots of scribal corrections makes it an historical treasure of elevated status among the scriptural works found in the Qumran caves.

Jeremiah

Six manuscripts of Jeremiah preserve parts of more than half of the book. Over the decades scholars have said that 4QJer^a and 4QJer^d have texts similar to the Hebrew underlying the LXX. In that case, their texts would have been shorter than the MT. Due to lack of space the phrase "to make cakes for the Queen of Heaven" does not fit in 4QJer^a 7:18. Evidence for a shorter text may be found in 4QJer^a 8:14; 18:20; 27:13–14; and 4QJer^c 33:19–20. 4QJer^c also lacks the phrase "and the moon and all the host of heaven" in 8:2, which is found in 4QJer^a, the MT, and the LXX.

In some manuscripts of Jeremiah the textual components have been rearranged.[7] 4QJer^a and the MT as well as 4QJer^b and the LXX present different sequences for several elements in 10:9. 4QJer^a and the MT preserve v. 10, which is lacking in 4QJer^b and the LXX. 4QJer^d 43 has several interesting variants. In 43:3 Baruch is mentioned, but the MT identifies him as "the son of Neriah." Verse 4 reads Johanan, but does not have "son of Kareah" in two places, as in the MT. 4QJer^d agrees with the LXX. In v. 6, however, one finds the appositional phrase "son of Akiham," but it lacks "son of Shaphan" as found in the MT. Sometimes one finds scribal corrections in the text. 4QJer^a 8:12 omitted the phrase "they had done," but inserted it above the line. In 4QJer^a 17:14 the scribe first penned "my praise" and later inserted "you" above the line creating the sentence, "You are my praise." In the very next verse he left out the word "not" and had to insert it above the line also.

Ezekiel

The six manuscripts of Ezekiel only preserve meager portions of ten chapters. Based on a lack of spacing it has been suggested that 11QEzek 5:13 may have had a shorter text than the MT. Either because of scribal error or an abbreviated text 4QEzek^a lacks 23:16–17: "When she saw them, she burned them and sent messengers to Chaldea for them. And the Babylonians went in to her to make love with her, and they made them impure with their harlotries, and they became impure through her, and then she got tired of them." Too little of Ezekiel remains to permit much speculation and reconstruction of its ancient text.

THE TWELVE MINOR PROPHETS AND DANIEL

Seven of the eight surviving Qumran manuscripts of the Twelve show that this was a collection that was copied as a unit. These manuscripts reflect typical scribal interventions, sometimes improving the text and occasionally creating difficulties for subsequent readers.

Hosea

4QXII^g Hos 11:8 reads: "He has turned back upon my heart." The MT is quite different: "My heart is turned over within me." Perhaps the most interesting variant from the MT appears in 4QXII^g and the LXX of 13:4, which preserves a long relative clause lacking in the MT. Although 4QXII^g is damaged, it can be completed with the Greek: "who fortifies heaven and creates the earth, whose hands made the whole host of heaven, but I did not show them to you to go after them, but I brought you up from the land of Egypt." This is probably a better reading than the one found in the MT.

Joel

The text of Joel is faulty in 4QXII^c 2:13, where the scribe wrote, "rend your hearts and not your goats." The MT and the LXX have the better reading, "garments" instead of "goats." The scribe seems to have accidentally omitted 4:6b–8a, his eyes jumping from the word "sold" to "sell."

Amos

The Qumran manuscripts of Amos prove to be more interesting. 5QAmos 1:3 and the LXX read "[because they have threshed] the pregnant women of Gilead." The MT lacks any reference to pregnant women. 4QXII^g 5:14–15 preserves a reading of significance for the ancient and modern reader. Whereas the MT has the commands, "Seek good and not evil!" and "Hate!" in 4QXII^g there is no second command, but rather the statement, "We hated evil and [loved good . . .]" In the last clause of v. 15 4QXII^g reads: "The God of hosts will be gracious to us, the rem[nant of Joseph.]" This sentence sounds rather contemporizing. At times manuscripts have differences in verb tense. 4QXII^g and the LXX of 7:8 have the past tense: "I have set a plumb line," whereas 4QXII^c and the MT use the present, "I am setting a plumb line." The latter alternative makes God active in the present.

Obadiah

Obadiah has no variants of major significance. In contrast, in 4QXII^g and the LXX of Jonah 1:9 the phrase "the Lord, the God of heaven" seems to be out of place, producing the sentence "I am a Hebrew, the Lord, the God of heaven, and I fear he who has made the sea and the dry land." The MT makes more sense: "I am a Hebrew and I fear the Lord, the God of heaven, who . . ."

Micah

Micah exists in two manuscripts. In 4QXII^g 2:3 one reads "their neck" instead of the MT's "your neck." The Cave 4 reading is probably better because the context addresses a "you." A very peculiar reading is found in 4QXII^f 5:1 where one reads, "out of you one shall not come forth to be ruler in Israel." This is startling because, it directly contradicts the positive announcement in the MT and LXX: "One shall come forth for me."

Nahum

Despite the much-discussed *Commentary of Nahum* (4QpNah), little of Nahum is extant.

Zephaniah and Haggai

Zephaniah has survived in three manuscripts and Haggai in two. None of the variant readings is particularly interesting. It is noteworthy, however, that 4QXII^a is considered the oldest manuscripts of the Minor Prophets in existence and that it has been copied, oddly enough, in a cursive hand.

Malachi

Only two manuscripts of Malachi were found in Cave 4. In several places 4QXII^a appears to have a faulty text. In 2:15–16 it seems to have lost the phrase "against whom you have dealt treacherously." In reference to the promised messenger 4QXII^a 3:2 asks, "Who can endure them. They come?" The MT and LXX sound better: "Who can abide the day of his coming?" In 3:9 one finds "You are looking on appearances." The MT says: "You are cursed with the curse." The LXX differs: "And you certainly turn your attention away." Although judging the best reading in context can be difficult, the MT's reference to the "curse" seems appropriate. Thus, in the case of Malachi, the traditional witnesses seem more reliable than the Qumran manuscripts.

Daniel

Compared with many other manuscripts of the Hebrew Scriptures, the eight surviving manuscripts of Daniel preserve most of its ancient text. Possibly, 1QDan^a reads: "In every matter of wi[sdo]m and under[standing]." This is better than the MT's "wisdom of understanding." Manuscripts disagree on the tense of the verb in 2:28. 4QDan^a says "He (God) is disclosing . . . ," which emphasizes the present power of God, whereas the MT and the LXX use the past tense, "and he has disclosed." 4QDan^a 3:2 calls King Nebuchadnezzar "Mechandnezzar" by error. In 3:25 the king speaks "to his officials," a detail lacking in other witnesses. In 5:7, 4QDan^a and the LXX mention "magicians." This is not in the MT.

Daniel 7:1 has traditionally been considered a controversial passage because it says that Daniel "wrote down the dream, he related the sum of the words" in the MT and some Greek manuscripts. 4QDan^b has a shorter text: "He wrote down the [dream]," and this shorter reading has now been incorporated into the New Revised Standard Version.

Daniel 10:16 is another difficult passage. Due to its fragmentary state, it will not be discussed here.

Daniel seems to have influenced or been influenced by other works that share some of its flavor.[8] These include the *Prayer of Nabonidus*, other Daniel texts, 4QFourKingdoms, and pap4QApocalypse. The mere mention of Daniel's dream interpretation causes one to think of the running commentaries or *pesharim* discussed above in chapter 6. Dan 12:10 is even quoted in the thematic commentary called *Florilegium*.

THE PSALMS

The most copied and used work of the Jewish Scriptures is the Psalms.[9] A total of 37 Psalms manuscripts were retrieved from the Qumran caves. Twenty-three were found in Cave 4, and six came from Cave 11. On the whole, the sequence of Psalms 1–89 follows the order of the MT, but in 4QPs[a] and 4QPs[q] Psalm 33 follows Psalm 31; and in 4QPs[a] Psalm 71 comes right after Psalm 38. Psalm 91 is attached to a series of exorcism psalms against demons in 11QPsAp[a] or 11QApPs. Based on the blank leather at the end of this scroll, Psalm 91 appears to have been the last piece recorded. 4QPs[b] preserves much of Psalms 92 and 94–100.

For decades study of the Qumran Psalms focused on the content and order of the psalms in 11QPs[a], also known as the Great *Psalms Scroll* (see the section on this scroll in chapter 3). This collection runs from Psalm 101 to the end of the Psalter. In numerous places this collection represents a reordering of chapters as well as the inclusion of a psalm known from the Syriac Psalms, several previously unknown psalms, and a narrative statement about David's final words and compositions. This rearrangement of chapters most likely served a liturgical purpose, as one sees in 93:1, "Peace be upon Israel" in 13:3, "for the children of Israel, for his holy people" in 149:9, "exalt our Lord" and "and in your midst O Jerusalem" in 135:2. Psalm 135:22 has been inserted after v. 12, just as Ps 136 includes 135:12b at some point before v. 23. The key liturgical phrase that recurs is "for his steadfast love endures forever."

In several other manuscripts one discovers different arrangements of verses. 4QPs[x] 89 preserves vv. 25, 22, 26–27, and 30, and in v. 26 it lacks the phrase "my God and the rock of my salvation," found in the MT and LXX.

Among the Psalms manuscripts one could list hundreds of variant readings. Throughout one finds words or formulations that make no sense and thus seem to be erroneous (5:10, 19:4, 33:7, 38:8, 20, 71:2, 49:12, 69:3–4, 88:15, 102:17, 19, 118:16, 104:2, and 122:2, 4). Some manuscripts disagree in terms of number. 4QPs^a reads: "Punish him." The context requires "Punish them," which is found in the MT and LXX. In 4QPs^x one finds, "with you." Considering the larger context, the MT's "with him" is a better reading. In 11QPsAp^a 91:2 the text reads "who says." The MT has "I will say," and the LXX has "he will say." The context suggests that the LXX has the best reading. In 11QPs^a 137:1 the scribe seems to have made a mistake when he wrote "there they sat down." The text is corrected and agrees with the MT in reading "We sat down," a much better contextual reading. Manuscripts also disagree on verb tense. In 1QPs^a one reads "[my ear] has heard." The MT and the LXX have "My ear will hear." 1QPs^a may preserve the better text.

The psalms traditions found in the Qumran caves confirm the existence of the 150 psalms known in the MT, but give eloquent witness to some readings that follow the LXX, the Syriac, and other independent pieces. Without doubt, the shape of the psalms manuscripts in the Qumran caves reflects the variations one would expect of a text used regularly for daily study and worship.

OTHER WRITINGS

Job

There are four surviving manuscripts of Job from Caves 2 and 4. Only a few minor variants appear in 4QJob^b. The Aramaic *targum* of Job was found in Caves 4 and 11.

Proverbs

Proverbs is represented by two very fragmentary manuscripts. Only portions of chs. 1–2, 13–15 have survived. Except for small variations, their texts resemble the MT and LXX. Other wisdom and instructional works that borrow from and enhance the scriptural book of Proverbs were found in Cave 4.

Ruth

Fragments of four manuscripts of Ruth contain chapters 1–4. The small variants are typically explanatory but seem to be of no great significance.

Song of Songs

Four manuscripts of the Song of Songs were discovered in Caves 4 and 2. In 4QCant[b] 2:12 the scribe wrote "the season of," but crossed it out and wrote "Look." Neither the MT nor the LXX have this. 2:17 reads "like a gazelle," whereas the MT and LXX are longer: "like a gazelle or like a young stag." Although 3:6–8 is found in 4QCant[a], 4QCant[c], the MT, and the LXX, it is missing from 4QCant[b]. 4QCant[b] also lacks 4:4–7. Scholars sometimes say that overly sensitive or prudish scribes must have removed these verses because of the reference to "breasts," but 4QCant[a] preserves the supposedly offensive word. At this point 4QCant[a] lacks 4:7—6:11, sometimes explained as due to its erotic nature, but 4QCant[b] preserves most of this passage.

Ecclesiastes

Ecclesiastes is witnessed by two extremely fragmentary manuscripts. In 4QQoh[a] 6:4 the scribe initially wrote "into darkness its name," because his eyes jumped from the first use of "darkness" to the second one. He erased "its name" and above the line he inserted "it goes, and with darkness its name." The same manuscript reads in 7:7: "[a bribe] perverts [the heart.]" Instead of "perverts the heart," the MT and LXX have "destroys." In the bottom margin, instead of on the line, one finds the word "worthless" from 7:16. Aesthetically speaking, 4QQoh[a] has a beautiful script.

Lamentations

In Caves 3–5 four manuscripts of Lamentations were found. 4QLam 1:7 has a command, "Remember, O Lord." The MT and LXX read: "In the day of her affliction and of miseries Jerusalem remembers." 4QLam 1:11 has the words, "her precious things as food to refresh her soul." The MT, LXX, and even 3QLam 1:10–11 preserve a different wording: "bring into your assembly. All her people sigh. They seek bread. They have given their soul." In 4QLam 1 one finds v. 16 after v. 17. In 5QLam[a] 4:19 one finds the present tense "are," whereas the MT and LXX have the past "were."

Esther

Not even a tiny fragment of Esther has survived. Scholars speculated that Esther was rejected either because its festival Purim was not Mosaic in origin, because Esther's marriage to a Persian tyrant was disgusting, because chapters 7–9 advocate retaliation and vengeance, or simply because the book never mentions God. One non-scriptural work has been dubbed "Proto-Esther" because of its setting at the Persian court (4Q550). It does not refer to Esther or other actors in the biblical book.

Chronicles, Ezra, and Nehemiah

Only a tiny fragment of 1–2 Chronicles was found. It has been suggested that even this fragment is not from Chronicles, but rather from a text like that of 4QSam^a that looks more like Chronicles that the MT of Samuel (2 Samuel 5–7, 11, and 24 in 2Sam^a). This fragment preserves a few words from 2 Chron 28:27—29:1–3: "son of Ahaz" ("his son" in the MT and the LXX)," . . . -ive years old, and . . . -ty nine years Aybah . . . He did what was right . . . father had done. And he, in the . . . yea . . . open the door. . . ." 4QEzra preserves 4:2–6, 9–11; 5:17; and 6:1–5. Nehemiah is also represented by a fragment of 3:14–15.[10]

CONCLUSION

Although most of the Qumran manuscripts survived in extremely fragmented form, they confirm the existence and use of the scriptural works found in the Jewish Bible and the Christian Old Testament. Some manuscripts seem to have few deviations from the MT and the LXX. Some passages reflect degrees of scribal independence from known written sources. Some manuscripts preserve lost passages as well as previously unknown works. All of the manuscripts show scribes copying accurately, inaccurately, correcting, rearranging the texts for whatever purpose, and preserving the written traditions that they valued greatly.

No one can ever again imagine the textual study of the writings of the Jewish scriptures without abundant reference to the biblical manuscripts among the Scrolls. As editorial committees become aware of the plethora of better and seemingly original readings from these manuscripts, they will decide to include more and more of these priceless ancient readings in our Bibles. One also expects that scholars of the Jewish Bible will become more cognizant and appreciative of the contributions of these ancient manuscripts for textual and literary studies.

No longer may one simply say that the Bible read by most Jews and Christians today hardly differs from the ancient Scripture of the Jews.

This is an oversimplification and a misrepresentation of the evidence. One must be willing to study carefully all the variant readings as well as the myriad of mistakes in the manuscripts and realize that these scrolls and fragments are the products of real authors, editors, scribes, and students who were hard at work down into the late Second Temple period preserving their treasured writings and supplementing them whenever they could.

Noah's Ark and the Flood

⊀SIX⊁

The Pseudepigrapha,
the Apocrypha, and the Scrolls

FROM MEDIEVAL CODICES TO fairly recent times, scholars have known about the world of pseudepigrapha, writings that concern the lives and words of ancient ancestors and heroes whose stories they recount. The pseudepigrapha serve a purpose similar to that of hagiography. Because of the discovery of the Scrolls, we now know that the production of pseudepigrapha was essentially a cottage industry during the late Second Temple period. The topics in the Qumran pseudepigrapha include the angelic world and its worship, the calendar and chronological concerns, purity laws, and the end of history and salvation. The pseudepigrapha among the Scrolls constitute a large percentage of the writings found in the caves.[1] To date there is no other literary discovery made in Israel that compares with the breadth, variety, and depth of the Dead Sea Scrolls.

THE BOOKS OF ENOCH

Before the discovery of the Dead Sea Scrolls, the book of *Enoch* referred to a collection of Ethiopic apocalypses preserving the wisdom that Enoch had received from the angelic world during his three hundred-year visit. Based on the Ethiopic version, *Enoch* divides into five parts: The Book of Watchers (chs. 1–36), the Book of Parables (chs. 37–71), the Book of

Astronomical Secrets (chs. 72–82), the Dream Book (chs. 83–89), and the Epistle of Enoch (chs. 90–108).

Evidence for an older Enochic collection written in Aramaic was retrieved from Qumran's Cave 4. Due to its absence, the Book of Parables seems not to belong to this Aramaic collection. The Book of Astronomical Secrets is longer and more detailed in Aramaic than the Ethiopic. Related to the Enoch collection, but perhaps an independent work itself, was the so-called Book of the Giants. The editor of the *Enoch* fragments, J. T. Milik, hypothesized that the Dead Sea book of *Enoch* began with the Astronomical Secrets.[2]

As every reader of Genesis knows, at the age of 365 God absconded with Enoch and nothing else is heard of him in the Hebrew Bible. *Jubilees* claimed that Enoch was the first human being to learn the art and skill of writing. Thus it was believed that Enoch was the progenitor of education and literary culture among the Jews. Supposedly, he spent six jubilees among the angels adding to his knowledge of heavenly secrets.

> Before these things Enoch was hidden, and no one of the children of men knew where he was hidden, and where he abode, and what had become of him. And his activities had to do with the Watchers, and his days were with the holy ones. And I, Enoch, was blessing the Lord of majesty and the king of the ages, and lo, the Watchers called me—'Enoch, the scribe'—and said to me: 'Enoch, thou scribe of righteousness, go, declare to the Watchers of the heaven who have left the high heaven, the holy eternal place, and have defiled themselves with women...ye shall have no peace nor forgiveness of sin ... (*1 Enoch* 12:1-6)

Ben Sira 44:3 praised Enoch. In the New Testament, Jude 14–15 quotes *Enoch* 1:9 concerning God's judgment against sinners. Similarly, Jude 6 refers to God's sending the Watcher's to the netherworld for punishment (*Enoch* 10:4–6, 12–16; 12; cf. 2 Pet 2:4–5).

Cave 4 preserved parts of the Book of Watchers that deal with the so-called fallen angels. Milik believed that these fragments once belonged to a work that also included the Book of Dreams, the Epistle of Enoch, and the Book of Giants.[3] However, one should recall that no one found a complete scroll of Enoch or even one of Enoch's several sections. In fact, chapters 16–17, much of chapter 24, chapters 72–75, and 80–81 are missing. As for the remaining forty-four chapters only a few brief portions have survived. In many cases not even a single sentence is extant. Overlaps with other Dead Sea manuscripts were found only for chapters 2–9, 31–32, 76–77, and 89. Palaeographers dated these manuscripts to the late Hasmonean and Herodian periods, which would make them the oldest Jewish apocalypses on record.

The Dead Sea fragments of Enoch recount the latter's translation to heaven, his journey to the four corners of heaven, and his vision concerning the fates of the Watchers and their children. Enoch is depicted as a righteous person who blesses both God and the righteous. Going beyond the vague statement in Genesis, Enoch tells the ancient reader that two hundred angels and their leaders had descended to earth and impregnated women, who bore their gigantic children. These monstrous figures were said to be three thousand cubits tall. Enoch also revealed that the angels taught their women industries such as making weapons of war, bracelets, cosmetics, sorcery, the casting of spells, and the cutting of magical roots. It was rumored that these giants devoured humans, and an outcry against them rose up to the ears of the archangels Michael, Sariel, Raphael, and Gabriel. Because these evil angels had destroyed the natural order of things, they were sentenced to remain bound for seventy generations until the day of judgment. Enoch was permitted to read a petition from the condemned Watchers to God, but Enoch was ordered to reprimand them. Suddenly, Enoch was whisked up in the presence of tongues of fire which encircled the house of God. During his travels Enoch was privileged to see mountains, trees, heavenly portals, the center of the earth, the paradise of the righteous, and even the tree of knowledge from which Adam and Eve had eaten.

Within the Enoch traditions, the story of Noah was recounted both literally and figuratively. At birth he was said to be wondrously white and red with a glow coming from his eyes. Lamech is assured, as in 1QGenApoc, that Noah was indeed his child, not the offspring of a watcher and Lamech's wife. One learns that the flood lasted exactly one calendar year (105:6). To make sense of this one has to assume that the author accepted a 364-day solar year.

Considered to date into the third century BCE, the Astronomical Book preserves heavenly calculations of the waxing and the waning of the moon in increments of sevenths and indicates how light entered and then emerged from various heavenly gates. The natures of the winds and other meteorological phenomena are explained. Another mathematical calculation using the number fifteen was also used.

The Book of Giants shows Enoch, the wisest and most pious of all mortals, explaining the dream of Ahiya, an offspring of the Watchers. Quite possibly this tradition developed out of earlier ones that claimed that Enoch had indeed heard the Watcher's petitioning God.

The Dead Sea's Aramaic manuscripts of *Enoch* not only detail Enoch's incredible heavenly travels, but turn him into a prophet who foretells doom and salvation. The *Enoch* writings are used as a pseudepigraphic vehicle by which to explain the relationship of the fallen angels and their relations with mortal women and the consequences of that relationship.

It has been forcefully argued that the *Enoch* writings were considered authoritative by some groups at this time.[4] CD cites *Jubilees* as a reliable reference work, and *Jubilees* treats at least some of the Enoch traditions as normative. Centuries later the *Book of Enoch* belonged to the canon of the Abyssian Church. A Persian Manichae named Mani knew well some version of the Book of Giants.[5]

Enough of the Apocalypse of Weeks remained in the Dead Sea caves to suggest that history was moving toward a time of increasing violence and bloodshed, which had started in the second week. In the eighth week the prophecy states that the unnamed righteous ones shall triumph over evil and the royal temple will be erected. In the tenth week the wicked will be judged. In the final analysis, *Enoch* is a book about the exaltation and wisdom of the righteous and the ultimate destruction of the faithless wicked.

THE BOOK OF *JUBILEES*

In the late eighteenth and nineteenth centuries Western scholars were fascinated by a book written in Ethiopic, which the Abyssinian Church considered canonical.[6] Portions of this book were already known in Latin. Fifteen fragmentary Hebrew manuscripts of this work were discovered in Caves 1–4 and 11 at Qumran. Close inspection of these Hebrew fragments shows that only about forty verses, only parts of about eight of its original fifty chapters, survived in the Qumran caves.

Known now as the *Book of Jubilees*, this work has sometimes been dubbed the "Little Genesis" for its use of pre- and post-flood stories from the book of Genesis. The *Zadokite Work*, which was discovered in the late nineteenth century in a synagogue in Cairo, Egypt, and later found anew in several Qumran caves refers to *Jubilees* as a work of some authority for understanding Israel's sinful activities.

> For that reason a man should oblige himself to return to the Law
> of Moses, for in it everything is established. And the exact de-
> termination of the times of Israel's blindness, behold, this is de-
> scribed in the book of the division of the times into their jubilees
> and their weeks. (CD 16:2–3)

The author's emphasis on the separation of times into longer periods of
jubilees and weeks sounds like a paraphrase of *Jubilees* 1:26. Unlike the
biblical book of Genesis, *Jubilees* consistently provides dates in terms of
months, days, and years for historical events from God's creation of the
world to the reception of the law on Mount Sinai. The author repeatedly
refers to forty-nine years periods called jubilees. *Jubilees* also emphasizes
Israel's former disobedience to God and shows Israel how it might avoid
infractions of God's laws in the future.

The book of *Jubilees* is a type of rewriting of Genesis and Exodus up
to chapter 14, beginning with Moses atop Mount Sinai receiving divine
revelation. "And Moses was on the mountain forty days and forty nights,
and God taught him the earlier and the later history of the division of
all the days of the law and the testimony" (1:4–5). The author wanted
his readers to understand the highpoints of Israel's story before moving on to the story of creation, paraphrasing the subsequent narratives
including the destruction of the Egyptians in the sea. Besides using the
organizing principle of jubilees, the writer needed to emphasize certain
points regarding history and religious law.

As *Jubilees* opens God tells Moses that he is about to learn about
Israel's past and future. Throughout the book other historical figures either receive an angelic message or see a vision about Israel's future. God
emphasizes that Israel will be disobedient choosing to follow the customs
of the Gentiles. Several passages warn the Israelites not to worship as
the Gentiles do nor to give their daughters to them (1:9, 13; 3:31–32;
15:34; and 30:11–14). A chief wrong mentioned is following the Gentiles
in using a religious calendar of 354 days, which runs counter to the heavenly calendar of angelic worship. According to Gen 7:11–14, the flood
started on the 17th of the second month of year 600 and ended on the
27th of the second month in the year 601. Writing from the perspective of the year of 354 days, *Jubilees*' author was saying that Noah's flood
endured for a year and ten days. According to his own calendar, the flood
lasted one year exactly. The *Book of Enoch* had also emphasized this.

Jubilees calls this calendar the rule of the sun (2:9, 17; 6:30–31). After all, after the flood it was the sun that had dried the earth.

> . . . command thou the children of Israel that they observe the years according to this reckoning—three hundred and sixty four days, and (these) will constitute a complete year, and they will not disturb its time from its days and from its feasts . . . for there will be those who will assuredly make observations of the moon— how (it) disturbs the seasons and comes in from year to year ten days too soon. (6:32–35)

This is, of course, a prediction-after-the-fact indicating a calendar dispute among Jewish religious and historical thinkers in antiquity. From the point of view of Jubilees certain Jews were following a Gentile calendar in their worship.

The author of *Jubilees* brings the role of angels in the life of the Israelites to the forefront. In 1:28 an angel of the presence is commanded to write down God's words about the divisions of the years for Moses. The same angel then tells Moses to record what he hears (2:1). In God's first act of creation he makes all kinds of angels, which are otherwise recognized as meteorological elements. Moses learns that angels celebrated the Sabbath day (2:18, 30) and the Feast of Weeks (6:18) and that they were created already circumcised (15:31). The angels of the presence represent the ideal priesthood of Levi in Israel (31:14). On one occasion an angel descends to bring Jacob seven tablets to read (32:21). Even Enoch, the first human to learn to write, spent six jubilees with the angels and witnessed against the so-called watchers, those angels who rebelled against God (4:21; compare Gen 5:21–25; 6:1–4). Cainam, the son of Arpachshad, discovered a writing containing the astronomical teachings of these evil angels (8:1–9). The author of *Jubilees* wanted his readers to realize that much more divine wisdom once existed than had been preserved in Genesis and Exodus. Who would have known, for example, that the patriarch Abraham had once been a student of astrology (12:16–26)?

The *Book of Jubilees* sometimes refers to "the spirit of Beliar" (1:20), a name which is very similar to Belial in the Qumran writings. Belial was a heavenly being who served as God's nemesis, an adversary that God would permit to manipulate human beings until the appointed time when God would create the world anew. In *Pseudo-Jubilees* the prince of Mastema (known in the Qumran writings as Belial) stands behind

Abraham accusing him as he is about to sacrifice Isaac. The scriptural books of Job and Tobit are two other works in which angels play a more explicit role. The apparent dualism, very similar to Persian views in some Quman texts, is not quite so pronounced in *Jubilees.*

In retelling the early history of God's people, *Jubilees'* author was writing hagiography. He clearly desired to paint many of the patriarchs from Adam to Jacob as pious individuals who often interrupted their travels in order to erect altars, sacrifice to God (2:22; 3:27; 4:26; 6:1; 7:1–7; 13:3–4, 25–26; 14:11–13; 15:1; 22:1; 24:23; 27:21; and 44:4), and pray for the salvation of Israel. Very often even before sacrificing, these patriarchs had received a vision. In 30:8 Levi and his children are chosen to be priests at Bethel. This is the only priesthood advocated in the book of *Jubilees.* The reader learns that Jacob's father had given him certain books which Jacob then passed on to his son Levi.

A work of some authority among the Qumran scrolls, *Jubilees* stands within the tradition of ancient Jewish haggadah. It was simply a retelling of a story emphasizing issues of concern and urgency for the wise people of his time and those of the future. The author wanted to show that much angelic wisdom had already been available to the humans but was subsequently lost.

As Moses stood atop Sinai, he was told that he would learn about the earlier and the latter history up to the erection of the temple. Jubilees itself concludes with the incident at the Red Sea and a chapter about observation of the Passover at its proper time. In 50:4, the writer reveals when he lived but not his own name: "There are forty-nine jubilees from the days of Adam until this day, and one week and two years. And there are yet forty years to come for learning the commandments of the Lord." The author rounds out his book by emphasizing the sacredness of the Sabbath day (50:13). He certainly knew that he was explaining his version of early Jewish history to a sympathetic audience. Instead of speaking of a human oral tradition alongside written scripture, the author of *Jubilees* boldly stated that his wisdom was not at all new and had come from the angels.

THE *GENESIS APOCRYPHON*

When the *Genesis Apocryphon* (1QGenApoc) was discovered it was dry and brittle.[7] The beginning of the scroll was damaged and its end was missing. All that was left were four sheets of leather that had been sewn together. In total, there were twenty-two columns in Aramaic. In recent years advanced image enhancement techniques have helped to decipher several difficult passages. It has been conjectured that this scroll may have originally been much longer.

Initially, the scroll was named the *Apocalypse of Lamech* for the father of Noah. In 2:3 Lamech admits worrying that his wife, Bitenosh, had been impregnated by one of the angels who came down to the earth in search of women. Lamech asked his father to have this situation investigated. In Genesis 4 Lamech takes two wives, Adah and Zillah, neither of whom was the mother of the famed Noah. Although Genesis mentions that Lamech fathered Noah when he was 182 years old, nowhere does it talk about Noah's mother. This question is answered in the book of *Jubilees* (4:28).

In the next recognizable section Noah's ark has landed on the mountains of Hurarat (Genesis: Ararat), where Noah immediate erects an altar, burns incense, and atones for the entire earth. Then one learns the names of Noah's grandchildren. The author not only mentions the sons of Japheth but even his four daughters, another tradition not in the Bible. He adds that Noah and his sons tilled the earth and that Noah planted a vineyard on Mount Lubar (compare the *Book of Noah*). Instead of presenting the odd and controversial biblical story about Noah's drunkenness and a presumed case of incest, in 1QGenApoc Noah talks about the first wine festival occurring of the first day of the fifth year after planting his vineyard. During this wine festival Noah and his extended family blessed the Lord of Heaven, the God Most High, and the Great Holy One, for their deliverance from the flood. The author repaints the Noah after the flood as righteousness and names his vineyard. Column 17 apparently deals with the apportionment of the then-known world among Noah's children.

The best preserved section of the scroll retells the journeys and adventures of Abram known already from Gen 12:8—15:4. Abram dwelled for two years in Hebron until a famine smote the land. Then he departed for Egypt. After crossing the border Abram fell asleep and dreamed about a cedar and a palm tree. In this dream he saw some men trying to cut down the cedar but left the palm untouched. The palm tree cried out to the Egyptians not to cut down the cedar pleading that it belonged to her family. Upon awaking Abram told his nightmare as well as its interpretation to his wife Sarai. The trees obviously represent

Abram and Sarai. Abram insists that Sarai identify him as her brother. After spending five years in Egypt, Abram the foreigner became known as a wise man with a lovely wife. One day three Egyptian princes came bearing gifts, and Abram read to them from the book of *Enoch*. At first, the Egyptians seemed to be smitten by Sarai's beauty, which is described in language similar to that used in the biblical Song of Songs. When one of the princes, a certain Hyrcanus, tells Pharoah Zoan about her dazzling beauty, the pharaoh orders that she be brought to his court. Abram prayed that God not permit the pharaoh to have sexual relations with her. God heard Abram's prayer and sent chastising spirits against the pharaoh and his family. As these plagues increased, the pharaoh sent for all his wise men, wizards, and healers to help him, but the scourging spirits attacked them as well. Prince Hyrcanus requested that Abram come to pray for and heal the pharaoh. Lot counseled his uncle Abram that he should only do this after Sarai had been released. The pharaoh was healed, and Sarai was given much wealth and the handmaid Hagar.

The actual healing of the pharaoh recalls Abimelech's healing in Genesis 20, but the pharaoh's sending for his own wise men reminds one of Joseph in Genesis 40 and Daniel in Daniel 2. Genesis 12 speaks of Sarai's beauty, and the 1QGenApoc added several details. Perhaps most importantly the question was answered whether Sarai had been sexually defiled by the pharaoh. One is even reminded of the biblical scene where Potiphar's wife attempted to seduce Joseph in Genesis 39.

Columns 21–22 tell the story of Abram returning to Bethel, his separation from Lot, God's showing him the Promised Land, Lots' kidnapping, and Abram's saving him near Damascus. With some noticeable differences, this account parallels Gen 13:3—15:4. At Bethel Abram not only prayed but offered holocausts and offerings. The reader learns that Lot bought a house in the Jordan Valley rather than setting up his tent at Sodom. God appeared to Abram in a vision commanding him to go to Ramat Hazor to survey the land. When he arrived he looked around and beheld all the territory from the river of Egypt to Lebanon and Senir, from the Great Sea up to Hauran, all the land to Qadesh, and all of the Great Desert east of Hauran and Senir to the Euphrates. We are even told that Abram toured this area on foot. None of these details is biblical. Abram then recounted a list of kings, borrowing from Genesis 14 but with additional clarifications. Shinar, for example, was identified as Babylonia, Ellasar as Cappadochia, Goiim as Mesopotamia. Hobah, presented as a city north of Damascus, is called Helbon. After meeting Melkizedek, king of Salem, God appeared yet again in a vision to Abram reminding him of how much he had prospered in the ten years since leaving Haran. This time God promised him a son of his own loins.

Had no other scrolls been discovered in Qumran's Cave 1, 1QGenApoc would have been a treasure on its own. It shows that some ancient Jews viewed figures like Noah and Abram as models of sacrificial piety and prayerfulness. In particular, Abram was transformed into a wise healer, interpreting dreams, banishing evil spirits, and reading the book of *Enoch* to Egyptian nobles. It is also noteworthy that Noah, Lamech, and Abram are permitted to speak in the first person (at least up to Gen 14:21).

1QGenApoc is much more than a mere paraphrase of parallel sections in Genesis. It is an extensive pious retelling of parts of Genesis accenting prayer, sacrifice, faith in God, and dream and vision interpretation. Compared with the 1QGenApoc the biblical account looks like a skeletal version. The author freely adds details and eliminates embarrassments as much as possible. He might be accused of superb hyperbole and obscure detail at times, but his narrative reflects the views of a writer influenced not only by the literary world of Genesis, but at the same time a person dependent in some way on the ideas found in the *Book of Enoch* (chs. 56–57) and the *Book of Jubilees*.

GENESIS COMMENTARY

The *Genesis Commentary* survived in 29 fragments (4Q252–254). The easiest one to study is 4Q252, which preserves parts of four columns.[8] The columns have different dimensions. Column I has 22 lines; in the following columns fewer lines are preserved. Columns I–II of 4Q252 represent commentary smoothly inserted into a resume of the flood. The biblical material comes from portions of Genesis 6–9 and 15. Several key features of this text immediately strike the eye. The writer added chronological and calendar data in order to show that the flood lasted exactly one year of 364 days from the day it had started. He even inserted the days of the week when something happened, revealing in particular that the ark also rested at the end of the sixth day (biblical quotation in italics).

> [in the] four hundred and eightieth year of the life of Noah came their end. . . . until the end of the flood. . . . *the waters arrived in*

the six hundredth year of the life of Noah, in the second month, on the first day of the week. . . . *and rain fell . . . forty days and forty nights* until the twenty-sixth day of the third month, the fifth day of the week. . . . *the waters prevailed . . . a hundred and fifty days* until the fourteenth day . . . *the waters abated* two days, the fourth and the fifth day, and on the sixth day the ark came to a rest. . . . *the waters continued to abate until the [ten]th month, the first day,* the fourth day of the week. . . . *at the end of forty days,* after the tops of the mountains had been seen . . . *Noah opened the window of the ark* on the tenth day of the ele[venth] month . . . *she (the dove) came back to him with an olive leaf in her beak,* this is the twenty-]fourth [day] of the eleventh month, the first day of the wee[k] . . . [*it (the dove) did not*] *return again,* this is the f[irst] day [of the twelfth] month, [the first day] of the week. At the end of three [weeks after Noah had sent forth the dov]e which did not return to him, . . . this was *the first day of the first month,* . . . on the first day of the week. On that day *in the six hundred and first year of the life of Noah,* on the seventeenth day of *the second month that the earth was dry,* on the first day of the week, on that day *Noah exited* the ark at the end of a full year of three hundred and sixty-four days, on the first day of the week, on the seven[teenth of the second month . . . Noah from the ark at the appointed time of a full year.

The writer adroitly brought the chronology of the flood in line with a 364-day year calendar and showed that not only Noah, but even the torrential rains and the ark respected the Sabbath. Genesis 8:14 says: "On the 27th of the second month the land was completely dry." Reflecting a literal interpretation of Gen 2:2–3, the author of Jubilees emphasizes that God had kept the Sabbath before listing what God had created on the six previous days (2:1). Even the angels observed the days correctly in heaven (*Jub* 2:30–33). The expression "at the appointed time" probably means that Noah was simply acting according to divine scheduling.

Undoubtedly, the 4Q252 and *Jubilees* share an interest in a particular calendar whose leading principle was the observance of the Sabbath. Their language is not identical: the commentary is concerned with days of the week and dates *Jubilees* speaks of the "new moon" of a particular month. *Jubilees,* when speaking about the 150 days and nights of continued raining, refers to this as five months. Obviously, *Jubilees* is responding to a serious polemic among certain Jews in the time of the

Second Temple concerning the use of a 354-day calendar or one like that of *Jubilees* and the 4Q252 based on 364 days (*Jub* 6:30–38).

The author of Jubilees eliminates much of the narrative found in Genesis 6–11. Missing are the stories about the angels who descended from heaven, took women, and had children, the origin of evil in the earth, stories about Noah and his family, some of the divine speech, building the ark, the collection of animals, building an altar, worship, and Noah as vintner. Clearly, in the portion on Noah the writer overlay the biblical flood with a template based on a 364-day year and keeping the Sabbath, divine wisdom and law that may have been lost during the flood or even earlier.

In the section following the flood, Noah awakens from his drunken stupor to discover his sons covering up his nakedness. The youngest son Ham had seen his father's private parts, but since he had already been blessed, Noah officially cursed his grandson Canaan (Gen 9:24–25). In this case, the author clarifies the ambiguity of the biblical passage. Fragment 1 from another manuscript (4Q253) mentions Israel, the ark, and uses the phrase "to make known to Noah." The traditional Bible does not introduce Israel until Gen 32:28 long after the flood, but *Jub.* 6:10–11 inserts Israel right after the flood. In a third context (4Q254a frags. 1–2), the dove sent out by Noah is mentioned before reference to the dimensions of the ark. In ancient Jewish tradition, the dove foresaw the future. Fragment 3 reports that Noah exits the ark on the 17th of the month and a raven sent forth by Noah returned to make something known to latter generations. This may be the oldest Hebrew reference to the raven's ability to see the future.

The author skips other narratives so that he could arrive at Abraham, another of those favored by God. The biblical material that is lacking includes the list of peoples in the world, the tower of Babel, the generations from Noah to Abram, and even Abraham in Egypt (Gen 10:1—15:7). *Jubilees* 6:17–22 notes that the Feast of Weeks had been celebrated up to the time of Noah, was forgotten by Noah's children, and reinstated during the time of Abraham.

Without a smooth transition the author writes: "He gave the land to Abram, his beloved. [Terah] was one hundred and for[t]y-five years old when he . . . ," that is, Abram departed Ur for Haran. The ex-biblical comment continues: "Now Ab[ram was se]venty years old and for five years Abram dwelt in Haran. And afterwards Abram left for the land of

Canaan." This concern with the age of a patriarch, echoes similar language about Noah and the flood, is simply inserted before and after the biblical words. This turns the history of the patriarchs into a treatise on world chronology.

In two manuscripts, which are thought to belong to 4Q252–253, there is reference to the *yaḥad*. In 4Q252 4:3–5, after mentioning the coming of the messiah of righteousness, the branch of David, the text reads: "to him and his seed is granted the covenant of kingship of his people . . . the law with the men of the *yaḥad*. . . ." The text of this fragment has no obvious connection to cols. 1–3. Fragment 4 of 4Q253a has a related context: "two sons of oil . . . keepers of God's commandments . . . for the men of the *yaḥad*" (ll. 2–4). The two sons of oil suggests two messianic figures that are somehow connected to a body of orthodox individuals who followed the law.

OTHER WORDS OF THE FAMOUS

Besides *Enoch, Jubilees*, 1QGenApoc, and 4Q252, which show that biblical motifs and traditions could be expanded based on current ideas of angelology, revelation, the calendar and world history, and the Law, there are also manuscripts of apocryphal works attributed to or about the archangel Michael (4Q529, 6Q23), Enosh (4Q369), Noah (1Q19, 4Q534–536, 6Q8, 19), Moses (1Q22, 4Q375–376, 377, 390), Levi (4Q213–214, 1Q21, 4Q537–541), Naphtali (4Q215), Joseph (4Q371–372), Qahat (4Q542), Amram (4Q543–548), Joshua (4Q378–379), Samuel (4Q160), Elisha (4Q481A), David (11QPs^a, 4Q522, 5Q9), Zedekiah (4Q470), Jeremiah (4Q384–385B), Ezekiel (4Q385–391), Nabonidus (4Q242), and some fragments called "Proto-Esther" (4Q550).[9]

These "Words of the Famous" were intended to offer lessons for the people of Israel on the past, the present, and the future. Typical topics are the heavenly tablets, festivals, Sabbaths, judgment, the fallen angels and the giants, angelic speeches, prayer, the coming messiah, the prophet who preaches treason, the dominion of Belial or Satan, the temple, violence in the holy city, the piety of King Zedekiah, the lamentations of Jeremiah, the healing of a foreign monarch, a parable of the kingdoms, the wars at the end of days, and the allegiance of the Persian king Darius to the Jewish God. These works and their ideas represent some of the greatest thinking of the ancient Jewish intelligentsia and must have also been shared by the less educated believers in the society.

THE *REWORKED PENTATEUCH*

The *Reworked Pentateuch* (RP) is the name given to about 186 fragments from four manuscripts running from Genesis to Deuteronomy
and interspersed with additions, omissions, and novel textual sequences
(4Q158).[10] Some experts on the Scrolls believe that this work originally
measured between 22 and 27 m. This supposition is doubtful or at least
problematic, because much of the pentateuchal text is missing or has
been lost from these manuscripts.[11] Another manuscript dubbed *Biblical
Paraphrases* (4Q158) is often said to belong to the RP. In earlier years it
was called the Pentateuchal Paraphrase.

The key authorial strategies used in creating the RP are topical
juxtaposition, whereby passages on a particular subject are brought together, and free composition. Both approaches have the twin purposes
of making the biblical text easier to understand and to ensure that it is
more edifying. Topical juxtaposition obviously unites passages on a certain theme, but this approach also eliminates or subordinates passages
that were not to the point. In free composition the author speaks anew
for God. 4Q364 frag. 3 includes a 'blessing' inserted just before Gen
28:6. This combination appears in no other version of the Jewish Bible.
Another fragment, 23a-b col. 1, joins Num 20:17–18 with Deut 2:8–14.
This connection had already been made in the Samaritan Pentateuch.
Vestiges of a poetic interlude somewhat reminiscent of the Song of
Moses (in Exod 15:1, 7, 10) preceded Exod 15:22–26. Fragment 23 also
has an extensive addition to Lev 23:42—24:2, which presents a sequence
of tribes bringing the wood offerings for sacrifice. This fragment may
have belonged to another copy of 11QT^a 23–24 or have been an independent source for the 11QT^a. Fragment 28 combines Num 4:47–49 and
7:1, since they both concern the service within the temple. In the same
fashion, two passages about the feast of booths (Num 29:32—30:1; Deut
16:13–14) are brought together. Especially because of their combination
of topically similar passages, the manuscripts 4Q364 and 4Q365 have
been designated as "proto-Samaritan" or "pre-Samaritan." In fact, this
scribal approach typifies parts of 4QExod^m and 4QNum^b.

TARGUMS TO LEVITICUS AND JOB

Ezra 4:4 and Neh 8:8 recount an occasion when Ezra gave a public
reading of the Law in Jerusalem. As he read from the text, groups of

Levites, apparently expert in such matters, were dispatched to explain his readings to an unknowledgeable audience. Almost immediately study sessions were scheduled to clarify the biblical text further. From this context arose the term *targum*.

The word *targum* refers typically to an Aramaic rendering of a biblical book. After the Second Jewish Revolt (132–135 CE) against the Romans, there is plenty of evidence for the composition of *targumin*. Targum Onkelos was written to provide a reader for Aramaic speakers. Later, the Palestinian Targum and Pseudo-Jonathan added expansive *midrashim* (commentaries) on classical biblical traditions. Luke 4 also describes how scriptural readings were often followed by a spoken Aramaic translation or interpretation in the synagogue.

Brief portions of an Aramaic *targum* on Lev 16:12–15, 18–21 (4Q156) prove that legal interpreters created such works during the Second Temple period, thus confirming the essential factuality of Ezra and Nehemiah. The few extant verses from Cave 4's *targum* on Leviticus dealt with the Day of Atonement and the purification of the Temple.

Rabbinic tradition tells how a Rabban Gamaliel once hid a *targum* on the book of Job. This was the same Gamaliel known as the teacher of Paul of Tarsus (Acts 22:3). In Qumran's Caves 4 and 11 two such *targumin* were discovered.[12] The Cave 4 *targum* preserves Aramaic texts for Job 3:5–9 and 4:16—5:4. In Cave 11, however, a well-preserved manuscript of a *targum* on Job (11Q10) was found. In a lovely Herodian hand, this manuscript contains an Aramaic rendering for Job 17:14–42. This translation is literal in general and based on a traditional Hebrew text. On occasion words have been added to clarify the meaning of a single word, phrase, or the context. Two other long and well-kept scrolls were also discovered in cave 11—the famous 11Ps[a] and the 11QT[a]. A fragment found in Cave 4 that reads "[the] interpreter (*trgmn*) is he who was . . ." (4Q254, frag. 16). The Qumran evidence for *targumin* proves conclusively that the translation of texts was needed much earlier than the time of the Second Revolt against Rome in the 130s CE.

THE *TEMPLE SCROLL*

The story of the discovery and acquisition of the *Temple Scroll* (11QT[a]) sounds like something out of a great adventure novel.[13] It involved intrigue, deception, money, and national pride. The eventual editor, Yigael Yadin, received several Hebrew fragments. One of them read, "If the high priest . . ." Dead Sea Scroll scholars immediately thought of a conflict in other scrolls between a Teacher of Righteousness and a Wicked Priest, presumably a controversy between a former high priest and another who had been placed in his position illegitimately. During the following years Yadin learned of a 45-foot scroll for which his lawyers made an offer of $130,000. Although he had already made a down payment of $10,000, Yadin waited until Israel had won the Six-Day War in 1967 and therefore Jordanian territory in East Jerusalem to dispatch a trusted captain in the Israel Defence Forces to retrieve this lengthy scroll from the famed antiquities dealer Kando. Several fragments had been hidden behind family photographs in the home of Kando's cousin. One of them read, "seven complete weeks . . . you shall count fifty days." 11QT^a was discovered below the floor in Kando's house in a shoe box wrapped in cellophane and a towel. Kando meant to protect it and in due time was compensated with $105,000.

After carefully unrolling and cleaning the scroll, handwriting experts confirmed its antiquity noting that this scroll, which Yadin had named the *Temple Scroll*, had been copied in two Herodian hands. The script of cols. 6–66 belonged somewhere between that of 1QM and 1QGenApoc, and thus could be dated roughly to the end of first century BCE. Columns (1) 2–5, which replaced the original beginning of the scroll, was copied later. However, a fragment in the Rockefeller Museum (43.366) bearing a text like that in 11QT^a 23 was penned in a script like those of the Isaiah A manuscript from Cave 1 and a Deuteronomy manuscript from Cave 4 (4QDeut^a). This suggests that the 11QT^a or at least its sources were copied as early as the second century BCE. 11QT^a was pre-canonical, pre-Christian, and certainly worth more than the compensation paid to Kando.

Upon inspection 11QT^a turns out to be a law book of some apparent status. That is at least the impression it is meant to give. Its sources have been expertly edited in order to present a rather complete law book, which one could have imagined having been delivered to Moses on Sinai. The contents of the scroll are as follows:

Col. 2	covenant on the mountain
Cols. 3–12	temple and its furnishings
Cols. 13–29	festivals and offerings
Cols. 29–45	temple and courts and gates
Cols. 45–47	sanctity of the temple and the temple city

Cols. 48–51	unclean animals, cemeteries, and purity laws
Cols. 51–52	judges, officers, idolatry
Cols. 53–56	vows, oaths, pledges, prophets, and enticers
Cols. 56–59	king, army, king's bodyguard, council, king's wife, wars, curse and blessing
Col. 60	priestly and levitical dues
Cols. 60–63	abominable practice of the foreigners, false prophets, single witness, war, and the captive woman
Col. 64	rebellious offspring and cases of treason
Col. 65	marriage and incest laws

Several writers were involved in creating 11QT^a, but certainly a later redactor made major decisions in sculpting this law book. This redactor chose to eliminate historical narratives altogether. While the law-giving at Sinai is clearly assumed, and this presupposes the role of Moses, the redactor avoided giving him a prominent role in this masterpiece. An oddity without explanation is that such a valuable piece of ancient historical law remained incomplete in antiquity. The scroll ends abruptly without a clear conclusion.

11QT^a has often been categorized as a pseudepigraph, since God often speaks direct in the first person while legislating. Scholars believe that this fiction proves that the author of the scroll intended that his audience view it as the authentic words of God. Others think that the 11QT^a was written to rival the known Pentateuch. Still others, like Yadin, felt that 11QT^a was composed by a member of Qumran's Essene community.

Because of its sheer length and relatively comprehensive nature, 11QT^a has been studied from a variety of historical and literary angles. Yadin saw the dependence 11QT^a on the Pentateuch throughout, but allowed for turning God into the sole speaker. Several ancient editors culled and united laws on the same subject from various places, often eliminating apparent contradictions, modification of biblical commands, and the insertion of entirely new sections. Source analysis of the scroll has suggested that an editor had simply connected several pre-existent sources—a temple source, a source of laws for the polity, temple-related laws, a temple source, and a purity source, gluing the sections together with his redactional passages.[14] Certainly, Exodus, Leviticus, Numbers, and Deuteronomy are its chief ancient sources from which perhaps other sources were created. This is most obvious in cols. 13–29 (the so-called Calendar Source).

The 364-Day Calendar

Month	I					II					III				
Day	(1)	(8)	15	22	29		6	13	20	27		4	11	18	25
	(2)	9	16	23	30		7	(14)	21	28		5	12	19	26
	(3)	10	17	24		1	8	15	22	29		6	13	20	27
	(4)	11	18	25		2	9	16	23	30		7	14	21	28
	(5)	12	19	(26)		3	10	17	24		1	8	(15)	22	29
	(6)	13	20	27		4	11	18	25		2	9	16	23	30
	(7)	(14)	21	28		5	12	19	26		3	10	17	24	31
IV						**V**					**VI**				
1	8	15	22	29		6	13	20	27		4	11	18	(25)
2	9	16	23	30		7	14	21	28		5	12	19	(26)
3	10	17	24		1	8	15	22	29		6	13	20	(27)
4	11	18	25		2	9	16	23	30		7	14	21	(28)
5	12	19	26		(3)	10	17	24		1	8	15	(22)	(29)
6	13	20	27		4	11	18	25		2	9	16	(23)	30
7	14	21	28		5	12	19	26		3	10	17	(24)	31
VII						**VIII**					**IX**				
(1)	8	(15)	(22)	29		6	13	20	27		4	11	18	25
2	9	(16)	23	30		7	14	21	28		5	12	19	26
3	(10)	(17)	24		1	8	15	22	29		6	13	20	27
4	11	(18)	25		2	9	16	23	30		7	14	21	28
5	12	(19)	26		3	10	17	24		1	8	15	22	29
6	13	(20)	27		4	11	18	25		2	9	16	23	30
7	14	(21)	28		5	12	19	26		3	10	17	24	31
X						**XI**					**XII**				
1	8	15	22	29		6	13	20	27		4	11	18	25
2	9	16	23	30		7	14	21	28		5	12	19	26
3	10	17	24		1	8	15	22	29		6	13	20	27
4	11	18	25		2	9	16	23	30		7	14	21	28
5	12	19	26		3	10	17	24		1	8	15	22	29
6	13	20	27		4	11	18	25		2	9	16	23	30
7	14	21	28		5	12	19	26		3	10	17	24	31

1/1–7(8)	Priestly Ordination	6/22	Feast of New Oil
1/14	Passover	6/23–29	Feast of Wood
1/26	Waving of the Barley Sheaf	7/1	Day of Remembrance
2/14	Second Passover (?)	7/10	Day of Atonement
3/15	Feast of New Wheat/Weeks	7/15–22	Feast of Booths
5/3	Feast of New Wine		

Taken as a whole, no one can deny that 11QT[a] is a very original and impressive work of Jewish jurisprudence, no matter how it was put together.

11QT[a] has been described in numerous ways—as a veritable Torah (Law) of the Lord, a divine code of laws, an exegetical monument inspired by God, a realistic fantasy, an authoritative addition to the Pentateuch, a commentary on the Law, a sixth book of the Torah, a study text, the work of a creative legalist, rewritten Torah, a utopian vision, a blueprint, an independent revelation, a constitution, a pseudepigraph, an expression of the will of God, a new book of the Law to stand alongside the Mosaic Torah, a more perfect Torah, a re-presentation of biblical law, the last attempt at the meta-narrative within scripture, the true religious codex of the Qumran sect, a vision, and an ideal description. It seems that most of these descriptions fit the scroll quite well.

One fascinating feature of 11QT^a is that it opens apparently on Mt. Sinai and moves quickly to the temple's altar for burnt-offerings, structures, and furnishings before presenting the sacred calendar that would have dominated most activity at the temple. Along with the regular morning and evening offerings, the Sabbath offering, the offerings for the beginning of the month and year, the Temple presents the consecration, Passover, the waving of the barley sheaf, the first-fruits of wheat, wine, and oil. In the calendar section, the waving of the barley sheaf serves as the legal precedent for three more first-harvest feasts at fifty-day intervals.[15]

> And count seven complete Sabbaths from the day when you offered the sheaf (of barley) . . . count, until the day following the seventh Sabbath, count fifty days and offer a new cereal offering (wheat) for Yahweh from your dwellings (18.10–12). And count for yourselves from the day when you brought the new cereal offering for Yahweh, the bread of the first fruits, seven weeks, seven complete sabbaths until the day after the seventh sabbath, count fifty days and then bring new wine for the drink offering. (19.11–14)

These harvest festivals also require their own animal sacrifices and give attention to priestly portions.

The calendar section concludes with a rather exciting first-person divine speech.

> I will sanctify my sanctuary with my glory for I shall cause my glory to dwell upon it until the Day of Blessing/Creation when I create my sanctuary to prepare it for myself for all time according to the covenant which I made with Jacob and Bethel. (29.8–10)

This divine statement has been characterized as a redactional element inserted to connect what preceded it with what followed it. It remains a very intriguing appeal to the Jacob/Bethel traditions.

11QT[a] reads as if an entire section devoted to the calendar had been spliced between two sections on the temple itself. The second part on the temple includes instructions for the outmost area of worship— the building of a staircase tower, a structure for the laver, another for the altar vessels, the slaughtering area, and a columned area on the west side. Then one reads about the inner or priestly court, the gatehouses, the wings, the porches, and the cooking areas. The middle court is for all males qualified to serve at the temple. Reference is made to those who are permitted and not permitted to enter this court, the required sin-offering, the gatehouses, and the wings. Finally, the author deals with the outermost, Israelite court and its structures. The remainder of the scroll deals with cases of impurity, officials, vows, false prophets, laws related to the king, priestly and levitical dues, witnesses, war scenarios, treason, and inappropriate sexual intercourse, much of which was extracted from Deuteronomy and rearranged.[16]

While 11QT[a] can be characterized as an original composition, its various sections are dependent to distinct degrees on classical biblical laws. Lacking any definitive narrative framework, the scroll invites speculation about its authorship, the date of its compilation, and its use. Scholars are still concerned about who wrote 11QT[a] and for whom was it authoritative in antiquity. For Yigael Yadin, who presented 11QT[a] to the scholarly world, the author of the scroll was the Teacher of Righteousness. This mysterious figure has been identified with a certain Zadok who lived in the early second century BCE.[17] Still, the human enterprise that created the scroll has left few if any clues as to its authorship.

THE *NEW JERUSALEM* TEXT

Based on fragmentary manuscripts found in five Qumran caves, the *New Jerusalem* (11QNJ) presents a guided tour of an immense, imaginary city, which some see as only an ideal model and which others suggest was meant to be the Jerusalem of the last days.[18] It appears similar to the pictures laid out in Ezekiel 40–48 and Revelation 21. If handwriting specialists are right, the 11QNJ came from the late first century BCE to the first century CE.

Perhaps this urban vision came from a planner or surveyor's pen. The work deals in measurements and dimensions. A block of residential housing is calculated at 51 reeds square (with one reed equaling 7 cubits and a cubit measuring approximately the length from the elbow to the fingertips). Surrounding this housing block there was a passage for movement 21 reeds wide. And between the blocks the streets were six reeds wide. The eastern and western avenues measured ten feet in width. Another avenue running north of the temple was 18 reeds in width. Avenues stretching from south to north are measured at 9 reeds and 4 cubits wide. A thoroughfare ran through the center of the city which was 13 reeds and 1 cubit wide (an estimate is that it would have measured 132 feet or 40 meters in width). That is easy to calculate, but difficult to fathom. The city's streets would be paved with white stone, marble, and jasper.

This fantastic city would have eighty side entrances, each two reeds wide and supported by two one-reed blocks of stone. In addition to these lateral doors, there would be twelve main entrances measuring three rods each in width. On each side of these doors, towers measuring five reeds square would be erected. The author backtracks in order to give measurements for the entrance to the blocks of houses and thresholds. Additional stairways are also mentioned. The houses are then described along with their dimensions. Then come the dining rooms, each furnished with twenty-two couches and eleven windows. At this point, the text has broken off, and the vision seems to end.

Other fragments of 11QNJ text suggest that its description may have started with the gates of the temple and radiated outward including an ideal city for housing the perfect temple. Such a city would have impressed locals and visitors alike. Although some interpreters have suggested Near Eastern parallels to this city, it is far from typical. It was designed to highlight a magnificent communal area for living and dining within broad and leisurely boulevards.

Perhaps the author simply envisioned and hoped to see such a city within his lifetime. Nowhere does the visionary name this city. Nor does he make an allusion to or comparison his city with Jerusalem. This is equally true for the city of the temple in 11QT^a, which practically every modern interpreter still associates with ancient Jerusalem.

THE *APOCRYPHON OF JOSHUA*

Many of the seventy fragments that constitute the two manuscripts of the *Apocryphon of Joshua* (4Q379) preserve so little of the text that reconstruction is difficult.[19] Certain fragments of 4Q379 use language from psalms, praise, and prayer (frags. 12, 18, 22, and 27). Others mention cities connected with the story of Joshua—Aroer (frag. 2; see Josh 12:2; 13:9, 16; Num 32:34); Bethel (Joshua 8). Fragment 1 refers to several of Jacob's sons starting with Levi.

Two fragments of this work still preserve enough of the narrative context so that one can at least understand some of the author's concerns. Fragment 1, paralleling Josh 3:13–16, mentions crossing the Jordan river in the first month of the forty-first year of the exodus from Egypt. As in the Book of Jubilees, the scribe notes that this occurred during the wheat harvest of a jubilee year.

> . . . they [cr]ossed on dry ground in [the fi]rst month of the forty-f[irst] year of their exodus from the land of Egypt. That was a jubilee year at the beginning of their entry into the land of Canaan. And the Jordan overflows its banks from the f[our]th month until the wheat harvest. (4Q379 12)

The presence of this chronological entry demonstrates a concern to date accurately the major historical and theological event of crossing the Jordan, reminding one of a similar concern in the 4Q252 regarding the chronology of the flood. Unfortunately, other similar glosses are now lost.

Fragment 22 ii reflects Josh 6. Modern editors have used *Testimonia* (4Q175 21–30), which refers to Joshua's prayer and curse on persons who would rebuild the city of Jericho, to reconstruct the 4Q379.[20] 4Q175 says that blood would reach "the ramparts of the daughters of Zion and within the boundary of Jerusalem." It is possible that the writer of 4Q175 quoted from the 4Q379, treating it just as authoritatively as he had his extracts from Deuteronomy and Numbers.

Another manuscript of the *Apocryphon of Joshua* (4Q378) is represented by twenty-nine fragments. Most of them seem to be more closely connected with Deuteronomy than Joshua. In frag. 14, the Israelites are mourning the death of Moses. Fragment 22 mentions Moses, Joshua, and God's promise to Abraham. Fragment 26 notes that Moses was a man of God who shared God's desires.

PSALMS FROM THE QUMRAN CAVES

The discovery of multiple manuscripts of the Psalms as well as liturgical pieces in the Qumran caves emphasizes the fact that this literary genre comes close to imitating the voice of man before God, pleading, thanking, expressing hope, anguish, dismay, and exultation. The Psalms were clearly the most copied and used part of the Jewish Bible, because they brought people closer to God and to each other. Over three dozen manuscripts of the Psalms were discovered in the caves.

The Psalms Scroll *from Cave 11*

The *Psalms Scroll* (11QPs^a) reflects a collection of psalms that contrasts often with the traditional book of Psalms known in the traditional Masoretic text.[21] One sees this both in the arrangement or sequencing of the psalms and the appearance of psalms known from other collections such as the Syriac Psalms. There are also psalms that were previously unknown until the discovery of these scrolls and other cave 4 fragments. ASOR purchased the copyright to this partial scroll, which was edited in about 13 months by James A. Sanders and a number of collaborators and published two years later in 1965.

11QPs^a consists of 27 columns and 5 fragments written in a very legible middle to late Herodian script. The divine name Yahweh was recorded in paleo-Hebrew. The preserved scroll entails about 51 Psalms: 101–103, 109, 118, 104, 147, 105, 146, 148, 120–132, 119, 135–136, a work titled *Catena*, 145 plus a superscript, 154, a plea for deliverance, 139, 137, 138, Ben Sira 51, an apostrophe to Zion, 93, 141, 133, 144, 155, 142–143, 149–150, a hymn to the creator, a prose section concerning the literary compositions of David, 140, 134, 151A, and 151B. This listing of psalms indicates a collection of the last third of the known book of Psalms arranged quite differently and given a seal of approval as something like "the Psalms of King David."

Known in the Syriac Bible as Psalm 2, Psalm 154 is a call to assembly, wisdom, prayer, and meditation, forms of worship just as respectable in God's eyes as burnt offerings at the Jerusalem temple. Sandwiched between Psalms 154 and 139, the plea for deliverance includes the elements of humility, praise, sinfulness, confession, and a request for forgiveness. This plea for deliverance is also a novelty previously unknown.

Ben Sira 51 was indeed part of the Jewish tradition before the discovery of the Dead Sea Scrolls, but it had never before been part of a collection of psalms. In 11QPs^a Ben Sira 51 has been inserted between Psalm 138 and an apostrophe to Zion, whose idealistic language contrasts sharply with the impression given by the Qumran *pesharim* and other scrolls.

Psalm 155, which includes a confession and a request for cleansing and forgiveness, is known in the Syriac as Psalm 3. The hymn to the creator appears between Psalms 150 and 140. It speaks of God's creative act of separating light from darkness, the angelic praise upon witnessing this act, and God's creation of the heavens and other meteorological elements.

One of the most cited portions of this psalm scroll tells us that David was a scribe perfect in all his ways. God's anointing of David imbued him with the spirit that enable his prolific production of 3,600 psalms, 364 songs for the daily sacrifices all year long, 52 songs for the Sabbath offerings, 30 songs for the new moons, feast days, and the Day of Atonement. David wrote 446 songs in all, four of which served to palliate those suffering from some evil attack or incubation. Without the divine spirit David would never had composed 4,050 psalms and related verses. The compiler's intention was perhaps to have David outshine or at least complement Solomon's prolific 4,005 proverbs and songs (in the Hebrew). Josephus referred to Solomon's 4,005 poems and parables. The Greek speaks of Solomon's 3,000 proverbs and 5,000 songs.

The number of Davidic compositions obviously reflects the use of a solar calendar of 364 days, 360 calendar days plus four intercalendary days, and thus a period of 52 weeks.

The non-MT portions of this psalm collection share several themes. The David psalms and perhaps all of the psalms were meant to convey the spirit of prophecy with which Samuel had anointed David (the apostrophe to Zion, the Davidic prose tradition, and Psalms 151A and 151B). The spirit of wisdom recurs in psalms 154, the hymn to the creator, and the Davidic prose. Both prophecy and wisdom come from the Most High God who is mentioned in psalms 154, the apostrophe to Zion, the hymn to the creator, and the David's prose section.

11QPs^a ends with Psalms 151A and 151B (according to the Greek psalms). In combination, these two psalms form Psalm 1 of the Syriac tradition. In terms of content, they recount God's selection of David the shepherd boy, the prophet Samuel's physical anointing of David, and David's demonstration of extraordinary courage and strength after his anointing in his confrontation with Goliath. Unlike the proto-rabbinic Psalms collection, this one leaves no room for doubting that it should be considered a Davidic collection. This emphasis appears at the conclusion of the Greek psalms, but is placed at the beginning of the Syriac psalms. In contrast to the traditional book of Psalms, whose superscriptions situated within the history related in the books of Samuel, 11QPs[a], the Greek, and the Syriac emphasize that the collection was Davidic wisdom.

Scholars continue to discuss the nature of this beautiful psalms scroll, which seemed quite unusual until the discovery of similar written psalms manuscripts found in Cave 4. Some argue that 11QPs[a] was the Psalter of the Qumran community or that it was a liturgical collection, but not an authoritative collection. Others emphasized its authority and usefulness for study and worship. Above all, 11QPs[a] proves that ancient Jews appealed to the psalms regularly and in a variety of ways in order to express their devotion and proximity to the deity.

Other Manuscripts of the Psalms

In Cave 4 alone 23 manuscripts of the Psalms were found.[22] Six more were discovered in Cave 11. Three survived in Cave 1, and Caves 2, 3, 5, 6, and 8 each preserved a single psalm manuscript, bringing the total to 37. They have all been dated from the mid-second century BCE to the presumed time when the Romans captured Khirbet Qumran in 69/70 CE. Besides the traditionally known and used psalms, Caves 4 and 11 yielded fourteen others. Eight, perhaps nine of them, seem to be new compositions and thus function more or less as originals.

For Psalms 1–89 the traditional sequence seems to have survived with a few variations. For instance in two Cave 4 manuscripts (4QPs[a] and 4QPs[q]), Psalm 31 is followed by Psalm 33. In 4QPs[a] Psalm 38 is immediately followed by Psalm 71. Scholars suggest that five differing sequences for Psalms 90–150 are preserved in the Qumran scrolls: (1) the sequencing of the MT, (2) that of 11QPs[a], (3) an arrangement of Psalms 91 preceded by four psalms against demons (11QapocrPs), (4) another of Psalms 91–103 plus Psalm 112 (apparently excluding Psalms 92–111), and (5) a highly unusual collection consisting of Psalms 22, 107, 109, and three new psalms—the apostrophe to Zion, an eschatological hymn, and an apostrophe to Judah (4QPs[f]).

Perhaps most important of all is what the ancient scribes intended to accomplish with their various combinations. 11QPs[a] elevates the figure of David to that of prophet, scribe, and master of wisdom. In the case of 4QPs[n], the combination creates a different focus and tone. Psalm 135:12b is followed by 136:22a, a familiar refrain. According to the modern editor, this new combination or transition shifts the movement from a survey of God's saving deeds in Israel's history in the voice of the third person (135:8–12) to a personal story that includes the voice of the first person ("who remembered us," v. 23; "he rescued us," v. 24). This scribal reformulation produces a more personal and at the same time liturgical text.

The Psalms were the most reproduced, studied, and revised of all the biblical books. This accords well with the belief that psalms and prayers offered with the best intentions are just as good as whole burnt sacrificial offerings (1QS 9:4; 4Q258 7:3–6). In conjunction with that, one who immersed himself in the study and reading of such psalms as were found in the Qumran caves could certainly consider themselves the successors of their pious and wise King David.

Even More Psalms

The Dead Sea Scrolls augment greatly the number and variety of ancient psalms, prayers, and poetry beyond any other known biblical canon. Some of these new psalms were composed to continue traditional forms used in Jewish worship. Some were written to praise Israel, Judaea, Zion, Jerusalem, and the creator. Occasionally, a previously unknown psalm is attributed to a person known from Israel's or Judaea's history or even to a foreigner.[23] There is a psalm of Obadiah, one of an unknown man of God, a prayer of a king of Judaea, and a prayer of Manasseh. Many of these psalms belonged in a private setting of worship, some were probably presented aloud at the temple, and in other group settings. Some were even created to be read or recited on certain days and evenings of the week, for Sabbaths, and for festivals such as the Day of Atonement and the Day of the First-Fruits. There are blessings at sunrise. Others were composed as incantations to drive off all types of evil spirits. This is also reminiscent of the scribal activity of one like David in 11QPs[a].

Collective confession and historical retrospective are combined in the *Words of the Heavenly Lights* (4Q504–506, compare the *Confessional Ritual* 4Q393). The *Angelic Songs of the Sabbath Sacrifice* (4QShirShab, 11QShirShab) paint a world of angelic worship before God in the heavens. These songs were apparently meant to be read on specific Sabbaths within a three-month or thirteen-sabbath period. This work is witnessed in Caves 4, 11, and at Masada. 1QSb contains blessings of the chosen ones, the high priest, the priests, and the prince of the congregation. The *Prayer of Nabonidus* (4Q242) reminds one of monarchs who praise God in the book of Daniel.[24] It was written to show that God even sheds his mercy on a foreign king if his heart turns. A highly provocative manuscript preserves a praise of God which mentions his redeeming his poor ones from their oppressors and his selection of Jerusalem (4Q448).[25] In the same manuscript, this praise seems to be interpreted as referring to King Jonathan and God's people, Israel, wherever they may reside in the four corners of the universe. Scholars have suggested that the monarch King Jonathan be identified with either Jonathan Maccabeus or Alexander Jannaeus.[26]

Published very early, the personal hymnic devotion of the *Thanksgiving Hymns* (1QH, also 4QH) demonstrated the importance of individual hymns that resound with the unmistakable voice of a leader, a teacher, and perhaps a martyr.[27]

> I have been a snare to those who rebel but healing to those who repent, prudence to the simple ones, and steadfastness to fearful of heart. For traitors you have made me a mockery and scorn, but a counsel of truth and understanding to the upright of way. (X, 8–9; previously II, 8–9)

Within the broader collection there are also collective confessions, sometimes combined with an historical retrospective as in the *Words of the Heavenly Lights* (4Q504–506; cf. the so-called *Confessional Ritual* 4Q393).

The greatest contribution of the psalms from the Dead Sea caves is to show that personal piety consisted not only in using traditional psalms as received, but in reinventing them or even by adding to collections that already existed. Simple forms of spoken piety obviously found their way into various literary compositions. Even 1QS, a sort of community handbook, concludes with a thanksgiving hymn (1QS X 8–23). Poetic prayer also has its place in the 1QM (10:8–16; 12:10–16; 14:4–17; and 19:22–8). These psalms and hymns reveal a great degree of ideological and literary freedom beyond what is found in the classical biblical psalms.

WORKS OF WISDOM AMONG THE DEAD SEA SCROLLS

The word "wisdom" is often used in biblical studies to refer to a short list of works dealing with practical wisdom in one's daily life, with reflections on the meaning of life and one's fate, with meditations on why the past occurred as it did, and insights about God's creative act, actions in history, and in one's own life. Wisdom is what one generation passes on to the next. Typically included in the list of biblical wisdom works are Proverbs, Ecclesiastes, Job, and Ben Sira. Many other works of wisdom were preserved among the Scrolls. Some offer practical advice. Some tell the reader to contemplate "the secret of being" and to accept of one's place in the scheme of things.[28]

Instruction

Starting from the practical side, one encounters words of counsel for daily life. This wisdom, which usually appears in the form of a father's or a sage's advice to his son/s, is well known in the book of Proverbs. Initially, some of these Qumran manuscripts were called *Sapiential Works*, but that designation was changed later to *Instructions* (4Q416–417, 420, 424). Some of the key topics, as in Proverbs, are money, wealth, luxuries, dealings with one's neighbors, and daily work:

> If in your need you borrow money from people do not delay (. . . in repaying it). Do not exchange your holy spirit for any wealth, for no price is worth it . . . Do not fill yourself with bread and wine while there is no food. Do not seek luxury when you lack bread. Do not touch it (a deposit of money), [if someone entrust it to you], lest it burn up and your body (also) be devoured by its fame.

These instructions encourage the wise one to use common sense. Other counsels warn the wise one to avoid dealings with certain evil types of individuals.

> Do not humble yourself to one who is not your equal. Do not strike someone who lacks your strength, lest you stumble and increase your (own) shame greatly. Do not entrust a sleepy man with something delicate, for he will not treat your work gently . . . Do not [send] a grumbler to procure money for your need nor put your trust in a man with twisted lips. Do not put a stingy man in charge of your money. A man who judges before investigating . . . do not put him in charge of those who pursue knowledge. Do not send a blind man to bring a vision to the upright.
>
> Likewise, do not send a man who is hard of hearing to inquire into judgment, for he will not smooth out a quarrel between people.

The wise one should always be careful with whom he associates and protect his own station in life as well as his possessions. The assumption is that he has much control over his own life. If he is not prudent, he may contribute directly to his own destruction.

A Parable

One parable is reminiscent of Old and New Testament language. "Wise men, consider this: A man has a good tree (growing) up to heaven, to the lengths of the lands, yet it (pro)duces thorny fruits" (4Q302ᵃ). In its present form, it recalls Psalm 1; Matt 3:7; and Mark 4; but no doubt an ancient audience might have thought about the trees in the garden of Eden. The lesson here is to shun the bad tree or the people whose behaviors are not acceptable. Anyone could understand the instruction and parable mentioned above.

Meditation on the Mystery

Within this wisdom the wise one is told to meditate on the *raz nihyeh.* This expression has been translated as "the secret of being," "the secret of existence," or "the secret of what is to be/will be." The course of one's life and history should be contemplated in order to grasp the coming salvation (4Q417). If one's status improves one should remember the mystery of the beginnings of the world and the creation. Sometimes it sounds as if the writer is counseling one to reflect on the natural order, especially when he tells the wise one to honor his parents, for one day he too will be a parent (4Q416). The wise one is told to meditate on the mystery of being and to study it regularly so that he can know the distinction between what is good and what is evil: "because the God of knowledge is the foundation of truth, and by means of the mystery of being" God accomplishes all things (4Q418). The wise one is not given a well-formulated key to understand life, but is encouraged to use his own mind and heart to understand his place within God's plan. The details of the plan remain a mystery to be revealed in the unfolding of time.

Cave 1 preserved two of these mystery texts (1Q26–27). The wise man is told that iniquity is not located solely among one people but in every nation, just as are pieces of truth. In due time righteousness and knowledge will envelope the world wiping out all forms of evil and wickedness in its wake. The mysteries texts speak of or allude to God's foreknowledge and predestination of all history events and plans. The ideal wise person remains patient and focuses on the eternal secrets and the origins of wisdom, unlike magicians and soothsayers who utter senseless parables. Although the mystery seems to be unfathomable, one can discover clues to understanding it in God's creation and his ongoing orchestration of natural events. In *Meditations on Creation* (4Q303–305) the writer suggests that one take the heavenly lights as a point of orientation for understanding God's creative acts. One must also strive to understand the past. In this context the wise disciple is told not to hold a grudge.

Another mystery text (4Q301), formulated in the first person and apparently addressed to a group, deals with God's goodness toward his elect and his willingness to punish the wicked. God rules and judges from his "temple of the kingdom." Several manuscripts similar to the mystery texts (4Q415–423; 1Q26, see above), repeatedly speak of the poverty of the listeners or readers. The wise teacher advises them not to beg for food, to pay back loans quickly, and not to be mirthful during a time of mourning. They are told not to humiliate themselves with someone who is not of their status, not to strike a weaker person, not to hold on to deposits from friends and acquaintances, and not to accept things from a stranger. One should not associate with the blind, the deaf, the unjust person, a person who hates, one who has a fat heart, and a greedy man. All of these types of people may also be understood in a spiritual sense. The audience of men is told to rule over the spirit of their wives and to carefully monitor their vows and freewill offerings.

One manuscript written in an esoteric script speaks of the fruits of listening well, understanding the design of God's creation, accepting one status in life, following the rules, maintaining a life of virtue, and meditation on the ages of the world. The writer is speaking to the "sons of dawn," sometimes thought to refer to the novice members of the Qumran community, but very reminiscent of the "sons of light" mentioned by Jesus in Luke. A *Composition on Divine Providence* (4Q413) is similar to the previous text: "let me instruct you wisdom." Then the writer urges his audience to meditate on "the former years and contemplate the events of past generations as God has revealed." This hortatory language recalls passages in CD (1–8), 1QS 3:13–25, and the epilogue 4QMMT. One can know about what will happen in the future by studying the past and the present time in which one lives. A text called *Ways of Righteousness* again recalls 1QS: "he shall bring his wisdom, his knowledge, his understanding, and his goodness" (4Q421 frag. 1a I line 2). The wise person hears and understands before responding, because he is aware that his words have consequences.

Although wisdom texts may use the admonition, the rhetorical question, and vague references to the mystery, creation, and the future, wisdom certainly may appear in metaphorical dress. The text called *The Seductress* or *Lady Folly* (4Q184) describes a harlot who displays her goods within the city gates. Her beauty, clothing, and even her internal organs serve a single purpose—to entice righteous men into her traps. This female figure certainly does not represent all women, but rather is an attractive and alluring woman whose sole purpose is to entrap the wise and righteous. She should be avoided whether she appears literally on the streets of a city like Jerusalem or Jericho or whether she arrives in the form of wealth and power. This feminine representation of wickedness derives directly from the biblical book of Proverbs (5:3–9; 6:24–29; 7:7–23), which concludes ironically with praise for a good woman (31).

Beatitudes

A work known as *Beatitudes* (4Q525) shows one how to recognize or be a "blessed one." One needs a pure heart and a tongue that does not slander. One lives according to the Law of the Most High and does not abandon that Law, accepting punishments, and avoiding a life of folly. This is reminiscent of Ps 1, where one reads "Blessed is the man who walks not in the counsel of the wicked . . . but his delight is in the Law of the Lord, and on his Law he meditates day and night" (Ps 1:1–2). In form and general content Matthew's beatitudes are similar. Perhaps 4Q525 and Matthew 5 (cf. Mark 4; Luke 6 and 8) shared a common source. They share expressions like "the poor," "those who mourn," "they shall inherit," "the pure in heart," "light," "good works," and "righteousness." This little amount of comparison suggests that some wisdom was often packaged in the form of a sermon or a lesson.

APOCRYPHAL TEXTS

Texts are usually classified as "apocryphal," if they belonged to the Christian Catholic Old Testament, but not to the Jewish Bible. Historically, the list included 1 Esdras, 1–3 Maccabees, Tobit, Judith, Ben Sira, the Wisdom of Solomon, 1 Baruch, the Epistle of Jeremy, the three additions to Daniel—the Prayer of Azariah and the Song of the Three Children,

Susanna, and Bel and the Dragon—and additions to Esther. Only a few of these works turned up in the Qumran caves: they are Tobit, Ben Sira embedded in psalms, and portions of an epistle of Jeremiah. The rest either did not survive in the caves or never belonged to Qumran collection.

Tobit

Before the Qumran finds, Tobit was included in the Greek Bible of the Christian Church. Now it is clear that Tobit was already read in Aramaic and Hebrew in the Second Temple period. The most complete manuscripts of Tobit (4Q196–197) have been dated to the middle of the first century BCE. Parts of eleven of its fourteen chapters survived.[29]

Tobit is always a delight to read, because it seems to have been composed to mix traditional piety with a light-hearted sense of humor. Besides that, its narrative contains little known references to traditional folk medicine and witchery. To summarize the story, a pious Jew living in Nineveh named Tobit interrupts a feast to bury a fellow Jew. When he fell asleep, bird droppings fell into his eyes and blinded him. After this his son Tobiah or Tobias has to travel to retrieve his father's money and find himself a suitable wife. As he travels to Media northeast of the Tigris River in the Persian empire, he is accompanied by Raphael, a guardian angel in human form, and even a dog. Along the way Tobiah catches a fish. Raphael tells him to preserve its gall, heart, and liver—the latter two for his wedding night since the smoke of these fish organs will prevent the demonic attacks of Asmodeus and the gall can curse Tobit's blindness. Of course, the demon Asmodeus was thwarted on Tobiah's wedding night, and Tobit received sight. The story is enhanced with wisdom instruction, prayer, thanksgiving, and almsgiving.

Tobit and Tobiah were not known biblical personalities. In fact, Tobit is presented simply as an understanding, pious citizen, trying to give a Jewish brother a proper burial outside the city walls. Found alongside hundreds of biblical and non-biblical works in Cave 4 and later in the Christian Bible, Tobit seems to have been popular in antiquity.

Ben Sira

This work is named for a Jewish teacher who put together a book of wisdom sayings and instructions in Hebrew in the early second century BCE (ca. 190 BCE). It belongs to the Old Testament portion of the Greek

Christian Bible. A goodly portion of Ben Sira was discovered in the Cairo Genizah, which also had leaves from the *Zadokite Work* (later *Damascus Document*, CD). Two copies of the work and a poem using some lines from Ben Sira cave from the Qumran caves. Fragments of chapters 1 and 2 came from Cave 2. In 11QPs^a 51 one finds Sir 51:13–30.[30] In Ben Sira itself these verses follow the epilogue. Perhaps Sir 51:13–30 had circulated independently and was easy to attach to other works. The plain meaning of the text is sensual, but if understood metaphorically one might also think it was alluding to someone's longing for the Law.

The Epistle of Jeremiah

Inspired by the text of Jeremiah 10, the epistle is an exhortation on the senselessness of idol worship. One usually finds the Epistle of Jeremiah printed as Baruch 6. The thumb-nail fragment written is Greek (7QpapEpJer gr).[31] Although not even a sentence survived completely, scholars identify this fragment with 6:43–44.

Greek Fragments from Cave 7

In Cave 7 many tiny Greek fragments were discovered (7Q3–19). Since then scholars have tried to connect these fragments with various Greek texts. 7Q5 has been identified as Mark 6:52–53, parts of 2 Sam 4–5, Zechariah 7, and *1 Enoch* 15. 7Q2 was said to be from the Epistle of Jeremiah 43–44, Numbers 14, Job 34, and *1 Enoch* 103. 7Q6 frag. 1 has been connected to Psalms 9; 34; 50; and Proverbs 7. 7Q6 frag. 2 has been identified with Isaiah 18. 7Q8 with *1 Enoch* 103 and several chapters from the Jewish Bible.

These seventeen fragments illustrate brilliantly the difficulty of making secure identifications of texts when the evidence is so sparse. 7Q3 preserves 26 Greek letters. 7Q10 has only ten. All of the fragments preserve only 130 letters. Of all the fragments, 7Q19 alone preserves the words "of the creation . . . in the writings." These Greek letters show only that Greek was one of the languages used by the people living at Khirbet Qumran.

The pseudepigrapha and other writings from the Second Temple times witness a scholarly and scribal interest in the "Words and Deeds of the Famous" in ancient Jewish traditions. In one way or another all of these writings reflect wisdom lost and rediscovered that served as models for legal, narrative, poetic, and philosophical interpretation. They reveal how ancient Jews saw themselves ideally and how they hoped to speak and act before God and with other human beings. Sometimes these ancient works intend to entertain their audiences while emphasizing the very best of ancient Judaism. Some of these texts seem to preserve the philosophical musings of wisdom teachers who had found no simple answers to Israel's special dilemmas and who advocated that one focus on God's acts in creation, history, and at the end time in order to find one's spiritual stability in this world. The new writings from the Qumran caves are now an indispensable component of the intellectual history of ancient Judaism.

Map of Ancient Jerusalem

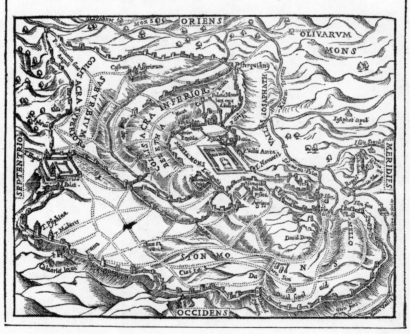

⚔SEVEN⚔

The Community Scrolls

THE *DAMASCUS DOCUMENT*

IN 1896, A CENTURY before the discovery of the Dead Sea Scrolls, Cambridge University's Solomon Schechter went to a synagogue in the old city of Cairo, Egypt, and proceeded to salvage thousands of medieval manuscripts from the synagogue's storage area. Two manuscripts penned in the tenth and twelfth centuries were of special interests for they seemed to refer to an ancient Jewish group with allegiance to the Zadokite priests and the city of Damascus. In fact, these pages came first to be known as the *Fragments of a Zadokite Work* and later as the *Damascus Document* (see chapter 1 above). Now scholars use the abbreviation CD to refer to the *Damascus Document* and fragments of the same work from other caves.[1]

Over half of the two medieval manuscripts is legal in nature (pages 9–16; 4, 12b–8, 10a). Among the laws were those concerned with using the divine name when swearing oaths, swearing oaths outside the presence of judges, witnesses, the fulfillment of vows and free-will offerings, leprosy, contagion and purity, sexual intercourse, relations with the Gentiles, observation of the Sabbath and other holy days, a deranged individual, the role of priests, Levites, the guardian of the community, and a rule that required members to donate at least two days wages to support widows, orphans, and the poor.

The other section of this work reads like a collection of sermons about obedience and repentance. It is a theological exhortation basing its key points on biblical citations. The first page presents a Jewish group that views its founding during the Babylonian exile. Its chronological notes suggest that this group emerged during the early second century BCE. During the time it takes a boy to become a man, this group was joined by someone they called their Teacher of Righteousness, and he was opposed by a dark figure known as the Liar. Presumably this group had formed a new covenant in the land of Damascus (pages 6, 7, 19, and 20) and cast a critical eye upon the lax religious practices in Judaea and Jerusalem. On the surface this community seems to have consisted of Jewish expatriates who had moved from Syria to Israel. They accuse Jerusalem's leadership of fornication, accepting stolen wealth, profaning the temple, failing to observe the purity laws, and not caring for the downtrodden and the outsider. The elite of this group called themselves "the men of perfect holiness" (20:2). They advocated strict observance, apparently according to their own interpretations, of Mosaic Law and rejected the Hellenistic practices during the hegemony of an evil deity called Belial.

Once Qumran Caves 4, 5, and 6 had been cleared and studied, experts realized that this medieval work was at least a thousand years old and that it had been a foundation work for those who settled at Khirbet Qumran. Several partial manuscripts have been linked loosely with the medieval pages (4Q266–267, 269–270, 272–273). The fragments from Cave 4 deal with fornication, defiling ones holy spirit, the ancient activities of Belial, the avoidance of incest, keeping the Sabbath, anger, rebuke, swearing oaths, sexual intercourse in the city of the temple, the preaching of apostasy, and the types of people may not enter the community. Two manuscripts, 4Q266 and 4Q270, preserve texts similar to 1QS 7.

CD's first editor, J. T. Milik, believed that the original work consisted of an admonition, a lengthy list of laws, which might have been greatly expanded by the Cave 4 fragments, and a concluding liturgy for the Annual Feast of the Covenant Renewal.[2] Philip Davies emphasized the covenantal structure of the work's narrative and legal sections.[3]

The writer of CD culled the expression "New Covenant" from Jer 31:31–34.

> Behold, the days are coming, says the LORD, when I will make
> a new covenant with the house of Israel and the house of Judah,
> not like the covenant which I made with their fathers when I took
> them by the hand to bring them out of the land of Egypt, my
> covenant, which they broke, although I was their husband, says
> the LORD. But this is the covenant which I will make with the
> house of Israel after those days, says the LORD. I will put my law
> within them and I will write it upon their hearts.

The former covenant had become invalid, and this new covenant assumed that the true house of Israel knew and embodied God's law.

In this work the New Covenant is tied to the land of Damascus (6:5, 19; 7:15, 19; 19:33–34; 20:12). The proper name "Damascus" is never equated with any other geographical region. Historically speaking, Israel and Judah had always had connections with Syria and Damascus. The same is true in the periods of Ptolemaic, Seleucid, and the Roman dominance. In fact, Damascus had a thriving Jewish community for centuries.

In the legal section (p. 16), the writer mentions the book of *Jubilees* as a source for understanding when and how Israel and Judaea had strayed from God's laws. It is called "the Book of the Divisions of the Times into their Jubilees and Weeks" (CD 16:3–4). This citation is juxtaposed with the statement, "And on the day that a man swears to return to the Law of Moses, the angel of persecution will stop following him, assuming that he keeps his promise. Therefore, Abraham circumcised himself on the day that he knew" (CD 16:5–6).

CD preserves the most detailed Sabbath Code in antiquity (10:14—12:6; cf. 4Q265 frag. 7:3–8). It prohibits work, talk about work, walking to do business and sending foreigners to do business, walking beyond one thousand cubits of the town where one lives, improper speech, the making of loans or other decisions about money, preparing food, picking up food or drink away from the camp, and using a vessel to draw water. No one may wear dirty garments on the Sabbath, mingle with others, pasture an animal more than two thousand cubits from his town, nor strike that animal nor force it in any way. Nothing may be brought into nor brought out of a house or booth. He may not open a vessel nor carry perfumes. He may not lift stones nor dust where he lives. He may not carry a child nor admonish a servant. He may not help an animal give birth nor pull it from a cistern or pit. No one may pass the Sabbath near foreigners. If someone falls into water, he may only be helped with a ladder or rope.

He may not send the Sabbath offering by unclean persons. Proverbs 15:8 is quoted to support prayer as a substitute for physical sacrifices and offerings. When a man goes to the house of worship, he must be clean. He may not interrupt the Sabbath service. He may not have intercourse with a woman in the city of the temple. Without doubt, the members of this community were quite restricted on the Sabbath. They were required to know and adhere strictly to the stipulations of the Sabbath Code.

A SABBATH PRIMER

1. End all work before any part of the sun sinks below the western horizon.
2. Stop all irreverent talk and activities related to tomorrow's business.
3. Stop all activities related to the exchange of money and property.
4. Walk no farther than 1000 cubits beyond your town—even when tending your animals.
5. Eat only food already prepared in advance in the camp.
6. Fill no waterskins or vessels with water for a journey.
7. Send no foreigners to do your business.
8. Wear clean clothes.
9. Keep away from all non-assimilated foreigners and non-believers.
10. Carry nothing out of or into your dwelling, including vessels, foods, children, stones, dust, and perfumes.
11. Open no sealed vessels, and lift nothing in your dwellings.
12. Chastise no one, not even your servants and hired help.
13. Save no animals that fall into a pit or cistern.
14. Assist in no birth of animals.
15. Save a person only by using a ladder or rope.
16. Offer only the Sabbath burnt-offering.
17. Send only clean people to the altar.
18. Come to the house of worship clean and on time.
19. Sleep with no woman in the city of the temple.
20. Place in custody those who profane the Sabbath and the feasts.

THE *RULE OF THE COMMUNITY*

About 1 km north of Khirbet Qumran in the wall of a cliff the bedouin discovered the first batch of scrolls that for years, and perhaps until today, have represented the central documents of an ancient Jewish group, perhaps Essenes, perhaps of mixed affiliations, but a body of people who apparently lived a rigorous religious life. Among the first scrolls scholars discovered a scroll called "Rule for the *Yahad*," called here the *Rule of the Community* (1QS).[4] The word *yahad* has always been understood as referring to a community or religious order. Another work referred to the *Rule for the Congregation of Israel* (1QSa),[5] and a third is titled *Words of Blessing for the Wise One* (1QSb).[6] These three texts were copied together on a single scroll.

Because of presumed similarities to Christian writings like the *Didache*, the *Didascalia*, the *Apostolic Constitutions*, and the modern Methodist Manual of Discipline, scholars sometimes attributed 1QS to a monastic group contemporary with the early Christians. The comparisons are quite vague. Other scholars also noted similarities with the ancient Essenes described by Josephus (*War* 5.128–132; 7.137–143). 1QS was understood as the key communal document for understanding the ideological and disciplinary nature of the Qumran Essenes. Copies of this work from Cave 4 also indicate that both the community and its foundational document had evolved over time.

1QS provides a reminder or a manifesto of the ideals of the members of this community. Those who enter this *yahad* pledged to adhere with strong conviction to God's laws and not to succumb to the pressures of Belial during this period of evil dominance (1QS 1:16–17). The annual covenantal ritual involved both a prayer and a curse on Belial, a satanic figure (1:1—3:12). In this ritual the priests recount God's favor and bless those who do God's will and the Levites curse those who belong to Belial. The actual covenant renewal may have taken place in the third month (4Q267 frag. 18 col. 5:17). 1QS includes a list of virtues and vices of those led by the forces of light and darkness, that is, of good and evil. The good are known as humble, patient, giving, understanding, and wise. Those belonging to Belial are said to be greedy, untruthful, arrogant, of bad temperament, insolent, lustful, stubborn, and uninterested in acquiring righteousness. Until a divinely designated time in the future these two groups will remain in opposition. Those who enter the community are expected to love all the children of light and hate the children of darkness.

Much has been written about the process of entering the community and achieving full membership. A person joining the *yahad* pledged that he was returning to the covenant. That is, he admitted having wandered from its ways. His deeds and understanding were examined upon entering and again annually. If he was considered acceptable after living one year in the community, the congregation permits this member to hand over his property and earnings to the treasurer of the congregation who assigned the man's wealth to his own personal account. After that first year, he could share the pure meal of the congregation. He would be examined again after completing a second year and ascribed a communal status. His property was then merged with that of the community. At this point he could participate in the drink of the congregation. Describing the Essenes, Josephus presents a similar three-year period of probation and prayer reminiscent of 1QS 10–11 (*War* 7.137–143; 5.128–132; Philo, *Apologia* 6), but his description is also quite different in its details.

Columns 10–11 serve as a prelude to the discussion of disciplinary and behavior concerns within the community. One reads that wherever there are ten men in the Council of the Community, a priest must be there to bless the first fruits of bread and new wine. Wherever ten men gather, they are to study the Law. Other members of the congregation are also told to "read the book and to study the Law and to bless together" (6:6–8). It is not at all clear which book is meant. When there is an assembly of the congregation, priests sit at the front, then the elders, and finally others according to some ranking system. Some of the rules for regular meetings included taking turns to speak, requesting permission to speak, accepting the authority of those who admit a new member. The disciplinary concerns involve lying about property, obstinacy and insults toward a fellow, deception, mentioning the holy name, anger toward priests inscribed in the book, failure to care for a brother, foolish words, sleeping during the assembly, nakedness, spitting, laughing, misuse of the left hand, and speaking against the authority of the community. The consequences are rather strict—expulsion for lying about property or questioning the authority of the community, a year exclusion for acts against a fellow, sixty days for irresponsibility with a fellow's property, interrupting a fellow while speaking gets ten days of exclusion. Members can also be expelled for sharing food or other items with someone who has been removed from the community.

The purpose of the leaders of the community was to study, know, and practice the Law. 1QS 8 says that they atone for sin by their deeds. They were chosen to "atone for the land and pay the wicked their reward" (8:5–7). They are called the "precious cornerstone" mentioned in Isa 28:16. They are described as "an agreeable offering," to use an expression from sacrifice in the temple. 1QS gives the impression that the leaders and all those members who have lived two years of exemplary and acceptable life according to the community's rules are part of that "cornerstone" which Isa 40:3 says will prepare God's way in the desert (8:14–16). They are to live by the revelations found in the books of the prophets. The members of the community were instructed in the ancient laws and expected to be responsible to follow them until the coming of the prophet and the messiahs of Aaron and Israel (9:9–11).

1QS is a rather complex document that moves forward, doubles back taking up topics mentioned earlier, and even adding text that may amend what was said earlier. This sometimes makes its disciplinary pronouncements difficult to understand. For instance, in 8:21–23 the author refers to the Holy Council saying that anyone who belonged to this Council but who violated even one word of the Law of Moses purposely and through negligence shall be expelled and never return to the Council. Then it says that in the case of inadvertently violating a Mosaic law, this person is removed from the pure meal and council for two years, may perfect himself, and return (8:24–27). Based on these two seemingly contradictory statements, it is not clear whether inadvertence equals intentional violation of a law.

In col. 9 one again reads the community functions as a human atonement for Israel's sins without the meat and fat of animal sacrifices. In fact, prayer is interpreted as a favored free-will offering along with its "aroma of righteousness." This recalls the citation of Prov 15:8 in CD 11:20–21, where a just man's prayer equals a sacrificial offering.

The wise one, for whom or by whom 1QS was written, lives according to God's revelations. He evaluates the children of righteousness, judging each person according to his spirit. This person should not argue with" the men of the pit" and reveal knowledge only to those who have been chosen and refined within the community. The *maśkil* should praise and bless God at certain times of the day and night and during the year. Perhaps appropriately, 1QS 10:5–26 concludes with a lengthy thanksgiving hymn similar to those found in the *Thanksgiving Hymns* (1QH). To a large extent this prayer echoes what is said less poetically toward the end of col. 9 and the beginning of col. 10.

The Cave 4 manuscripts of 1QS are not only shorter, but also preserve a somewhat different content. At least two of these manuscripts lack the text of 1QS 1–5, 10–11. Consequently, they lack the dualistic thinking, the annual covenant ceremony, the lists of virtues and vices, and the concluding hymn. Whereas 1QS 5:2 mentions the authority of the Zadokite priests and the men of the community, 4Q^c 1:2 refers simply to the authority of the congregation. Two manuscripts (4Q^d and 4Q^e) also lack any reference to the prophets and the messiah of Aaron and Israel mentioned in 1QS. Some of the manuscripts of CD are connected ideologically with 1QS, in particular those manuscripts that refer to the penal code (CD 14:19-20; 4Q266 frag. 10; 1QS 7:4, 9–15).

The first line of 1QSa speaks of the "last days" when certain people adhere to the Law of the Zadokites. In both columns we hear about women and children. Males shall be taught the "Book of Mediation for ten years." No one these days really knows which book that was. When a man turns twenty-years old he may satisfy his obligations to his family and within the congregation. He may then become involved in hearing legal decisions. At twenty-five he begins his service to the congregation in earnest. At thirty he participates in court cases and judgments. As he grows older, he is given duties appropriate to his age and abilities. If he is a simpleton, he may neither participate in legal decision-making nor direct others in foreign wars. Those called to the Council of the Community, an expression reminiscent of passages in 1QS (3:2; 5:7; 6:3, 10, 12–13; 7:2, 22; 8:15, 18, 21), remain under the authority of the Zadokite priests. No one who has physical or mental disabilities may belong to this Council.

The final passage of 1QSa envisions the presence of a messiah, the mere mention of whom conjures up visions of a special military leader selected by God. His function in this work, however, is to wait until the priest has blessed the first fruits of bread and wine, and then he, the messiah, does the same (2:20–21).

This trilogy of sorts that started with 1QS concludes with the *Blessings* (1QSb) to be said by the *maśkil*. First, he is to bless those who fear God. Then he pronounces blessings upon the high priest and Zadokite priests. The *maśkil* says: "May you be like an angel of the presence in the place of holiness" and "holy among his people." This high priest seems to have one foot in heaven and another among the earthly congregation of God. The final blessing falls upon the prince of the congregation, who will care for the poor, render justice fairly, and combat the ungodly, doing all this through his righteous spirit. This person will be served by all the nations (1QSb 5:27–29).

A RULE-DAMASCUS HYBRID

A dozen fragments form what appears to be a hybrid of 1QS, CD, and other material. Fragment 1, whose preserve text is minimal, includes a penal code similar to the one in 1QS 6–7. In the *Hybrid* (4Q265) one novelty is a reduction to half-rations in some cases. There are fifteen- and thirty-day periods of punishment instead of the more extreme sentences of a year, six months, three months, and sixty days in 1QS. Interestingly 4Q265 has the punishments before the description of the initiation (cols. 1–2; 1QS 6). It also says that the inspector will teach him the community's interpretation of the Law. This is absent from 1QS.

Fragment 2, which quotes Isa 54:1–2, seems to have no connection to the penal code. Fragment 4 asks the question why someone betrays his brother and why a man and a woman eat (perhaps leavened bread) during the Passover. These questions also lack a context for interpretation, but show that the behavior of women was important for this writer and his group.

4Q265's Sabbath Code is similar to the one in the CD XI, but with noticeable differences. Several stipulations are missing, perhaps because the fragmentary hybrid starts with the prohibition of wearing dirty garments. This is followed by the prohibition to remove vessels and foods from one's tent. Possibly the reference to living in tents refers literally to the lifestyle of the people for whom the hybrid written. The saving of life on the Sabbath is clarified by saying that garments may be used and not utensils like the ladder and rope mentioned in CD. One reads the word for "army," but there is no context. A new stipulation says that the Aaronite priests may not sprinkle people with purifying waters on the Sabbath. 4Q265 permits one to walk one's animals for 2000 cubits, which raises the question whether this meant 2000 cubits round-trip. Another new stipulation says that defective animals must be kept at a distance of thirty stadia from the temple. Based on the Roman stadia, this would be 5,550 meters/18,210 feet (5½ km/3½ miles). This language sounds like the 11QT^a 52:17–18 or its source.

4Q265 also shares with the 1QS a council of the community, but this in 4Q265 reference follows the Sabbath Code in 4Q265. 1QS mentions being extremely knowledgeable in the Law, while 4Q265 adds the prophets to this curriculum. 1QS refers to twelve men and three priests. 4Q265 simply speaks of fifteen men. These are subtle, but certainly important distinctions in self-definition, breadth of learning, and organizational leadership. If priests are not necessary, this is a lay community making its own decisions.

Following the mention of the council of the community, one finds a reference to the first week after creation, to the garden of Eden, and to the bone out of which God would make Eve. Then Lev 12:2 and 4 are quoted to make the point that a woman remains unclean for seven days plus thirty-three days after bearing. If the child is female, the period of impurity is seven days plus sixty-six more, according to Lev 12:4–5. During these times after birth, the mother may not touch anything sacred nor enter the temple. This is another indicator that 4Q265 legislated for both men and women.

One sees in 4Q265 how an ancient Jewish writer modified and combined legal material from two key community documents and used quotations to form a new work. Unfortunately, very little of this work remains.

THE *RULE OF WAR*

Among the Dead Sea Scrolls, the *Rule of War* or *milḥamah* (1QM) provides a bellicose and nationalistic description of a war to vanquish the forces of Belial.[7] Scholars do not agree entirely on how to understand this scroll, in large part because it is a complex juxtaposition of several parts. Its compositional logic is not linear, but much more circular. It should probably be classified as a vision of the final war that will lead to Israel's triumph. In sections it tells how Israel will combat the forces of Belial and emerge triumphant. Although numerous enemies are listed, the name Kittim probably originally meant the Seleucids in the time of the Maccabeans and Romans later (see Dan 11:3). Fragments of this work were also discovered in Cave 4.

There are clear links between 1QM and some other texts from the Qumran caves. As in 1QS, the divine and human worlds are made up of good and evil forces. The dualism is most prominent in 1QS. 1QM also assumes a liturgical calendar year of fifty-two weeks, that is, one having three hundred sixty-four days. This work was compiled from hymns and prayers for battle, military formation and strategies, and descriptions of weaponry. Only a few biblical passages are quoted (Deut 20:2–4; Num 10:9; 24:17–19; Isa 31:8). Scholars believe that some traditions in 1QM can be traced back to the Maccabean campaigns in the mid-second century BCE. Thus, the designation *Kittim* originally referred to the

Seleucids. An oddity within the scroll is mention of "the shield of the Prince of the Congregation" (5:1), who is nowhere depicted as leading or participating in the battles. The strategists and directors of the battles are clearly the priests who manage to stay well out of range of the polluting blood of the fallen.

1QM 1 presents a brief overview of the initial seven-year campaign to eradicate the Ammonites, the Moabites, the Edomites, the Philistines, the *Kittim*, and wicked Jews from the holy land. The Levites, the Judaeans, the Benjaminites, and the "exiles from the wilderness" combine forces to battle the children of darkness and the army of Belial. In three major battles the sons of light will be victorious. In three further battles the sons of darkness shall emerge, but in the seventh battle God's hand settles the matter in favor of his sons of light. Columns 2–9 concern the remaining years of this forty-year war plan. In observant fashion even during war, the holy ones shall keep each seventh year as a Sabbath. The remaining years are for combat. Various battle maneuvers, which scholars some-times describe as Roman, are used. Pious triumphant messages are to be inscribed on the banners, the trumpets, the shields, and other weapons. Trumpets will be inscribed with slogans such as "The Called of God," "The Princes of God," "The Peace of God in the Camps of his Holy Ones" (3:2–4). The large standards will carry the words "The People of God," the names of Israel, Aaron, and the twelve tribes of Israel (3:13–15). On the standard of Merari is written "The Votive Offering of God" (4:1). On the javelins one will write "Shining Javelin of the Power of God" and "Bloody Spikes to Bring Down the Slain by the Wrath of God" (6:2–3). On the shields that make up the battle towers will be written the names of the angels, Michael, Gabriel, Sariel, and Raphael (9:14–16).

Age limits are set for specific war duties (7:1–3). Men of the army are forty to fifty-years old. The inspectors of the camps are between fifty and sixty. Officers are forty to fifty as well. The plunderers, the cleans-ers of the land, and those with provisions will be twenty-five to thirty-years old. No boys, women, or handicapped will be permitted in the war camps (7:3–4). Latrines must be established two thousands cubits away so that no filth or nakedness is seen by the angelic troops (7:6–8). 1QM is even concerned with the clothing of the priests. It should be made of flax and embroidered with blue, purple, and scarlet thread. They shall wear mitered turbans. The priests wear this into battle, but remove it before entering the temple (9–12).

Numerous liturgical pieces make up cols. 10–14. God is blessed for his plans and deeds as are those who serve him. Belial is likewise cursed as are his minions. They represent the darkness that will be overcome by God's army of light (13:3–5).

In the final five columns of 1QM the writer details the first seven-years of confrontation between the opposing forces or light and darkness. When the Israelites are ready, they will establish their camp opposite the king of the *Kittim*. The high priest, the priests, the Levites, and the soldiers recite "the Prayer in Time of War" and other hymns. Then a priest appointed for the occasion encourages and heartens the warriors. The priests sound the trumpets as the foot-soldiers advance. Once all of the actors are in place the trumpet will be sounded to take up arms. The priests again blow on their trumpets to initiate battle. As a second formation advances, the high priest announces that this is the day designated for the destruction of the prince of the kingdom of wickedness by the power of Michael and his forces. The trumpet will sound the second attack on the *Kittim*. A third attack will occur. A seventh and apparently final advance will bring the promised defeat of the *Kittim* and the forces of Belial.

THE *THANKSGIVING HYMNS*

This collection of prayers, meditations, and hymns was named the *Thanksgiving Hymns* (1QH, 4QH) because of the repeated use of the expression ʾ*odekah* ('I thank you').[8] Much of the collection seems to reflect the true feelings of an individual who finds himself to be a vile sinner unworthy of the mercy for which he is thanking God. A goodly portion of this realism contributes to the creation of one praying or writing poetry before God. For decades the collection has been divided into hymns composed and recited by the Teacher of Righteousness and hymns representing the collective adoration of the worshiping community. Scholars still view 1QH as a cohesive collection, but are less certain about connecting the very personal hymns to the psychology of a leader of the Qumran community.

Many of these meditations speak about matters that concern all human beings. Repeatedly, one reads about the worthlessness of all people, sinful vessels shaped of clay, whose fates have already been decided by divine decree. How much more self-effacing could the one praying be?

> I, a shape of clay kneaded in water, a foundation of shame and
> source of contamination, a melting pot of wickedness and a
> structure of sin, a straying and perverted spirit lacking under-
> standing. (1:27–33)

The praise of God that follows this self-loathing contrasts the creator
with his lowly creation and shows that all good things depend ultimately
on God's grace and marvelous, yet unfathomable mysteries.

> By your mercies and by your great goodness, you have strength-
> ened man's spirit in the face of adversity, and have purified [. . .]
> of a multitude of sins, that it may declare your wonders before all
> your creatures. (1:29–45)

Throughout the hymns the writer points out that God's wisdom is
discernible already in his creation of certain forces of nature. Unlike the
creation story in Genesis 1, 1QH insist that what eventually happens
on earth was first a thought in the mind of God. Everything that exists,
even elements in nature, operates according to divine forethought and
design. The mighty winds existed according to divine law even before
those winds became angels. The heavenly lights function according to a
divine mystery. The stars faithfully travel their heavenly paths, and thunder and lightning are only fulfilling their duties (1:2–5, 8–21).

The poet says he is no more than a worm without God's grace.
Many of the themes interlacing these hymns nicely with the interests of
the other so-called Qumran sectarian scrolls, especially the imagined
life of the Teacher of Righteousness known primarily from the commentaries known as *pesharim*.

Many scholars believe that several hymns came from the Teacher
of Righteousness (2:1–19, 31–39; 3:1–18; 4:1—5:4; 5:5–19; 5:20—7:5;
7:6–25; 8:4–40) who is mentioned in other texts.[9] The ancient writer, no
matter who he may have been, expressed the unbearable abuse that he
suffered simply for sharing God's wisdom to others.

"They have cast toward the pit of life the man whose mouth you
have confirmed and into whose heart you have placed instruction and
understanding, that he might open a fountain of knowledge to all men
of insight" (2:18–20). The writer feels himself full of spirits that God
placed in him. These spirits are the source of his ability to tell others
about God's majestic deeds in creation and history. It enables him to
recount his own evil deeds and sins (4:17–20).

This language echoes a key passage in the *Commentary of Habakkuk* (1QpHab 2:7–8), which speaks of the faithful at the end of time who refuse to believe the priest whom God inspired to interpret the prophets. The writer of the 1QH never refers directly to such a priest nor does he name his adversaries. Instead, he paints his enemies in stereotypical terms as deceitful, false interpreters, seekers of smooth things, and considers them a realm of ungodliness and evil. He presents his own deliverance in various ways appealing to the images of childbirth, fear upon a storm-tossed sea, warfare, hunting, and the life of the silversmith. The writer constantly thanks God for saving him from these trials.

In 4:8–9 the writer says he had been driven from his country and away from his family and friends. This expulsion has been compared with passages in 1QpHab and 4QpPs 37. In 1QpHab 9:4–8 one reads that a wicked priest pursued a teacher of righteousness to his place of exile. In 4QpPs 37 4.8–9 a wicked priest tried to kill the righteous one.

How should one interpret these seemingly realistic depictions of human aggression in light of the voices in the Thanksgiving Hymns? Should one understand the two prophetic commentaries as concrete manifestations of the generalizing language of the hymns? Should one take the statements made in the commentaries as real history that has been personified in the hymns? The choice is not easy. Because so much of 1QH is a patch-quilt of biblical phrases, one cannot tell where the literacy artifice ends and the human suffering really begins.[10] In 10:29 references to "the net" and "the trap" which his enemies have spread for him ultimately derive from Pss 9:15; 35:7; and 142:3. The writer even makes a connection to 1QM when he says confidently that God created the wicked for their day of destruction (7:18–19; cf. 11:35–36; 14:29–31).

These meditations and hymns are genuine and represent a continuation of the Bible's individual songs of lament and thanksgiving. The personal suffering and personal love for God seem rather excessive, but the repeated use of the first person pronoun "I" permits one to share the pain, torment, and turmoil of the author. The hymns are based on one's need for God's saving grace as well as insights into divine wisdom. Above and beyond any possible historical connections, which cannot be proved, the religious and human sentiments expressed in the hymns gives them their enduring value. These hymns were meant to be recited and heard as one discovers in 9:34–38:

Hear, O you wise man, and meditate on knowledge.
O you fearful, be strong!
Increase in wisdom [. . .].
O just men, put aside evil!
Hold fast [. . .],
O all you perfect of way [. . .]
Be patient and despise no righteous judgment!

In 20:12 the writer says, "I, the *maśkil*," identifying himself with a learned teacher. He may describe himself as wise only by virtue of all that God has done at creation and continues to do within him. 1QH and its 4QH fragments represent key witnesses to the personal piety of a person who loved God and racked his brain to think of language to talk about him.

THEMATIC COMMENTARIES

Several works have usually been classified as thematic commentaries, because, instead of creating a narrative based a consecutively running prophetic text, one finds in these tractates themes that are built up out of scriptural texts. The writer makes his argument using one or more central prophetic texts and then bolsters his exposition with other prophecies. Sometimes this is called proof-texting. *Florilegium*, *Testimonia*, and *Melchizedek* are the three main works of this type.

Florilegium

The little treatise, *Florilegium* (4Q174) preserves quotes from seemingly unrelated scriptural passages in order to express its author's views on events and people living in the last days.[11] These passages are 2 Sam 7:10; Exod 15:17–18; 2 Sam 7:11–14; an allusion to Amos 9:11; Ps 1:1; Isa 8:11; Ezek 44:10; Ps 2:1; and Dan 12:10. Probably the author used 2 Samuel 7 and Psalm 1, both of which are 'Davidic.' He draws on other passages to buttress his case.

In quoting 2 Sam 7:10–14 the writer wanted to emphasize that God's promised house to David, which will be a refuge from Israel's enemies and the children of Belial, is a royal house. In order to stand at the end of time, this Davidic monarch will be accompanied by an interpreter of the Law. The topic of "house" connected 2 Sam 7:10–11 and Exod 15:17–18. The ancient writer believed that the book of Moses revealed information about events in the last days.

Psalm 1:1 was inserted to illustrate that God had chosen a group that would not follow the ways of the peoples. Isaiah 8:11 and Ezek 44:10 are cited to show that this elect group will stand in the trial at the end of days. The language of the text suggests that they will be Zadokites. Rounding out his anthology, the writer identifies those *maśkilim* who understand God's words and deeds as the children of light. This group will exist as a symbolic temple, practicing "the entire Law" so as to send up sweet aromas of human incense and works of the Law to God.

The writer has proved himself masterful in demonstrating the contemporary relevance of scriptures from 2 Samuel to Exodus to the Psalms and to Daniel, collapsing any past time into a vague period known as the last days. In essence, he has recruited the words of prophets from Moses to the end of scriptures to clinch his argument. This is a sign to him and his readers that the last of the final days has indeed arrived, and Israel's enemies will be prevented once and for all from destroying the human temple that is obedient to the law. If reference to "the branch of David" should be taken literally, and this is not certain, the monarch will be guided by an interpreter or multiple interpreters of the Law. These interpreters are the *maskilim* of the children of light. Certain parts of 4Q174 make one think of the 11QT^a 29:7–10, where God promises the erection of a temple on the day of creation. One also thinks of the King's Law in cols. 56–59, where priests, not the *maśkilim* or children of light, are obliged to teach the monarch God's laws and prevent him from committing errors in his life.

If the compiler of 4Q174 had been correct, a day would have come when Israel would no longer have been confronted by enemies, would not ever have had to be concerned about the impurities of the foreigners, and God's law would be executed flawlessly. A house will emerge where one should have rest and comfort from the vicissitudes of life. Throughout 4Q174 one reads about "the place," "the house," "the sanctuary," and even "the tent" as places of promise. A similar approach to understanding scripture is found in the work on Melchizedek.

Testimonia

Among the thousands of fragments salvaged from Cave 4, one of the most beautiful and intriguing has been titled a *Testimonia* (4Q175), a series of quotations collated to make some theological or historical point. The title *Testimonia* derives from a comparable phenomenon in

Christian literature. 4Q175 contains five such biblical quotes on what looks like a page from a codex. Sometimes this work is also known as a messianic anthology.

Physically the text is laid out in four paragraphs. At the beginning of the first paragraph four dots represent the name of God. This also occurs toward the end of the third paragraph. As in many of the other scrolls, 4Q175 preserves written pericope markers. Although it is believed that the scribe who copied a manuscript of 1 Samuel from Cave 4 also copied 4Q175, it should be noted that the latter contains several interventions to correct misspellings and to insert word interlinearly. This first scribe copied carelessly. The first paragraph constitutes a little more than seven lines. The second paragraph has five lines (the third is indented), and the third paragraph contains six lines. The fourth paragraph is nearly as long as the second and third combined. However, roughly one-third of the bottom left corner has broken off and disappeared.

The first biblical quotation is that of Deut 5:28–29. God speaks to Moses of the upright heart of the people and their future blessedness. The writer juxtaposes the famous passage in Deut 18:18–19: "I will cause to rise up for them a prophet like you from their brothers . . ." This passage continues to warn the people to listen to and obey this prophet. The second quotation is a very enigmatic one culled from Num 24:15–17 that historically was applied to foreigners and Jewish leaders alike: "a star shall come from Jacob and a scepter shall arise from Israel." He is a military leader who will destroy Israel's enemies. The third passage, taken from Deut 33:8–11, is about Levi or the Levites who had traditionally been observant and faithful to the covenant. The Levites will burn incense, and execute burnt offerings. To this point 4Q175 is creating a list of heroic figures—the prophet, the leader in war, and those who serve God at the altar.

The fourth paragraph quotes Josh 6:26: "Cursed be the man who rebuilds this city, laying its foundation on his first-born and erecting its gate upon his youngest." In stark contrast to the previous three paragraphs this one contains an extensive explanation of Joshua's words. Taking the curse literally, various identifications have been suggested for the father and his two sons: Mattathias and his sons Judas and Simon Maccabeus, Simon and his sons Judas and Mattathias, John Hyrcanus and his sons Aristobulus I and Alexander Jannaeus, Alexander Jannaeus and his sons Hyrcanus II and Aristobulus II. The figures in 4Q175 ll. 22–24 have also been identified with Jonathan and Simon Maccabeus.

No doubt, the ancient writer and his audience probably had certain historical actors in mind, but the language is prophetic and quite nebulous, tempting each new generation to equate an evil tyrant of their times with the prophetic passage.[12]

Testimonia *and the* Apocryphon of Joshua

Soon speculation arose that the creator of 4Q175 had used an unknown text of Joshua that referred to his praying and giving thanks. It turned out that such a version of Joshua also lay not far from where 4Q175 was in Cave 4. Scholars immediately wanted to compare the two texts. Both 4Q175 and the *Apocryphon of Joshua* (4Q379 frag. 22 ii) are damaged at critical points preventing a complete reconstruction of either of these ancient texts. Oddly enough, 4Q175 had been used to restore missing portions of 4Q379, although both were damaged. There is doubt, however, that both works preserved precisely the same basic text in antiquity.

Most scholars have argued that the 4Q379 must have preceded 4Q175 since the latter is a collection of prophecies from authoritative sources.[13] Despite its fragmentary condition, 4Q379 seems to have been an independent composition. The strongest argument for its priority appears in l. 7, which reads "Blessed be Yahweh [God of Israel]." Although 4Q175 concludes with an allusion to Joshua worshiping, the quotation itself has been extracted from some other larger context. 4Q379 provides such a possible context.

Perhaps 4Q379 was written by a scribe in a non-Qumran context. 4Q175 has a phonetic or full Hebrew spelling and was written in a Qumran-type script. The scribe wrote rather carefully, unlikely the person who inscribed the text of 4Q379.

As one learns from so many of the works from the Qumran caves, 4Q379 shows once again that versions of scripture existed in Jewish antiquity that had been lost from the historical record for two thousand years until the discovery of the Scrolls.

Melchizedek

The name Melchizedek appears only three times in the Jewish and Christian Bibles.[14] He is identified as the "king of Salem" and priest of

"God Most High," to whom Abraham gave a tithe (Gen 14:18). In Ps 110:4 the king is acknowledged as "a priest forever according to the order of Melchizedek." One assumes a connection between the latter and former references, but both are very mysterious. The name Melchizedek is also associated with worship in the heavenly temple in the *Angelic Songs of the Sabbath Sacrifice* (4QShirShab, 11ShirShab). Apparently, this rarely mentioned tradition held a special meaning for the author of Hebrews 5–7, who presents Jesus as a high priest like Melchizedek.

The text is preserved partially in ten fragments, of which only can be read to any degree. Partial reconstruction of the text is possible because they contain known biblical texts. The Melchizedek work (11Q13) is a thematic commentary like 4Q174, but it uses both "as it was written" and "its interpretation" (*pishro*) to introduce the commentary. The theme of the preserved fragments is the heavenly high priest Melchizedek's deliverance of Israel after a Day of Atonement sacrifice. As a consequence of this, the wicked will be destroyed.

The author is essentially an anthologist creating his narrative by selecting and interpreting scriptural passages. He uses Lev 25:13 and Deut 15:2 to pinpoint chronologically when the deliverance will occur. Deuteronomy calls this time "a year of release." Then Isa 6:1 is cited to emphasize that freedom will be proclaimed in "the year of the Lord's favor." The *pesher* interpretation clarifies the situation further: the captives will join the heavenly beings and the party of Melchizedek at the beginning of the tenth jubilee.

> . . . this will (occur) in the first week of the jubilees that follows
> the nine jubilees. And the Day of Atonement is the e[nd of the]
> tenth [ju]bilees, when all the sons of [light] and the men of the lot
> of Mel[chi]zedek will be atoned for. (11QMelch 2:7)

The writer then announces that "this is the day . . . of which Isaiah the prophet spoke: how beautiful upon the mountains are the feet of the messenger" (Isa 52:7). The mountains are interpreted as the prophets, and the messenger is the prince anointed by the spirit as foretold in Dan 9:25. This person is then identified as "the bearer of good tidings" (Isa 52:7) and "the comforter" (Isa 61:2–3).

As if coming full circle, the writer cites Lev 25:9 to present the image of the blowing of a horn to announce the year of jubilee. Although fragmentary, the few remaining words present "the devouring of Belial

with fire" and "the ramparts of Jer[usalem]" (col. 3). The author of
11Q13 wanted to present an argument and description, based on scripture, of the ultimate deliverance of God´s people from the forces of evil.
This concern is similar to the calculation of world history into periods of
multiple jubilees in *1 Enoch* and Daniel 9.

RUNNING COMMENTARIES ON THE PROPHETS

The discovery of these commentaries on prophetic writings literally
dominated the study of the Scrolls and the history of the community
behind the Scrolls for decades. These commentaries, known as *pesharim*
among specialists, represent a plodding style of contemporizing interpretation familiar primarily from the caves at Qumran. In the commentaries
the writer quotes a verse of scripture or even a small portion of a version and then introduces his understanding of the text with the Hebrew
word *pishro,* which means "its interpretation." In this context *pishro* was
probably understood to represent a special interpretation of scripture.
Uppermost in the mind of the interpreter is that the historical context of
the scriptural passage had lost its value and refers to a later reality.

This is, of course, nothing new. Scripture has always been treated as
predictive. One thinks of the Joseph's dream interpretations for Pharaoh
and Daniel's for Nebuchadnezzar and Belshazzar. The use of *pishro* certainly derives from two narratives, Genesis and Daniel. The running
commentaries from Qumran completely disrupt their narrative, prophetic context to bring a message that the average reader would not have
foreseen. Although the *pesher* interpretation is applied to known prophetic works, the *Commentary on Psalms 37* (4QpPs 37) also shows that
the writings of "David" were assumed to be prophetic as well. Perhaps
one could say that Qumran's continuous commentaries are based on the
idea that scripture looks forward and not backward. They illustrate that
prophecy sometimes requires much more time to be fulfilled.

The interpretation within the running commentaries is largely
atomistic, that is, the interpreter selects nuggets within his text to interpret. Contiguous verses may have no real connection in the interpretation. The interpreter is concerned to present a story involving the
human forces of good and evil. To what degree one can associate the
characters and events mentioned with public history varies. The running *Commentary on Nahum* (4QpNah) mentions historical figures. The
Commentary on Habakkuk 1-2 (1QpHab) and 4QpPs 37 are less clear,

consistently using code names to sketch the outlines of an intriguing competition between two or more religious leaders. Modern historians usually mine these three running commentaries for clues to the history of the group that lived at Khirbet Qumran from the late second century BCE to the first century CE.[15]

The Commentary on Habakkuk

1QpHab is the longest and most publicized of the *pesharim*. In the interpretation God has told the ancient prophet what would one day occur, but had not given him a precise date for the end. In 6:13—7:5 God orders the prophet to record a vision (Hab 2:1–3) about "the final generation." It turns out that the prophet Habakkuk was just God's secretary, so to speak, for it was a person centuries later called the Teacher of Righteousness who knew how to interpret the mysteries found in the words of the prophets.

Although Bible scholars understand Habakkuk's prophecies against the international history of seventh century BCE, the author of 1QpHab interprets the righteous and wicked as the Teacher of Righteousness and the Wicked Priest. He places them squarely in the time of *Kittim*, probably the latest Seleucids to be involved in the history of Jerusalem and Judaea. However, the story of the Teacher and his nemesis is not dated nor are specific names given. This has led naturally to much speculation about the identities of these characters. Based on descriptions such as wealthy, violent, in cahoots with the Gentiles, persecuted the Teacher, and died an ignoble death, scholars have spent much of their lives arguing that the Wicked Priest was this or that public figure. He was typically identified with one of a series of high priests in Jerusalem. The Wicked Priest's pursuit of the Teacher to his safe house on the latter's day of fasting (11:2–8) suggested strongly, along with lots of previously unknown calendar texts, that the Wicked Priest and the Teacher observed different liturgical calendars. After decades of rigorous historical research and debate, scholars are much more reluctant to associate the details of these theological texts with public history. References in 1QpHab to "seekers of smooth things" were often interpreted as Pharisees. Therefore, the conflict between the Wicked Priest and the Teacher was about legal interpretations and the applications of the laws. The solution may in fact be simpler. The broader context for understanding this commentary is a world in which some Jewish leaders opted for accommodation with the Hellenistic world, while others radically rejected that connection because the true and correct interpretation of God's prophets was that God would soon save his chosen ones and demolish all the forces of evil, including the wicked foreigners.

The Psalms Commentaries

In 4QpPs 4:5–12 the reader learns that the Wicked Priest attempted to kill the Teacher because of a law that the latter sent to the former. Scholars have speculated on whether that law was a lawbook like the 11QT^a or specifically it's "Law for the Monarch," or 4QMMT, but it is utterly impossible to make any identifications because the writer stops short of giving readers the details needed to make sense of the story. The ancient interpreter knew what happened, but could not or did not wish to be more explicit. If that is true, his commentary was for himself and some unknown group for which the commentary may have made perfect sense.

The Nahum Commentary

This commentary on the text of Nahum immediately brings one close to public history. The commentator interprets Nah 2:11 in the following way:

> The lion entered there, the female lion, the baby lion, [. . . ; its interpretation is about De]metrius, the king of Yawan who wanted/ tried to enter Jerusalem on the request of those who seek smooth things (1:1–2) [. . .] the Greek kings from Antiochus until the emergence of the leaders of the Kittim. (4QpNah frags. 3–4, col. 1:1–3)

Nowadays scholars are virtually unanimous in identifying Demetrius with Demetrius III, who responded to the Pharisaic request to intervene in Jerusalem power struggles c. 90 BCE. The "furious lion cub" has been identified with the Hasmonean ruler, Alexander Jannaeus, who crucified 800 Pharisees in a major public spectacle for betraying him to the Seleucid Demetrius. One might conclude that the exegete was arguing that no foreign leaders had captured Jerusalem for roughly a century from the time of Antiochus IV in 176 BCE up to Roman domination starting in 63 BCE. Although this apologist was concerned to defend the invincibility of Jerusalem within the context of a public history, he, too, failed to offer sufficiently specific information for understanding his text. The authors of the 1QpHab and 4QpPs 37 seem to be recounting a rather personal or unknown history whose connection to public history still remains unclear.

Other Commentaries on Prophets

The six fragmentary *Commentaries on Isaiah* (4Q161–165, 3Q4), the prophet of prophets, use expressions like "prince of the congregation" and "sprout of David" when talking about a non-priestly messiah, but there is neither a private story told nor one that connects to public history. It remains a vague prediction about the last days and the rise of a messianic figure from the house of David. Fragments from *Commentaries of Hosea, Micah, Zephaniah,* and *Malachi* are too fragmentary to yield helpful information.

ORDINANCES

These three manuscripts have sometimes been called *Commentaries on Biblical Law* (4Q159, 4Q513–514).[16] Their texts are reminiscent of the legal portions of CD from Cave 4, 11QT^a, and other fragments from Cave 4.

In 4Q159 it says that a poor Israelite is permitted to gather for himself and his family at a threshing-floor or wine press. In contrast, he may consume corn if he is in someone's cornfield, but he may not carry what he gathers home. This is based on Deut 23:25–26.

The next law says that each Israelite man shall pay the half-shekel money of valuation once in his lifetime. This is often understood as a sly interpretation to circumvent paying this individual valuation annually.

> Each person counted in the census will give this—half a shekel according to the shekel of the sanctuary—the shekel is twenty gerahs, half a shekel as an offering to the Lord. (Exod 30:13)

> We also place upon ourselves the duty to pay yearly the third part of a shekel for the service of the house of God. (Neh 10:32)

It seems much more likely that this interpretation provided an amelioration of the law for the less fortunate. Matthew 17:23 provides an entertaining anecdote about the half-shekel tax. At Capernaum the tax collectors asks Peter if his teacher did not pay the tax, and he answered affirmatively. Matthew has Jesus ask Peter from whom the kings exact tribute, from their sons or from others? Peter answered that the tribute was taken from others. Jesus then says that the sons, that is, God's children are free from the tax, but in order not to offend anyone Jesus tells him to catch a fish, remove the shekel from its mouth, and pay it to the tax collectors.

After this reinterpretation of the valuation requirement, the reader is provided an equivalency scale enabling one to compare the value of talents, minas, and shekels (4Q159). The text says that a total of 600,000 people would contribute 100 talents, which was equivalent to 300,000 shekels of the temple—according to the half-shekel interpretation. 4Q513 seems to continue the topic of the half-shekel valuation, explaining that the half-shekel equals two zuzim, which are sources of uncleanness. Then the topic shifts to a clarification that an ephah and a bath are the same thing and equal to ten issarons, although one is a dry measure and the other is liquid. A bath of wine is equated with an ephah of corn. The seah is defined as one-third issaron. The most obvious context for understanding this terse form of accounting is in a situation where dry products can be exchanged for liquid ones or vice versa. This would also make sense if someone were presenting an offering at the temple.

Another law prohibits Israelites from selling their own people to the Gentiles as slaves (4Q159, frags. 2–4). This is again a humanitarian law serving to protect the indentured and their families. A similar statement is found in Lev 25:35–42. The next law refers to a twelve-member judicial panel that deals with cases of treason and rebellion. They investigate the cases and sentence the guilty persons to death. This law bears some connection to the context of Deut 21:18–21, which does not mention a group of judges. After this comes a law prohibiting men and women from wearing each other's clothes. This is practically word-for-word the text of Deut 22:5.

The final law of 4Q159 is an abbreviated form of the law of the accused virgin in Deut 22:13–21. If a woman's husband accuses her of not being a virgin when they married and it turns out that he was correct, she was to be executed. If the husband was wrong, he had to pay her two minahs/one hundred shekels for her humiliation and was not permitted to divorce her. The same issue and interpretation is also found in 11QT^a 65:7–15.

In 4Q514 one learns that a person remains unclean for seven days and then washes and cleans himself on the day of his purification from his "fount" or penis. After that he was permitted to eat pure bread, that is, partake of a sacred meal.

The laws mentioned above probably arose from actual controversies and practical considerations. As in some biblical legislation, some of these laws help the destitute to survive without violating the civil law. In the case of slavery and the accused wife, one can also understand the laws as providing for the survival of the weak. Perhaps these laws come from a community of impoverished persons and possibly even couples who needed extra sustenance in their humbled state. One recalls certain wisdom sayings that urge one to continue to acquire knowledge and wisdom even in a state of poverty (4Q416).

THE CALENDAR TEXTS

Already in the book of Genesis the catastrophic flood lasted 354 plus ten days, the length of a round solar year of fifty-two weeks. This 364-day year contrasted and conflicted with the 354-day calendar that had alternating months of 29 and 30 days and no added days. Several manuscripts discovered in the Qumran caves focus on the question of the correct universal or liturgical calendar.[17]

The books of *Enoch* and *Jubilees*, Second Temple works known before the discovery of the Scrolls, were written in part as heavenly wisdom used to show that the 364-day calendar was the best calendar for the Jewish people to follow. The Ethiopic *Book of Enoch* claims that Enoch learned about this calendar during his long stay with the angels. Enoch states that the "future" flood on earth will last exactly one year. In tandem with *Enoch*, *Jubilees* condemns those who strictly adhered to the 354-day calendar. Yet, God knew that his people, the Israelites, would stray from the "rule of the sun" (2:9, 17; 6:30–31) and follow the year of the Gentiles. According to Jubilees, the earthly and heavenly calendars must be synchronized so that the Jews keep the Sabbath and the festival of weeks at the same time.

Among the Scrolls, 11QT^a, 4QMMT, 4QShirShab/11QShirShab, a narrative section in the famous 11QSPs^a, CD, a *Commentary on Genesis* (4Q252), and a few other pieces are based on the premises laid out in *Enoch* and *Jubilees*. Some works speak of phases of the moon as mentioned in the *Astronomical Book of Enoch* (chs. 72–82; 4Q209; 4Q317). In another work each year is assigned a priestly name for a period of seven jubilees (4Q321). The days of the year are also harmonized with the signs of the zodiac, and meteorological signs announce the advent of historical events (4Q318).[18] In fact, in one work the 364- and 354-day calendars are correlated so that one can know the correct rotation of priests into and out of the temple during a six-year cycle (4Q320).

The writer of 4Q317 synchronized his list of lunar observations with the 364-day solar calendar. This scientist-cum-exegete obviously favored the type of heavenly observations known from Enoch's *Astronomical Book* (chs. 72–82). 4Q318, classified as a *brontologion*, predicts the future based on signs within the natural world, including those in the heavenly realm.[19]

> Adar. On the first and the second (days), the ram. On the third and on the fourth, the ox. On the [fifth and on the sixth and on the seventh, the twins . . .] (col. 2)

No other Dead Sea manuscript uses the Babylonian names for months and associates dates with concrete zodiac signs given in Aramaic. Based on the Roman tradition the ram is of course Aries, the ox is Taurus, and the twins are Gemini. In this brief passage the writer wanted to correlate heavenly signs and historical events. In fact, this *brontologion* may come from the oldest Jewish handbook on astrology in existence. It bears some similarity to the Enoch traditions, but advances Enoch's ideas by presenting omens about very imminent occurrences.

> [If] it thunder[s . . .], a siege against [. . .] and adversity for the nation and violence [in the court] of the king, and among the nations in [. . .] shall be. Concerning the Arabs, [. . .] famine, and they will plunder each oth[er . . .]. If it thunders in the twins, panic and sickness because of foreigners and [. . .]. (col. 2–9)

Thunder serves as the sign for national and international difficulties. It signals war, violence, illness, confusion, famine, and chaos.

Another much more prosaic set of fragments preserves specific dates for priestly duties at the temple. These dates are also related to events of public history. Although the miserable condition of these fragments prevents one from grasping much of the context, one does read about Gentiles, prisoners, Nabateans, Shelamzion, Hyrcanus, Aristobulus, Aemelius, and the high priest Johanan (4Q333). The writer is apparently referring to Jewish civil strife and the role of the Roman general M. Aemilius Scaurus in this conflict. One fragment reads: "Amelios killed" (4Q324ª, frag. 2, l. 4). The sparse contextual clues suggest that this Aemilius had killed someone in the seventh month. It is not possible to determine the precise year when this happened, but it has been suggested that this murder occurred around the time of the Day of Atonement and the Feast of Booths. Optimistic modern interpreters might suspect that the Roman general was the Wicked Priest who tried to kill the Teacher of Righteousness on a Day of Atonement according to 1QpHab. If this were true 1QpHab concerns the role of a Gentile leader in killing a leader of the Jewish community, perhaps at the behest of another Jewish faction.

Astronomical and priestly concerns are combined in a work that tabulates the conjunctions of the sun and the moon during established jubilee periods when the years are named for priestly families (4Q319). The second through seventh jubilees are represented. Reflection on Gen 1:14–19, which recounts God's creation of lights of the fourth day, permits the writer to imagine that the two dominant lights coordinating their efforts in a grand dance of time.

> And God said, "Let there be lights in the firmament of the heavens to separate the day from the night. And let them be for signs and seasons and days and years. And let them be lights in the firmament of the heavens to give light upon the earth." And so it was. And God made the two great lights, the greater light to rule the day, and the lesser light to rule the night. He made the stars also. . . . And God saw that it was good. And there was evening and there was morning, a fourth day. . . . its light on day four [. . . The conjunction at the creation of lights, on the fourth day of Ga[mul . . .]. (4Q319, frag. 1, col. 5, ll. 10–11)

The author seems to believe that both the sun and moon were created and began to function simultaneously, taking turns at their specified times.

The correlation of the astronomical knowledge with the fourth day of the priestly course of Gamul probably indicates that the pedigree of the family of Gamul is preeminent. The priestly courses or *mishmerot* for service at the temple are correlated in another work (4Q320). First Chronicles 24 already preserved a traditional roster order for service at the Jerusalem temple, which positioned Gamul in the final or twenty-fourth rotation. In the *mishmerot* work from Qumran, Gamul has been moved to the top of the list. Other priestly rosters appear in 4Q328–330.

Another six-year cycle with dated festival appears in 4Q325. This work unambiguously dates the Barley Festival to the twenty-sixth of the month on the day following the Sabbath. The Wine Festival follows on the third of the month, and the Oil and Wood Festivals fall on the two days after the Sabbath. Two other fragments give dates for several

Sabbaths and the First Fruits Festival according to the 364-day year (4Q327 and 4Q394).

Debates about the calendar are quite ancient. This is revealed in the biblical story of the flood. The books of Enoch and Jubilees continue this discussion in astronomical and narrative contexts. Other Qumran manuscripts reflect the use of a forty-nine year jubilee. There is an emphasis on the phases of the moon, as in Enoch. The Scrolls, however, take this topic farther by tabulating synchronisms between the solar and the lunar years and connecting this with priestly service schedules, the Sabbath, and dated festivals. The appearance of the Roman zodiac and the Babylonian calendar prove that the owners of the Scrolls were influenced by international standards. The reference to a Roman leader involved in the occupation of Judaea suggests that these calendar materials had some connection with both the Roman and Jewish elite.

1QS prescribes that the wise person should study any wisdom that may be discovered along the way with respect to the times (9:13). In light of the varied works falling under the rubric "calendar," it is fascinating that the rabbinic tractate *Rosh HaShanah* (II.8) reports that the famed Rabbi Gamaliel maintained a table of moon phases on the wall of his upper chamber. Roughly a millennium later Maimonides said that the ancient Jewish Sanhedrin observed the moon and made calculations (*The Code of Maimonides*, III.8, Santification of the New Moon). What is clear from Qumran's written traditions associated with the 364-day solar calendar was that Jewish thinkers were organizing their thoughts and lives in light of the proper calendar all the time and that the use of the correct liturgical calendar was of supreme importance.

SOME WORKS OF THE LAW

In the early 1950s batches of fragments from Cave 4 arrived at the Palestine Archaeological Museum. One group of fragments was written in a Hebrew that looked somewhat like the language of the Mishnah and was given the designation 4QMishn. Three decades later at a biblical archaeology conference in Jerusalem, editor Elisha Qimron presented some sentences from these fragments and characterized the work as a letter written by Qumran community's Teacher of Righteousness to his nemesis, the Wicked Priest.[20] In fact, both Qimron and John Strugnell, his co-editor, had originally advocated the view that in this "halakhic letter" the Teacher of Righteousness explained his flight to Khirbet Qumran. Although this overly precise interpretation still seems to be accepted rather tacitly, scholars believe that 4QMMT (4Q394–399) was definitely a document that revealed complex legal discussions among Jewish groups in the late Second Temple period. Twenty topics are mentioned.[21] The handwritings in the six manuscripts date between the early first century BCE and the early first century CE.

Manuscript	Contents	Palaeographical Age
4Q394	calendar	early Herodian
4Q395	purity	early Herodian
4Q396	sacrifice of mother and fetus on same day, those with a severed penis, Jerusalem, sexual intercourse between priests and non-priests	early Herodian
4Q397	separation, scripture, blessings, curses	early Herodian
4Q398	blessings, curses, Solomon, David, Jeroboam, Zedekiah	early Herodian

The first preserved section, which some scholars believe may not have belonged to 4QMMT contains a list of dated Sabbaths and festivals. The next part preserves what may have been a conclusion to the initial part: "and the year is complete—three hundred and [sixty-four] days" (A 19). This calendar is alluded to in CD, which mentions Jubilees as an authoritative book. It is assumed in 11QT^a to establish dates for festivals and in 4QShirShab/11QShirShab to schedule readings for specific Sabbaths.

Another of the key themes in 4QMMT is a critique of certain priests who permit Gentile offerings and sacrifices.

> the priest[s] should be cautious concerning this practice in order not to cause the people to bear punishment (B 12–13). These priests are also warned not to accept any items made of the hide and bones of unclean animals. (B 21–26)

It is the clergy who ultimately bears the responsibility and guilt when others do not adhere strictly to correct understandings of the Law.

The writer says "we have separated from the multitude of people . . . and do not follow them in matters of purity" (B 16). Most likely, the separation does not refer to total physical isolation, since the ultimate goal of the writer is to reform priestly practice. The tone of the writer of 4QMMT is not radical or severe. It is that of someone hoping to reform the current ways of the priests and the people.

Another purity concern deals with the interpretation of the ceremony of the red heifer found in Num 19:1–10. According to 4QMMT, those involved in this ritual did not become pure until the sun had set. Both this view and 4QMMT's opinion about liquid streams is sometimes called Sadducean (B 55–58).

The author of 4QMMT was particularly worried, as was Ezra, about intermarriage with foreigners, but he also felt that the blind and the deaf could easily contaminate the temple. He wanted the priests to enforce carefully all purity laws regarding lepers and other such people.

Not only should the priests avoid intimate relations with foreigners, the Aaronite priests are strictly forbidden from marrying daughters of the laity.

> They are holy, and the sons of Aaron are [. . .] However, you know that some of the priests and [the laity mingle . . . and unite with each other contaminating [. . .] seed [. . .] their own [seed] with women whom they are forbidden to marry. (B 79–92)

Similar to the concerns of the 11QT^a, there is an enhanced emphasis on maintaining stringent standards of purity for the temple and its personnel. Those who carry out God's laws within the temple, the priests, bear the responsibility for violations of purity standards. From them flows purity, and they above all human groups must avoid contamination with unclean people and things.

Certainly, part of 4QMMT appears to be addressed to priests at the temple, but another section is directed to an unnamed, but respected individual. The writer mentions his integrity and good reputation while encouraging the addressee to study carefully "the book of Moses and the books of the Prophets and David" (C 9–11). Because the writer refers to former blessings and curses on Israelite and Judaean kings and asks his readers to recall their deeds, it has been suggested that the recipient of "the letter" 4QMMT was in fact a Judaean king. He is told to "recall

David, a pious man," a suggestion that makes one think of David, the psalms writer and pious man, recorded in 11QPs^a.

> We have sent you some of the specific laws of the torah according to our understanding, for your welfare and for the welfare of your people. For we have seen (that) you have wisdom and knowledge of the Torah. Consider all these things and ask him that he bolster your will and remove from you the plans of evil and the tricks of Belial so that you may rejoice at the end of time ... (C 26–30)

Whoever the writer and addressee may have been, it is obvious that the former believes in the addressee's capability of discerning the right things to do and passes on his blessing to him. The reference to the evil entity Belial suggests that at least this part of 4QMMT was connected to the writers of the communities' scrolls.

4QMMT does not give the impression of having been a lofty legal tractate, but rather a personal correspondence of some sort, very rare among the Scrolls, written to encourage proper behavior rather than to condemn any single person. Unfortunately, the names of the people who wrote, received, and read this supposed letter are lost. This forces one to speculate. Some scholars connect a few of the legal positions taken in 4QMMT to the Sadducees. It is clear, however, that the writer is condemning some priests who are open to social, religious, and sexual intercourse with foreigners. To the modern reader, some of the topics noted may seem rather trivial, but certainly these concerns were not unimportant to ancient Jews and particularly not to certain orthodox priests who believed in the presence of God in the temple. The writer of 4QMMT, who may have in fact been a leading priest, understood that priests are God's representatives on earth and are therefore to be held to higher standards within God's holy dwelling and within their lives.

The existence of 4QMMT in Cave 4 raises other issues. Why were so many copies of it stored there, if they had been sent to a particular Wicked Priest, thought to have been a high priest, or a monarch? Since the manuscripts were copied during the Herodian period, it seems likely that versions of this work either never left the community at Khirbet Qumran, or belonged to different people affiliated with that site, or perhaps they were sent to the community at Qumran from elsewhere. Only further manuscript finds might clarify these questions.

THE *ANGELIC SONGS OF THE SABBATH SACRIFICE*

In Cave 4 eight manuscripts of this work were found. Another was retrieved from Cave 11. Surprisingly, a manuscript of the same work was salvaged during the archaeological work atop Masada. Handwriting analysis of these manuscripts showed that the fascinating religious work had been copied at least 10 times from the first century BCE to the fall of Masada in 73 CE. Its initial editor, John Strugnell, named it *The Angelic Liturgy*.[22] He passed it on to his student, Carol Newsom, who called it *Songs of the Sabbath Sacrifice*.[23] Along with another scholar, Hartmut Stegemann, Newsom eventually reconstructed a sequence of thirteen songs or praises that had been dated internally to some of the first thirteen sabbaths of an ideal liturgical calendar.[24]

While some of the introductory formulae to the songs have disappeared, dates for the first, sixth, seventh, eighth, and twelfth sabbaths are at least partially discernable. The very first Sabbath was dated to the fourth of the first month. God is praised for establishing the angelic priest of the presence. These priests are called *elim*, which means nothing less than divine beings. The praise says that God "engraved his laws for all the spiritual works." These angelic beings are purified by God. They sacrifice on behalf of those who repent of their wicked deeds. God is depicted as royalty surrounded by the camps of *elim*, who are praising his greatness.

One Masada fragment of 4QShirShab/11QShirShab is reminiscent of a passage in the 1QS: "From the God of knowledge (is) everything that exists forever . . . He establishes the former things in their determined times and the latter things in their seasons." This explanation of all existence as divine deed based on a divine plan feeds into the song for the sixth sabbath of the ninth of the (second) month.

Then, in another fragment, one reads of tongues of princes exalting the God of the *elim*. Repeatedly, there is reference to psalms of praise, psalms of thanksgiving, psalms of exultation, psalms of magnification, and always seven wonderful words or songs. Seven princes bless those who praise God, the king, those who are determined to be righteous and knowledgeable, those who confess, those who wait for God, and those who exalt God's laws. The marvelous words of blessing are likened to sturdy shields. This imagery recalls the war towers formed by shields on which the names of Michael, Gabriel Sariel, and Raphael are inscribed in 1QM 9:15–16.

The temple's entrance vestibule is described as bearing the likeness-es of living *elim* with colors and chambers. Even the shapes of the *elim* praise God. Their speech is quiet. On the twelfth Sabbath, which prob-ably was calculated as the twenty-first of the third month, the cherubim worship before God.

> The cherubim prostrate themselves before him and bless. When they rise, a soft divine sound [. . .], and there is a den of praise. When they lower their wings, there is a soft divine sound. The cherubim bless the image of the throne-chariot above the firma-ment . . . there seems to be a fiery vision of the most holy spirits. (4Q405)

Experts say that these songs of praise provided a heavenly model upon which the earthly priesthood should model itself. Of course, hu-man priests find it ridiculous to compare themselves with angelic priests:

> [. . .] for how shall we be counted among them? For how shall our priesthood be counted in their dwellings? [How shall our] ho[liness compare with their supreme] holiness? How does the offering of our tongue of dust compare with the knowledge of the divine [one. . . .]

The author is not simply lamenting the futility of imitating angelic praise, he is also emphasizing the beauty of understanding and trying to reproduce angelic praise. In one fragment a few legible letters have led scholars to suggest that the chief angelic priest was none other than Melchizedek (4Q401 11, 3).

Scholars have speculated about whether these songs were read dur-ing a Sabbath ritual to legitimate the Zadokite priesthood of the Qumran community over a period of thirteen weeks. Others simply read the *Angelic Songs of the Sabbath Sacrifice* as descriptive of angelic worship in the heavenly temple. According to this view, the reader participates in his own private mysticism by reading the songs aloud.

Nothing like this vision appears in the Bible, but some traditional passages may have been influential. In Exod 24:11 Moses, Aaron, Nadab, Abihu, and the elders of Israel saw God and the paved work of sapphire stone under his feet (cf. Ezek 1:26). In Isa 6:1–3, Isaiah says that he saw God upon his throne, the six-winged seraphim who were saying "holy, holy, holy." The prophet Ezekiel reports his visions in chapters 1 and 3. Perhaps the reference to the "wheels" in 4QShirShab/11ShirShab have their origin in 1:15–21. In 3:12 Ezekiel is taken up and hears a voice saying, "Blessed be the glory of the Lord from his place." Daniel 7:9–14 provides another vision of God upon his throne. The prophet sees God's white garment, his hair like pure wool, his flaming throne and its wheels. In some ways Rev 8 seems closer to the tradition of these praises, because it mentions the seven angels, their trumpets, the altar, and the prayers. In *1 Enoch* 14 we read that Enoch dreamed that he had been taken up into the heavens where he saw a building of crystalline walls and tongues of fire. He saw God sitting up his throne there. Eventually, the mystical thinking which led from biblical and extra-biblical ideas about the heavenly kingdom was continued in the *Hekalot* writings of the early rabbinic period.[25]

PHYLACTERIES

No less important than the many fragments of lengthy manuscripts, in fact, was the discovery of about two dozen phylacteries or *tefillin* in the Qumran caves. Cave 4 preserved twenty-one; Cave 5 may have yielded three; Cave 8 had one, and four others said to come from undisclosed caves.[26]

Found in varying stages of deterioration, these phylacteries show that ancient Jews actually wore boxes filled with sacred texts on their foreheads and arms. The hand phylacteries contained tiny folded pieces of parchment with extremely minute texts from the Law of Moses. Those worn on the forehead consisted of four compartments for four different passages. According to later rabbinic tradition, the four mandated texts were Exod 13:1–10; Exod 13:11–16; Deut 6:4–9; and Deut 11:13–21. The Qumran phylacteries show no signs of adhering to that later standardization.

The content of Exodus 13 is the Passover, a time for consecrating one's first born of humankind and farm animals during a week-long celebration requiring one to eat unleavened bread and teach one's children the commandments. Deuteronomy 6 and 11 emphasize the teaching commandments. Chapter 11 assures one that God will provide rain for the crops. All four passages refer to signs on the hand and between the eyes (Exod 13:9, 16; Deut 6:8–9; 11:18–21). Deuteronomy explains that the phylacteries connected to the body are reminders of God's involvement in history and his promises for the future. Deuteronomy also requires that God's law be placed upon the doorposts of the house and the gates (Deut 6:9; cf. 11:20). This is "so that your days and the days of your children may be multiplied in the land . . ." (11:21). The *mezuzot* among the Scrolls included the Ten Commandments, which later rabbinic tradition rejected.

According to rabbinic tradition, males thirteen years of age and older should wear phylacteries (*m. Sebuoth* 3:8, 11), but not during festivals, on the Sabbath, or at night (*b. Menaḥoth* 36a-b). Apparently, they were attached for morning prayers. No such rules have been found for their use in Qumran's manuscripts, nor do the Qumran phylacteries reflect later rabbinic guidelines. In order to understand the nature of the most ancient phylacteries it helps to see the sequences provided by later writers.

Rashi	Rabbenu Tam
Exod 13:1–10	Exod 13:1–10
Exod 13:11–16	Exod 13:11–16
Deut 6:4–9	Deut 11:13–21
Deut 11:13–21	Deut 6:4–9

The medieval and ancient phylacteries have the same starting point. Rashi most clearly follows the biblical sequence.

The phylacteries from Cave 1 were published in the category of biblical works. One of them includes Deut 5:23–27; 10:17–18; 10:21—11:1; 11:8–12; and Exod 13:2–3, 7–9, and 15–16. Another from Cave 2 preserves Exod 13:1–10, 11–16; Deut 11:13–21; and Deut 6:4–9. In Cave 3 several phylacteries survived, but reflect a situation opposite that of standardization. In one case the sequence is Exodus 13, then Deuteronomy 11, 6, and 10. In another the sequence is Deuteronomy 10; Exodus 12; Deuteronomy 5; and Exodus 20. In a third case the order of passages is Deuteronomy 10, then 11, back to 10 and 11. Two Cave 4 phylacteries preserve the order Deuteronomy 11 followed by Exodus 12 (like 4QDeut[j] col. 9). The editor of the Cave 4 texts of Deuteronomy says that portions of the Ten Commandments and its framing text, Deuteronomy 11, and Exod 12:43—13:5 frequently appear in the Cave 4 phylacteries. The phylacteries from the Qumran caves are very individualistic, but show a tendency to harmonize Exodus and Deuteronomy when they share a certain topic. The sequence Exodus followed by Deuteronomy was apparently not sacrosanct in the manuscripts from the Qumran caves.

The *Letter of Aristeas* (158) says that the wearing of the hand phylacteries is a sign that one fears God and his works. Josephus traces the phylacteries back to Moses (*Ant.* 4.213). In the New Testament book of Matthew, Jesus ridicules external piety, self-adornment with phylacteries, and special clothing.

> The scribes and the Pharisees sit on Moses' seat; so practice and observe whatever they tell you, but not what they do; for they preach, but do not practice. . . . They do all their deeds to be seen by men; for the make their phylacteries broad and their fringe long. . . ." (23:2–3, 5)

There should be no doubt that Jesus' words reveal a controversy about external and internal piety beyond the Jesus group.

The evidence from the Qumran caves proves that phylacteries and *mezuzot* were used two thousand years ago following the injunctions in Deuteronomy. However, there seems to have been much flexibility about which texts could be copied and placed in the tiny capsules.

❧EIGHT❧

The Scrolls and Jewish History

T HE DEAD SEA SCROLLS are primarily religious literature, but occasionally they mention historical figures of known public history. In some of this literature writers refer to historical episodes that seem never to have recorded by the ancient historians. In that sense, the Scrolls potentially supplement the historical record.

PRAISE FOR JERUSALEM AND KING JONATHAN

A 15 cm by 7.5 cm fragment with a security tab to which a binding thong was attached was discovered among the Cave 4 texts (4Q448; see also 4QDamb). In contrast to the beautiful calligraphy of other manuscripts, this manuscript's cursive hand is difficult to read. Only a few words from about ten lines lead some scholars to see here part of an unknown Hallelujah psalm. Already known from the Syriac and 11QPs^a XVIII, the final verses of Ps 154 were written along the top left edge of the fragment (Column A). Below this psalm two more columns were penned in a rather tight fashion (Columns B–C). Perhaps this is from the hand of a second scribe.[1]

From the beginning it was a struggle to decipher the handwriting. One wondered whether ʿir qodesh ('holy city') or ʿwr qodesh' (awake of holy one) is correct (col. B, l. 1). Even the preposition ʿl, which normally means 'against,' may be 'over' or perhaps 'for' (l. 2). Scholars have disagreed about whether l. 2 reads 'over King Jonathan' or 'the king's happiness' (which would eliminate the proper name). The initial words of Column C, l. 1 are also perplexing. Does the text say "because you love Isr[ael (?)]" or "I will glo[ry in] your love"? Some scholars even doubt the possibility of reading the final word in Column C as "Jonathan."

The broadly accepted view is that someone at the Khirbet Qumran settlement had supported and prayed for a Hasmonean ruler, who was either Alexander Jannaeus, also known as Yanni. Some think it may have been Jonathan Maccabeus. As the hypothesis goes, this king was favored only as the military and political leader of the Jews. Later, when he granted himself high priestly functions, the Qumran community and its supporters censured him. Hartmut Stegemann thought that the text was a written congratulations to King Jonathan, that is, Alexander Jannaeus, who had defeated Demetrius III Eukarios around 90 BCE and prevented foreign conquest and control of Jerusalem (see 4QpNah I).[2] Geza Vermes thought that King Jonathan was the Maccabean after he had been recognized as a military and political personality. Vermes pointed out that Column B, ll. 3–6 mentions "all the congregation of your people Israel, who are in the four corners of heaven" and finds confirmation of this language in 2 Macc 2:16–18: "God . . . will gather us from everywhere under heaven into this holy place" (a letter from Judas Maccabeus and the people of Israel to Egyptian Jews on the occasion of the festive dedication of the Jerusalem temple.[3] This has been read in light of 1QpHab 8:8–9 which mentions the previously acceptable behavior of the person who was later called the Wicked Priest. In the final line of Col. C one can read "[o]n t[he] day war . . . to King Jonathan (?) . . ." One wonders whether this column may have originally mentioned a blessing on the warrior king Jonathan or whoever is meant in the text.

PERSONAL NAMES IN THE SCROLLS

Besides the traditional biblical name that one expects to find in manuscripts of scripture and related to scripture, some of the Scrolls preserve names that tell us two things—the extent of historical references, that is a range from this point in time to another point time, and specific names that can often be correlated with known public history.[4] 4QpNah preserves the Seleucid names Antiochus and Demetrius. These names appear in a context that claims that no foreigners have conquered the holy city Jerusalem from the time of Antiochus IV (ca. 176 BCE) until Demetrius Eukarios III (ca. 90 BCE). A Jewish faction had wanted Demetrius to intercede in their civil war, but the Seleucid was unsuccessful. This failure was probably seen as a sign that God was on the side of the anti-Seleucids. A short prayer for a certain King Jonathan has also survived (4Q448; see above). This Jonathan has been identified with Jonathan Maccabeus, Alexander Jannaeus, and John Hyrcanus. There are Jewish coins stamped with the name Jonathan, and this refers to Alexander Jannaeus.[5] Perhaps the connection to Jannaeus is the most logical, since 4Q322 mentions his widow, Shelamzion. The text mentions the 9th of Shebat, the 20th day of a certain month when Shelamzion came to see Hyrcanus, the king.

In the seventh month, in the week of Gamul, according to a calendric work from Cave 4 (4Q324b), a certain Aemilius killed someone. He was known to have massacred many Jews on the temple mount in Jerusalem in 63 BCE when the Romans were initiating their siege of Jerusalem. The text mentions the 9th of Shebat, the 20th day of a certain month when Shelamzion came to see Hyrcanus, the king. A second fragment from the same manuscript says "high priest . . . Johanan to bring to." Some of these historical figures had been connected with the nicknames mentioned in the commentaries on biblical works.

In an entirely different context, a palimpsest preserves the name Potlais or something similar (4Q468e l. 3). This person may have been connected with Pompey's governor of Judaea in 63 BCE or perhaps was a fellow traveler of Archaeleus, who ruled after the death of Herod.[6] If he is the latter, he is reported to have killed 3,000 rioters on the temple mount ca. 4–5 CE (see Josephus, *War* 1.162, 172, 180; *Ant.* 14.84, 93, 124).

One manuscript reports on the notorious vices of certain individuals (4Q471a).[7] This text has been interpreted as a record of rebukes. A certain Yohanan ben Ar was short-tempered and prideful. Hananiah Notos disturbed the spirit of the community. He loved his body or perhaps showed favoritism to his family relations. Another individual, Hananiah ben Simon, is mentioned, but the manuscript breaks off at this point (4Q477). Scholars speculate that these people were rebuked for their wayward behaviors publicly in communal assemblies. The name Notos has been taken to mean someone from the South. The penal code of 1QS and that of the *Rule-Damascus Hybrid* (4Q265) lead one to expect written evidence of those who were not living up to community standards and perhaps others who had been thrown out of the community, but the oddity is that practically nothing of the registry has survived of a community that presumably lived for two centuries at Khirbet Qumran.

On a pottery sherd dated to the Herodian period, one finds the names Honi, Eleazar ben Nahamani, and perhaps a slave named Hisday.[8] Although controversy accompanies the crudely penned Hebrew text, some scholars interpret the sherd essentially a deed of property promising the transfer of a slave and some property to the community at Khirbet Qumran. A separate sherd has the name Jehoseph ben Natan. Another has the name Eleazar scratched on to it. On a large jar one easily reads the name Jehonanan Hatela.

THE *COPPER SCROLL*

Less than a km south of Cave 1 and 2 km north of the ruins of Qumran, archaeologists had been searching approximately 250 caves and discovered among other things two inscribed rolls of oxidized copper stacked against a wall of what came to be called Cave 3.[9] In order to open and decipher these enigmatic rolls, they were eventually taken to Professor H. Wright Baker at the College of Science and Technology in Manchester, England, who devised equipment to cut the pieces of copper into 23 longitudinal slices. The lettering of the inscription was not like that found in the other known manuscripts from the caves. Its Hebrew was not the literary Hebrew of those manuscripts. Its language has been described as belonging to Mishnaic Hebrew, a linguistic development usually dated after the First Jewish War against the Romans. Broadly speaking, the scripts of 3Q15 have been dated between 50 and 100 CE. Several individuals were likely responsible for chiseling the detailed inventory, and it has been suggested they may have been illiterate and had no idea what they were inscribing.

The temple inventories of the isle of Delos, which were recorded on copper for longer preservation, use language similar to that in 3Q15 from the early second century BCE. The *lex coloniae genetivae juliae* was inscribed on copper (the 710th year after the founding of Rome = 43 BCE). Similarly, the *lex cornelia de XX quaestoribus* was recorded on a bronze tablet (the 673rd year after the founding of Rome = 80 BCE). The latter was discovered as a scroll in the ruins of the temple of Saturn. The *diplomata militaria* of the imperial period were also secured on copper, as were temple inventories in Egypt during the Roman period. From Medinet Habu came Demotic text CG 30691, which had been laid out in a two-column format. In terms of genre, these inventories are also quite similar to the 3Q15.[10] A key difference is that the latter preserves a record of approximately five dozen hoards, a rather large number of entries.

Sixty-four locations are mentioned where various amounts of gold, silver, coins, vessels both empty and those containing resin, senna, and aloes, priestly garments, and scrolls had been hidden. The text names a particular item, notes that it can be found under or even within architectural structures, in cisterns, courtyards, caves, tombs, and monuments, and gives relative distances to the hoards.

> In the tomb of . . . the third: one hundred bars of gold. (1:2)

> In the hill of Kokhlit, containers, sandalwood and ephods. The total of the offering and of the treasure: seven [talents] and the second tithe rendered unclean. At the exit of the canal on the northern side, six cubits, toward the cavity of immersion XAI. (1:9–11)

> In the courty[ard of] . . . in a southerly direction nine cubits: silver and gold vessels of offering, bowls, cups, tubes, libation vessels. In all, six hundred and nine. (3:13)

> In the tomb which is in the wady of Kippah from Jericho to Sekhakha, at its entrance from Jericho to Sekahkah, dig seven cubits, thirty-two talents. (5:26)

3Q15's extensive list of hiding places indicates that its author had an intimate familiarity with the area from south of Jerusalem into the Judaean Desert, north into Samaritan territory and even on the east side of the Jordan River. Repeatedly the place called Kokhlit appears (1:4; 2:12; 4:21; 12:64). The scroll concludes there.

> In the underground cavity which is in the smooth rock north of Kokhlit whose opening is toward the north with tombs at its mouth there is a copy of this writing and its explanation and the measurements and the details of each item. (12:64)

Some scholars speculate that Kokhlit was located in the Yarmuk Valley (northern Transjordan), where some Essenes had supposedly settled. The author of 3Q15 expected that his associates were familiar with the numerous and wide-flung locations. His final entry added that a copy of this work existed north of Kokhlit.

The hiding places were typical of locations where people fled with their possessions and took refuge throughout history. Caves are mentioned four times. Thirteen times water conduits or reservoirs are recorded. The most desirable caches were underground chambers or cavities; mentioned fourteen times. Tombs, monuments, and courtyards were also used.

A remaining oddity of 3Q15 are the seven passages where Greek letters conclude the treasure inventory. They have been interpreted as abbreviations of the owner's Greek names. According to one view, some of the treasures of 3Q15 represent the holdings of the royal family of Adiabene, who were recent converts to Judaism.[11] Bet ha-Qos is mentioned as the home of a priestly family known from late historical works of the Bible (1 Chr 24:10; Neh 3:4, 21; 7:61–65; Ezra 2:59–63; 1 Macc 8:17).[12]

In 1983, Bargill Pixner studied the topography of the scroll.[13] He determined that about a third of the caches (nos. 1-17) were connected with Mt. Zion. He associated at least four hiding places with Khirbet Qumran and Jericho (nos. 22–24, 26). The mother lode of thirteen caches was located at Batanea on the slopes of the Yarmuk River (nos. 35–47). Only one hiding place was found far north at Mt. Garizin (no. 60). Robert Eisenman also organized a survey, but no one has ever turned up the massive bullion and other artifacts. It is no wonder that several adventurers ventured to find these treasures. Many of them were presumably hidden in traditional areas such as the Vally of Achor, the valley of Sekhakha, Jericho, Doq, Siloa, Bet-Eshdatain, and Mount Gerizim. The Wadi edh-Daliyeh Samaritan letters from the fourth century BCE and the Wadi Murabba'at texts from the early second century CE were discovered to the north and south of Khirbet Qumran, where Jews had fled to escape the onslaught of their enemies.

Many scholars now believe that 3Q15 was a realistic, historical record of hidden deposits brought from Jerusalem and the temple treasury when the Romans were about to take the city. If the inhabitants of the settlement at Khirbet Qumran had nothing to do with the Jerusalem priesthood, it is difficult to imagine a connection with the owners of the Dead Sea Scrolls. If one admits that people did travel between Khirbet Qumran and Jerusalem, not to mention to other locations, both the inhabitants of Qumran and those who administered at the Jerusalem temple may have shared some connection to the treasures of the 3Q15.

DOCUMENTARY TEXTS

Among the Cave 4 fragments published in the 1990s were letters, debt records, property conveyances, grain accounts in Hebrew, Aramaic, and Nabatean. Since one has always thought of the Dead Sea Scrolls as collections of religious writings, these documentary texts came as a surprise.[14] Immediately, some scholars said the bedouin had discovered them elsewhere but mixed them in with fragments from Cave 4. In the official edition of texts from Seiyal, otherwise known as Naḥal Ḥever (30 km south of Khirbet Qumran), these documentary texts are included as an appendix. The editor of the documentary texts, Ada Yardeni, doubts that the fragments have anything to do with the Qumran caves.

Twelve manuscripts were written on hide and seven on papyrus. Yardeni, a specialist in paleographical analysis, dates one manuscript, a letter (4Q342), to the early first century CE. According to C-14 analysis, the dating range is 14–115 CE. This letter contains the names Yehudah, Eleazar, and Elishua. Another manuscript written in a Late Hasmonean semi-cursive and Nabatean hand (ca. 50 BCE) refers to Shimon, S'dlhy, and Beit 'Aphek (4Q343). A promissory note (4Q344) mentioning a certain Elezar bar Yehosef has been dated by C-14 to 72–127 CE. A deed mentioning Shimon and Menashe dates to the late first century BCE (4Q346). Written in a beautiful Herodian hand, another deed (4Q348) mentions several persons: Menahem, Eleazar, Shimon, Yehohanan, son of Yehosef, . . . son of Yehosef, Mattatyah son of Shimon, Eleazar son of . . . , . . . son of Hanan, Eleazar son of Shimon, son of Honi, son of Yehohanan, Yehosef, Menashe, and certain Shimon from Market or Beam Street. It also refers to a high priest who is not named. There is a deed written on papyrus (4Q359) in a Herodian or post-Herodian cursive script. Yardeni says that the manuscript 4Q360a was probably a literary text that referred to sacrifices.

The dating of a text that mentions the month of Elul, 30 silver denarii, and the names Yeshua', Hosha'yah, and Yishma'el son of Shimon turned out to be controversial. Yardeni dates it from about 50 BCE onward, while C-14 provides a chronological range 373–171 BCE. There seems to be no way to reconcile this obvious conflict. By virtue of their genres, age, and distance from Khirbet Qumran, Yardeni is convinced that the manuscripts 4Q343–346, 346a, 348, 351–354, and 356–360b never belonged to the Cave 4 collection.

Yardeni is correct in pointing out that one typically would not expect personal letters and other documentary texts among the Dead Sea Scrolls. Nevertheless, an ostracon discovered at Khirbet Qumran has been interpreted as a deed of property conveyance somewhat like some of the documentary texts (see above). The writing on this ostracon mentioned an individual from Jericho. A second ostracon mentioned people from 'En Gedi. In terms of their age, only three of the manuscripts apparently lie outside the date usually given for the demise of the Qumran community in 70 CE (4Q344–345, and 4Q359). Of course, thirty km is quite a distance from Khirbet Qumran, but it was also surprising to discover a manuscript of the *Angelic Songs of the Sabbath Sacrifice* as far south as Masada. Probably the origin of these documentary texts will continue to be discussed for some time.

HISTORY AND THE QUMRAN COMMUNITY

For decades scholars have developed narratives about the community that live at Khirbet Qumran from the second century BCE until the destruction of Qumran in about 69/70 CE.[15] In most cases, the reconstructed histories draw on a handful of comments in a few scrolls or fragments of scrolls. Establishing the chronology, scholars refer initially to CD 1:5–11, which mentions God raised up a faithful remnant 390 years after the Babylonian exile. A second passage then says that after twenty years a person called the Teacher of Righteousness appeared. In several other passages this Teacher is found in conflict with someone designated as the Liar and another character called the Wicked Priest. According to 1QpHab, the Wicked Priest pursued the Teacher to his place of exile on the Teacher's Day of Atonement because of some issue involving the Law. This passage makes several contributions to the historical reconstruction. It tells us, according to many scholars over the decades, that a serious conflict occurred between two individuals. The reference to the Law leads one to think that the two disagreed intensively over some matters of interpreting and practicing the Law. Explicit mention of the Teacher's Day of Atonement gives the impression that the Wicked Priest and the Teacher observed the Day of Atonement at different times and according to different calendars. The text mentions "his place of exile," which has been understood as the settlement at Khirbet Qumran.

Based on these pieces of information plus sources beyond the Dead Sea Scrolls, scholars have developed rather elaborate hypotheses about the identities of the people behind the code names used in 1QpHab, 4QPs 37, and 4QpNah. Although one hardly ever finds this proposal anymore, some scholars used to think that the Qumran community emerged after the murder of Onias III ca. 172–71 BCE. According to the slightly later Maccabean view, the Qumran community arose early in the second century BCE and involved the famous Maccabee family. The Wicked Priest was Jonathan or Simon Maccabeus. The Hasmonean hypothesis identifies the Wicked Priest either with Alexander Jannaeus or Aristobulus II. Some scholars read the texts against the background of the Roman period. Although one cannot be sure of the identity of the Wicked Priest, it has been even more difficult to find suitable candidates for the role of the Teacher of Righteousness. In more recent times, scholars are steering away from the specific identification of figures mentioned in the Scrolls, because the language of the Scrolls is very theological and quite ambiguous in terms of its usefulness for historical reconstruction.

Of all the works that have been used to recreate the history of the Qumran community, 4QpNah provides names of political figures that one knows from other sources. The context is public and international. The writer says that no foreign monarch was able to conquer Jerusalem from the time of Antiochus, probably the IV (ca. 176 BCE), up to the time of Demetrius Eukarios III (ca. 95–88 BCE), when a group of Jews requested that Demetrius help them take power in a Jewish civil war. The attempt was a failure, and Jerusalem remained unoccupied. At that time the Jewish leader Alexander Jannaeus crucified 800 Pharisees, which seems to be mentioned in 4QpNah 1:7–8. It is possible that Jannaeus was the Wicked Priest, who was initially favored by the persons who wrote 1QpHab and 4QPs 37? It has also been suggested that the short prayer for a king Jonathan (4Q448) refers to Alexander Hyrcanus, who is praised in this document and was considered an ally to the writer's group. These are two possible scenarios against which one can try to understand the mysterious language of the commentaries. Increasingly, scholars simply take for granted some version of the history of the Qumran community, but few of them are really involved in improving the reconstruction nor in defending a particular reconstruction.

THE SCROLLS AND EARLY CHRISTIAN THOUGHT

According to scholars the Dead Sea Scrolls were hidden in caves along the Dead Sea around 69 or 70 CE, when the Romans were approaching the settlement at Khirbet Qumran. Archaeologically speaking, the activities of John the Baptist, Jesus, Paul, and others were contemporary with the later history of the people at Qumran. It seems likely that the early followers of Jesus crossed paths in Jerusalem, at Khirbet Qumran, or other places. The Christian religion found supporters both inside and outside Israel. The same was apparently not true for the people of the Scrolls.

Scholars have long speculated on the possible Essene origins of John the Baptist and Jesus, but both of these figures apparently never founded or belonged to a known communal structure. Paul says that he had been a Pharisee until his conversion (Acts 23:6). The Jewish historian, Josephus, also emphasized connections with several Jewish groups, but acknowledged himself as a Pharisee (*Life* 12).

When one turns to the Scrolls and the New Testament, it is possible to find connections between the two in terms of language, ideas, and images.[16] On a grand scale both communities viewed themselves as the ideal people of God. In CD, the writer says he follows the interpretation of God's laws according to the New Covenant in the land of Damascus. Jesus was also understood as the essence of a new covenant. The early Christians were devoted to the person, power, and divinity of Jesus. The running commentaries called *pesharim* also refer to a Teacher of Righteousness, who may have been a charismatic personality like Jesus, but he seems to have never been considered a divinity.

None of the New Testament writings nor their sources were ever found in the Qumran caves. Some Greek letters found in Cave 7 were said to come from the book of Mark, but this cannot be substantiated (see Chapter 6). The Greek manuscripts of the Mosaic Pentateuch from Cave 4 reveal the presence of people at Khirbet Qumran who read and valued the Greek text of the Bible.

In terms of lifestyle, scholars agree that the people of 1QS advocated a communal lifestyle whereby members' assets are eventually merged into a sort of holding company. Acts 2:4–5 also says that members surrendered their property to the community. It is not at all clear who was in charge of the communities mentioned in the Scrolls. Some have equated "the guardian" with the bishop or overseer in Philemon, 1 Timothy, and Titus. The messianic banquet in 1QS 6 and 1QSa 2 bears some resemblance to the meals mentioned in Matt 26:26-29 and 1 Cor 11:27–30. Scholars believe that the leadership at Khirbet Qumran came from the priesthood at the Jerusalem temple. The early Jesus movement seems to reflect little if any priestly affiliation and interests.

11QTᵃ, 4QMMT, and CD preserve laws demonstrating that some Jews actually desired to apply laws for priests to everyone. The Jesus movement never seems concerned about this. Jesus himself emphasizes that one has to adjust one´s practice of the Law to current circumstances. God´s salvation had already arrived. Several works from Qumran reject or disqualify lepers, those with skin diseases, those defiled by their sexual organs, the crippled, the deaf, those without speech, and foreigners from participation in the divine service. Jesus was apparently involved in healing the handicapped and accepting such societal outcasts. Jesus healed lepers, but always told them to go to the priest and give his offering (Matt 8:1–4; Mark 1:40–45; Luke 5:12–16; 17:11–19). Perhaps this suggests that Jesus tried to conform to traditional practices and avoid injuring the sensibilities of the priests.

As he is depicted in the Gospels, John the Baptist offered baptism as an independent agent, but Jesus went to him for baptism thus giving his ministry divine sanction. The Gospels present John as a preacher of repentance. One has the impression that perhaps he had a significant number of followers. John was courageous enough to condemn the house of Herod for inappropriate and multiple marriage partners. It is clear that Jesus, his disciples, and later Paul often led very solitary lives away from their families and loved ones. There were also married members. This is true for the people of the community behind CD and other texts also.

The closest connection between the Scrolls and the New Testament seems to be in their shared language and imagery. Certain texts from both groups speak of the sons of light, the righteousness of God, the works of the Law, lawlessness, light and darkness, Belial, and the human temple of God. 1QS uses the expression "the many" to refer to one of its assembled bodies. Matthew 26:27–28 and Mark 14:23–24 employ similar language. The dualism of light and darkness in 1QS 3 and 1QM 4 is like that in Gal 5:2 and 2 Corinthians 6.

In terms of messianism and eschatology there are obvious similarities. Like 1QS 9, Acts 2 and Hebrews 10, refer to a prophet and a messiah. One manuscript from Cave 4 (4Q285) has been interpreted as referring to a "pierced messiah," although that translation has been questioned. 4Q286 speaks of a "son of God."

Scholars tend to agree that Qumran's thematic commentaries, which weave together various ancient scriptures, resemble thematic sections in the New Testament. One of the most popular texts seems to have been Isaiah 40. In 1QS this text is interpreted as referring to the birth of an elect community. In the Gospels, its referent is John the Baptist. The Melchizedek text (11Q13) from Qumran uses Isaiah 61 to proclaim the future redemption from evil. Jesus quotes this chapter in order to announce that scripture had already been fulfilled. Luke 4:16–22 presents Jesus in a synagogue in Nazareth reading from Isa 42:1, telling his audience that scripture had been fulfilled that very day. Just as in Acts 2:15–19, many passages in the Scrolls are interpreted to show that prophecy was relevant and a serious concern in the last days, a notion that was widespread. The Teacher of Righteousness and Jesus were both considered to be authoritative preachers or teachers in whom others felt prophecies had been fulfilled. Second Corinthians 6:14—17:1 refers to the human temple of the living God. 4Q174 (6–7) also mentions that God's salvation will be found in a human sanctuary, a select group of individuals who represent the temple and its sacrifices.

The 11QNJ text from Qumran describes features of an architecturally realistic city that is often interpreted as a future Jerusalem. Revelation 21, which speaks of "the holy city Jerusalem coming down out of heaven from God," paints a picture of a square city with high walls, twelve gates, but no physical temple. God is the temple. Revelation's concern with heavenly worship reminds one of angelic worship in the *Angelic Songs of the Sabbath Sacrifice*.

Besides sensationalism or piety, the primary reason that one finds parallels between the language, ideas, and images of some passages in the Scroll and parts of the New Testament is that both derive from the same world of thought and from the same time period. The Dead Sea Scrolls constitute a library of religious thinking that created fertile ground for various types of religious groups in Judaism. One or more of these movements is reflected in the Scrolls. Early Christianity also witnesses to growth of a movement led first by Jesus, James, Paul, and others. Much of the religious thought in the Scrolls emerges also in later Jewish literature.

WHO WROTE THE SCROLLS?

The Scrolls do not answer that question directly. Palaeography and carbon-14 analyses have demonstrated the antiquity of the scribes and their materials. The Scrolls are a little more than 2000-years old. In the Scrolls, one finds highly skilled, one might say, professional calligraphy.

Some of the scripts are less attractive and clumsy. Still, they testify to a plethora of individual scribal hands used over a period of about 300 years. Some manuscripts have been copied by skilled scribes, who are often presumed to have lived at Khirbet Qumran.

Probably the overwhelming majority of modern scholars believe that the Scrolls belonged to the group called the Essenes in Josephus, Philo, and Pliny. Josephus's description of the admission procedure for new members is astonishingly similar to the entrance requirements prescribed in 1QS. The groups and individual members behind the community scrolls are most likely responsible for the production, study, and preservation of some of the Scrolls.

The Essene identification has been challenged on several fronts. Josephus never presents the Essenes as a separatist group with its headquarters on the Dead Sea. On the contrary, he said that they lived throughout Palestinian Syria. If the scrolls came from the residents of Khirbet Qumran, certainly these inhabitants were highly literate—probably among the most educated in the society. The settlement at Khirbet Qumran may have been a center for the study of religious literature. It is not difficult to imagine people coming there to live would have brought their treasured scrolls along with them. Some scholars believe that the Scrolls were brought from libraries in Jerusalem during the war against the Romans and hidden in the caves. This is only one possible explanation of the great abundance of scrolls and scroll fragments of religious works discovered in the Qumran caves. These religious works could have been brought from various places in Palestinian Syria. It seems certain that many of the scrolls were copied in a distinctive scribal style, which probably suggests that they originated in a major center for such activity. One would automatically think of Jerusalem, Damascus, or other such locales.

The Scrolls testify to an intensive preoccupation with understanding and extending scripture. There were plenty of clues to this before the discovery of the Scrolls. Whoever the authors were, Essenes or otherwise, they were open to copying, rewriting, re-authoring, and expanding the scriptures of their day. Since Scrolls have been dated from the mid-third century BCE to approximately 70 CE, one can safely conclude that living with and unpacking divine texts was the chief goal of the owners of the Scrolls. Even in the early years after their discovery, one knew about a group that associated itself with a Covenant in Land of Damascus. This group organized and lived according to an interpretation given within that communal context. CD remained strongly attached to ancient scripture, and its communities were administered by someone with the title, the *mebaqqer* (the inspector or supervisor). Another direction is found in 1QS: its community is usually called the *yaḥad* (the United, the community). It often calls its leader the *maśkil* (the wise one, the well-informed one). One view says that the *yaḥad* broke off from the Damascus covenant. Another suggestion is that several groups broke off from the *yaḥad*. At some point, it seems that the Covenant in the Land of Damascus and the *yaḥad* joined forces or overlapped in membership. Another direction is represented by those who were perhaps satisfied with studying and learning from the sacred texts that had been passed down to them. A fourth direction is represented in the many parabiblical texts, most of which derived from Cave 4.

The interpretation of the Scrolls has almost always insisted that the Dead Sea Scrolls community separated completely from following ritual law at the Jerusalem temple, led by the Teacher of Righteousness, a code name for a high priest who left Jerusalem to found a demanding religious community on the shores of the Dead Sea. His nemesis was a certain Wicked Priest, who kept the high priesthood for himself. The Teacher and the Wicked Priest have been identified with various known historical figures from the early second century BCE to the first century CE. Only a handful of scholars read the Scrolls against the background of the Early Christian movement.

The caves in which all the Scrolls were discovered lies in the same general region, and some of them are located right next to the site Khirbet Qumran. Everyone knows that Cave 4, from which the vast majority of fragments were retrieved, is a natural hiding place. Caves 5-10 are also rather close. Caves 1 and 2 lie no more than 1 km (2/3 of a mile) to the north. Cave 3 roughly another 1 km (2/3 of a mile) north of Cave 1. Cave 11 is located roughly 1 1/3 km (1 mile) north of the ruins and maybe 1/3 km (1/4 mile) south of Cave 3. The caves were connected by the people who hid the Scrolls.

When one reads and studies the Scrolls, many of them seem to be connected in terms of their basic themes and doctrines. Like the traditional Jewish Scriptures of the times, the Scrolls show us that an intramural conversation was continuing. As much as written texts can said to be alive, the Scrolls represent multiple lively conversations about works of the past and ideas of the ancient present. Were the ancient authors

Essenes as most scholars believe? Were some texts Sadducean as a few now think based on some legal texts?

Since the discovery of the Scrolls scholars have identified the writers and owners of the Scrolls with Essenes, Pharisees, Sadducees, Zealots, or some other unknown group in the late Second Temple period.[17] If one takes Josephus seriously—certainly the best-known and most prolific Jewish historian of the first century CE—as a model, one can imagine how ancient sectarians functioned. Josephus claimed that he had joined all of the groups he mentioned as well as having spent time with a recluse named Banus before eventually declaring himself a Pharisee at the age of nineteen. If Josephus were typical of men of his socioeconomic class, and he definitely was one of the Jewish elite in the mid-first century CE, men and perhaps women as well were constantly in dialogue about their religious beliefs, often advocating a certain position one day and perhaps changing their minds on another occasion. No doubt, the admittance procedure of 1QS and the Essenes that he described was too restrictive for him. And under the circumstances of the First War against the Romans, in which Josephus was a military leader, each person was forced to decide whether he was pro-Roman or anti-Roman. Others would be involved in authoring new religious works and debating legal issues and eschatology. By the time Josephus wrote his famous works in Rome, he had had a chance to profit from not dying in battle and serving the Roman emperors. In good Deuteronomistic fashion, he counseled that the Jews were a peaceful, well-meaning people. Only a few bad seeds, he argued, had forced God to the side of the Romans.

In recent years it has been suggested that the tensions within the Scrolls reflects an ongoing struggle between Enochic and Mosaic forms of Judaism.[18] Both Enoch and Jubilees represent freedom in reflecting on and telling us more about ancient Judaism. The former emphasizes Enoch's reception of wisdom in the divine world and Jubilees offers an enhanced version of Genesis through Exodus 15 with an emphasis on schematizing history into jubilees and Sabbaths. In fact, the importance of established times for celebrating festivals can be traced back to the angels worshipping in heaven. *Enoch* retrojected chronologically certain Israelite-Jewish rituals into the antediluvian period and treated it spatially as a normal aspect of heavenly life. Many writings among the Scrolls prove the importance of the Lawgiver, Moses. The Enoch and Mosaic traditions are complementary rather than adversarial.

In the final analysis, few of the Scrolls support the simplistic view that the Dead Sea Scrolls came solely from the Essenes. Some of the legal viewpoints have been identified as Sadducean. Their interest in authoring, studying, and passing on familiar and previously unknown pseudepigrapha indicates that the owners of the Scrolls were concerned with collecting written traditions. The legal works are often imbued with priestly concerns that could be broadly applicable to anyone. Many of the wisdom texts suggest that the Scrolls come from a place of learning. The so-called community scrolls give the impression that those who wrote and read these works realized they were living in the last days and expected God to save the true Israel from the grips of Belial, a satanic figure, and his minions and restore Jerusalem and Israel to its deserved glory.

Although 1QS gives the impression that its community kept good records on its membership and discipline, little remains that would help those living in the twenty-first century to connect the Scrolls with one group to the exclusion of all others. Scholars often say that the Qumran community was anti-Pharisaic, but this too is based on little evidence. In fact, Pharisees, Sadducees, and Essenes probably seemed very much alike to outsiders. Most likely, members of these groups had opinions that evolved over time, sometimes divergent, sometimes convergent with others. The collection called the Dead Sea Scrolls is a scribal phenomenon reflecting the literary and theological interests of many highly educated Jews in the Second Temple period.[19] Giving each of the Scrolls' authors a name remains a task for the future.

The Convent of St. Saba

NINE

Epilogue

In 1939 Frederic Kenyon wrote: "There is, indeed, no probability that we shall ever find manuscripts of the Hebrew text going back to a period before the formation of the text which we know as Masoretic."[1] Eight years later the Dead Sea Scrolls were discovered. Five years later thousands of fragmentary pieces of manuscripts were found. A little more than fifty years later they had all been published. Scholars agree that the publication of all the Cave 4 materials has vastly modified how we understand the Scrolls and the people who held them dear.

In the first three to four decades after the first discoveries, those who have devoted themselves to studying the Scrolls and understanding their significance for Judaism "between the Testaments" saw the initial seven scrolls as the literary output of a small group of disgruntled separatists. Most scholars thought that the Scrolls belonged to and many were written or copied by the people who inhabited Khirbet Qumran from the second century BCE to the destruction of the Jerusalem temple in 70 CE. It is doubtful that the scrolls came from an isolated haven of malcontents, but rather from a larger religious movement in ancient Judaism. The sheer size of the collection that was retrieved from the Qumran caves argues against thinking that they come from any single Jewish group.

The Scrolls reflect the literary efforts of hundreds of authors and scribes, regardless of their denominational affiliations, who cared about their religious heritage. Besides the nearly complete scrolls known from Caves 1 and 11, as well as the inscrutable *Copper Scroll* from Cave 3, the 10,000 or so fragments from Cave 4 leave no doubt that the Dead Sea Scrolls still constitute the greatest archaeological discovery of ancient literature in Israel ever. If one may consider the collections from the various caves to be the vestiges of an ancient Jewish library, it would be the largest such library known in Jewish antiquity. No wonder that some scholars have suggested that the Scrolls belonged to the Jerusalem Temple's library, and many others are now saying that the Dead Sea Scrolls represented the heritage of Second Temple Judaism.

The presence of many writings, some biblical, some pseudepigraphical, some apocryphal, and many previously unknown, reveals a Judaism growing through its literary production. Some of the writings not found in the Jewish Bible could be found already in early Greek codexes of the Christian Old Testament. Some texts have been connected to the Syriac canon. Others are revered among the Ethiopians. Some found their way to Masada and to Cairo, Egypt. Although numerous the Dead Sea Scrolls lay outside the accepted Jewish canon, this collection has always been Jewish in origin and content—even when it had been lost for nearly 2000 years.

These writings show us the propensity to create Jewish hagiography in the late Second Temple period. This was certainly a phenomenon that developed in dialogue with Hellenism. There are vestiges of works attributed to or about figures of hoary antiquity. Some of these are Enoch, Enoch, Noah, Abraham, Levi, Naphtali, Joseph, Qahat, Amram, Moses, Joshua, Samuel, Elisha, David, Zedekiah, and other figures known from the Jewish Bible. These were heroes who had a message for later generations. In the case of King David, he becomes a model not only of the pious one, but of the classic composer of religious songs and poetry through the divine spirit. Some of these literary works reflect the words and actions of angels such as Michael, Melchizedek, Melchiresha', and the evil Watchers. The angel Melchizedek is God's instrument for destroying evil at the end of days. Belial is his nemesis. Such actors could easily compete with the divinities and personalities of Hellenistic and Roman mythology.

The Dead Sea Scrolls expand the number of exemplars of each type of writing known previously from the Jewish Bible. Pentateuchal works such as Exodus and Deuteronomy are read together as one often reads the New Testament Gospels, because they told the same story, even if one version often supplemented or supplanted the other versions. All of these variations, variants, and spin-offs coexisted in the ancient library of the Qumran caves, because they coexisted in the lives of those who owned, read, and mined them for wisdom. These works gave insight into the ancient present and near future so that one could know what God planned to do and through which individuals. This type of literature is related to the future-oriented apocalyptic works, but bears a strong similarity to use of Jewish scriptural quotation in the New Testament. The genre of wisdom literature was greatly enhanced by the production of additional instructions and secret knowledge. Some works were even penned in cryptic scripts.

The biblical or scriptural scrolls corroborate the list of books in the traditional Jewish canon, but expand it at the same time. The biblical manuscripts reflect the hands of many scribal hands, all seemingly well-skilled in penmanship. Because of the human factor and the individual talents and peccadilloes, some scribes were less skilled in copying another manuscript or taking dictation. In these scrolls one can see scribal corrections above the line, in the margins, and the use of dots for deletions and for the divine name. The Qumran biblical manuscripts sometimes agree with the MT, the LXX, the Sam, or other textual witnesses, but often preserve independent readings. These manuscripts from Qumran do, however, disagree with each other at points, showing that there was no editorial policy moving the scrolls monotonously toward an official standardization. These convergent and divergent readings at least prove the existence of competitive readings. Sometimes, as in the case of the paragraph about Nahash in 4Sam^a, a Qumran manuscript preserves a lost piece of scripture preserved also in the Greek text of the Jewish historian Josephus. Sometimes passages were lost due to a wandering eye or inattention. Perhaps a scribe may have excised a passage that did not suit him. Sometimes a scribe carefully copied his source text. One sees this in 4QExod^m, which has been described as Samaritan because of its tendency to juxtapose topically similar or identical passages from two separate works. If the Samaritan Pentateuch had not been known before the discovery of the Scroll, one might consider 4QExod^m an exegetical piece and not the Torah of a community. One recalls that the Scrolls preceded any known decree about canonization. These scrolls permit us to see God's words in the minds and hands of devoted believers.

Among the first scrolls found were the *Rule of the Community*, the *Rule of the Congregation*, the *Blessings*, the *Rule of War*, the *Thanksgiving Hymns*, the *Genesis Apocryphon*, and the books of Isaiah. Studying these scrolls was a new experience for all scholars. In a way, these ancient works showed us how individuals belonging to a very rigorous Jewish group interpreted scripture in order to help them understand their place in their world. The communities depicted in these scrolls had strict procedures for becoming a member and especially for maintaining oneself within the central decision-making committees. Members were evaluated annually, and their wisdom, behavior, and comments were monitored closely. In one work the community is described as a sort of human temple that offered up prayer that pleased God as much as bloody sacrifices. This is a major development, for it places a high value on personal piety and free-thinking. Some members of this community expressed their appreciation to God in touchingly personal hymns of thanksgiving. Other writers planned for the final battles before God would permit his people to reign supreme. Some individuals saw themselves in Abraham and other pious heroes of their antiquity. Still others sought to find God's plans for themselves in the predictions of the prophets.

The community scrolls reveal the existence of married and non-married members. They are concerned with numerous affairs of daily living and often express a hyper-orthodox lifestyle. CD includes rules for women's oaths, freewill offerings, Gentile judgments, laws of self-defense, lost property, witnesses, the counsel of judges, purification by water, the Sabbath, assemblies of the camps, slander, the disqualification of priests, misconduct at meetings, skin diseases, fluxes, menstrual impurity, and punishments. Purity has become a major focus of these groups.

In numerous scrolls the writers advocate or assume that the righteous lived their religious lives according to a liturgical year of 364 days. Some believed that all divine beings carried out their divine services according to this calendar, keeping festivals and Sabbath, just as should be done in the Holy Land or wherever Jews may have lived. The Sabbath was of utmost concern in some works, where one finds dates for the Sabbaths in the first quarter of the divine year. CD preserves the most extensive Sabbath code in Jewish antiquity. There are also astrological and zodiacal observations, showing that even these pious Jews were part and parcel of the spirit of their times.

In addition to the large number of extra-canonical psalms and hymns among the Dead Sea Scrolls, the large number of phylacteries to be worn during prayer and the *mezuzot* testify to the active personal religion of the owners of the Scrolls. Prayers and praise are woven into several of the non-liturgical texts as well. 11QPs^a represents a major liturgical restructuring of the traditional psalms collection and the acceptance of many psalms and other works that never belonged to any other known canon.

Still debated is the meaning and place of the *Copper Scroll* in the context of ancient Judaism and the Qumran community. It purports to be an inventory of treasures waiting to be retrieved. Some have thought it represented the assets of the Qumran community or the treasure of the Jerusalem temple. Metallic inventories were used in the Mediterranean world, but the Copper Scroll is the first to be found in Israel.

The Scrolls also belong to modern scholarship. They have added to our understanding of ancient Hebrew, religion, and history. They supplement the Bible, Josephus, the Maccabees, and other ancient Jewish writings in Greek. Now we know what ancient Hebrew, Aramaic, and Greek scrolls and writing looked like in the Second Temple period. The Scrolls have not rewritten public history for that age, but have added hues to the palette.

The desire to reconstruct, read, and understand the Scrolls better has led to discussions of ancient Hebrew and Aramaic paleography, improved carbon-14 analysis, the use of aDNA dating, and the application of new techniques in the field of photographic imagery.

In sum, the Dead Sea Scrolls, perhaps the greatest archaeological discovery of recent times, belong to the Jewish heritage, even as it morphed into rabbinic Judaism and Christianity and spread throughout the world. In that sense, the Scrolls belong to all those who care about the ancient scriptures. The Scrolls are the heritage of every outgrowth of ancient Judaism, for each one in its own way honors the sacred books of the ancients. They have also mined the ancient writings for their nuggets of wisdom for daily living and theological doctrines. Beyond that, many scrolls reflect the ongoing creation of religious literature in a period when it was thought to have ended.

The Dead Sea Scrolls appeal to those who care about origins and beginnings. In a more secular sense, the Scrolls belong to humanity and especially to those who care about the lost literary remains of ancient civilizations. In this new millennium there may and probably will be other such manuscripts discoveries that challenge our picture of ancient Judaism. We should never say never. The Dead Sea Scrolls are certainly an indicator that we can see from our position on the boat only the tip of an iceberg long submerged but gradually coming into view.

Notes

CHAPTER ONE: INTRODUCTION

[1] William F. Albright (letter to John Trever) quoted in VanderKam, *The Dead Sea Scrolls Today*, 8.

[2] Albright, *BASOR* [110 (1948) 3], quoted in VanderKam, *The Dead Sea Scrolls Today*, 11.

[3] Davies, *The Complete World of the Dead Sea Scrolls*, 16.

[4] Ibid., 20–21.

[5] Tov, "Some Thoughts about the Diffusion of Biblical Manuscripts in Antiquity," *The Dead Sea Scrolls. Transmission of Traditions and Production of Texts*, 151–72.

CHAPTER TWO: EDITING THE SCROLLS

[1] Davies, *The Complete World of the Dead Sea Scrolls*, 22–35.

[2] Ibid., 34.

[3] Vermes, *The Complete Dead Sea Scrolls in English*, vii–xii.

[4] Davies, *The Complete World of the Dead Sea Scrolls*, 29.

[5] Stegemann, "Methods for the Reconstruction of Scrolls from Scattered Fragments," 189–220.

[6] Newsom, *Songs of the Sabbath Sacrifice*. Newsom, "'He has Established for himself Priests': Human and Angelic Priesthood in the Qumran Sabbath *Shirot*," 101–20, especially 101–2, where she describes working with Stegemann in Jerusalem.

[7] Schuller, *Non-Canonical Psalms from Qumran*, 267–78.

[8] Stegemann, "Methods for the Reconstruction," in *Archaeology and History in the Dead Sea Scrolls*, 203–4. A more cautious view is presented in Callaway, "Limitations in Reconstructing Dead Sea Scrolls Manuscripts." *QC* 16/1–2 (2008) 37–48.

[9] Qimron and Strugnell, *Qumran Cave 4. V: Miqsat Ma'ase Ha-Torah*, DJD 10, 201–11.

[10] Davies, *The Complete World of the Dead Sea Scrolls*, 27.

[11] Wacholder quoted in Davies, *The Complete World of the Dead Sea Scrolls*, 27.

[12] Elgvin, "How to Reconstruct a Fragmented Scroll: The Puzzle of 4Q422," in *Northern Lights*, 223–36.

CHAPTER THREE: THE WORLD OF THE SCROLLS

[1] Sacchi, *The History of the Second Temple Period.* Hayes and Miller, *Israelite and Judaean History*, 435–677. Davies, *The Complete World of the Dead Sea Scrolls*, 38–44.

[2] Jonathan Maccabeus is one possible candidate for King Jonathan in 4Q448, *Praise for King Jonathan.*

[3] According to the *Commentary on Nahum* (4QpNah 2:2–7), Jerusalem remained unconquered for about one century from Antiochus until the advent of the rulers of the Kittim, the Romans. The Lion of Wrath, who has identified with Alexander Jannaeus, is mentioned in a context with Demetrius (probably III). Jannaeus slaughtered 800 Pharisees, "the seekers after smooth things," whose coalition requested the military aid of Demetrius (*Ant.* 13:372–83; *War* 1:88–89). This happened around 90 BCE.

[4] Simon has been identified as "the man of Belial" in 4Q175 23 (*Testimonia*). In what seems to be a list of priests, the name Simon appears after Jonathan (4Q245 frg. 1 1:10).

[5] John Hyrcanus is the other possible candidate for King Jonathan who is praised in 4Q448. He, too, has been identified as "the man of Belial" of 4Q175. Josephus said that Hyrcanus embodied the ideal prophet, ruler, and priest.

[6] Salome (Shelamzion) is mentioned in 4Q331 frg. 1 2:7 and 4Q332 2:4.

[7] See note 3.

[8] Many of those Pharisees who petitioned Demetrius III fled Judaea thereby saving their own lives. For many Jews he was an unsavory character. They emphasized that his mother had been sexually tainted in captivity. Because his own wife was the widow of his father, many Jews would have found that despicable.

[9] Hyrcanus II is possibly the one who rebelled in 4Q332 frg. 2 l. 6. Arabs (that is, Nabateans) may have been mentioned earlier in l. 2. The historical context would have been the Nabateans support of Hyrcanus II against his brother Aristobulus II.

[10] The Scrolls make no direct reference to Pompey. His subordinate, Marcus Aemilius Scaurus is said to have killed someone in 4Q333 1:4, 8.

[11] Dio Cassius, *Historia Romana* LXVIII 32:1–3. Ben Zeev, *Diaspora in Turmoil*, 116/117 CE. Smallwood, *The Jews under Roman Rule from Pompey to Diocletian*, 416–21.

[12] Benoit, Milik, and de Vaux, *Les grottes de Murabba'at*, DJD 2, 46–48.

[13] Davies, *The Complete World of the Dead Sea Scrolls*, 46–48.

[14] Besides the concern to rebuild the temple in the days of Ezra and Nehemiah, the Maccabees, Herod, and many others put much energy into protecting and rebuilding the temple. Among the Scrolls, especially 11QT[a], CD, and 4QMMT focused on the temple.

[15] This is evidenced by the phylacteries and *mezuzot* from the Qumran caves and Murabba'at. See Chapter 7.

[16] In addition to the biblical psalms, 11QPsa, *The Songs of the Sabbath Sacrifice* (4QShirShab/11ShirShab), *Liturgical Prayer* (1Q34 and 1Q34bis), *Prayers for Festivals* (4Q507-09), *Blessings* (1QSb), and a few other texts reflect liturgical concerns. Immediately, one thinks of the *Rule of War* (1QM), which includes psalms (10:8–18; 12:10–18; 13:1–17; 14:2–18; and 19:1–11) and refers to others—the psalm of return (14:2), the prayer in time of war, and all their hymns (15:4–5).

[17] A statement near the end of 11QPs[a] (27:2–11) says that David composed songs to be sung over the possessed. Two such exorcism pieces are found in 11QPsAp[a] 5:4–6:2 and Ps 91 in 11QPsAp[a] 91 and 4QPsAp[a] 91.

[18] A *Zodiac with Brontologion* (4Q318); *Horoscopes* (4Q186, 4Q534, 4Q561).

[19] *Calendar of Priestly Courses* (4Q320–30) and *Calendric Signs* (4Q319).

CHAPTER FOUR: THE CAVES, THE SCROLLS,
AND THE SITE KHIRBET QUMRAN

[1] Vaux, *Archaeology and the Dead Sea Scrolls*. For a good summary of the archaeological data and interpretations, see VanderKam and Flint, *The Meaning of the Dead Sea Scrolls*, 3–53. Davies, *The Complete World of the Dead Sea Scrolls*, 78–81 for a list of scrolls by cave.

[2] Saulcy, *Narrative of a Journey Round the Dead Sea and in the Bible Lands, in 1850 and 1851. Including an Account of the Discovery of the Sites of Sodom and Gomorrah*, I, 49–50. Clermont-Ganneau, "Kumran," in *Archaeological Researches in Palestine during the Years 1873–1874*, II, 14–16. Dalman, "Jahresbericht," *Palestina-Jahrbuch* 10 (1914) 9–12. Dalman, "Jahresbericht," *Palestina-Jahrbuch* 16 (1920), 40–41. Masterman, "Observations on the Dead Sea Levels," *Palestine Exploration Fund Quarterly Statement* (1902) 161, also several reports in the same journal (1902-03, 1917). Masterman, "Notes on some ruins and a rock-cut aqueduct in the wady Kumran,"*Palestine Exploration Fund Quarterly Statement* (1903) 267.

[3] Vaux, *Archaeology and the Dead Sea Scrolls*. For decades scholars have read de Vaux's popular book as scientific fact. One depended on whatever he wrote about Khirbet Qumran, whether in this work or in his articles. Still, it should not be forgotten that this book was a synthesis of the archaeological data interpreted in light of a few statements in the community scrolls. See also Humbert, *Fouilles de Khirbet Qumrân et de Aïn Feshka*.

[4] Davies, *The Complete World of the Dead Sea Scrolls*, 178.

[5] Magness, "The Chronology of the Settlement at Qumran in the Herodian Period." *DSD* 2 (1995) 58–65. Magness provides a revision of de Vaux with more information especially on the physical remains at Khirbet Qumran.

[6] Cross and Eshel, "Ostraca from Khirbet Qumran," *IEJ* 47 (1997) 17–28. Yardeni, "A Draft of a Deed on an Ostracon from Khirbet Qumran." *IEJ* 47 (1997) 233–37. Callaway, "A Second Look at Ostracon No. 1 from Khirbet Qumran," *QC* 7/3 (1997) 145–70. For reflections on the context in which the ostracon was found, see Callaway, "Future Prospects of Scrolls and Khirbet Qumran Research: A Prophecy of Concrete Realism." *QC* 8/1 (1998) 35–36.

[7] Reich, "*Miqwa'ot* at Khirbet Qumran," in *The Dead Sea Scrolls: Fifty Years after Their Discovery: Proceedings of the Jerusalem Congress*, July 20–25, 1997, 728–31.

[8] Vaux, *Archaeology and the Dead Sea Scrolls*, 29.

[9] Robert Donceel and Pauline Donceel-Voûte, "The Archaeology of Khirbet Qumran," in *Methods of Investigation of the Dead Sea Scrolls and the Khirbet Qumran Site*, (eds.) Michael O. Wise, et al, 27–31.

[10] Ibid.

[11] Ibid., 7–13.

[12] Ibid.

[13] Hirschfeld, "The Architectural Context of Qumran," in *The Dead Sea Scrolls: Fifty Years After Their Discovery*, 673–83. Hirschfeld, *Qumran in Context*, 183–210.

[14] Patrich, "Khirbet Qumran in Light of New Archaeological Explorations in the Qumran Caves," in *Methods of Investigation of the Dead Sea Scrolls and the Khirbet Qumran Site*, 91 and figure 11 on 85.

[15] Schulz, "The Qumran Cemetery: 150 Years of Research." *DSD* 13 (2006) 194–228.

[16] See note 6.

[17] Callaway, "What Have 'En Gedi and Jericho to do with Qumran?" *QC* 8/3 (1999) 169–70.

[18] Allegro, *The Dead Sea Scrolls and the Christian Myth*, 235–40, pls. 16–17. Charlesworth, *The Discovery of a Dead Sea Scroll (4QTherapeia)*.

[19] Naveh, "A Medical Document or a Writing Exercise? The So-called 4QTherapeia," *IEJ* (1986) 52–55, p. II. Naveh, "341. 4QExercitium Calami C," in *Qumran 4. XXVI: Cryptic Texts*, 291–93.

[20] Callaway, "Some Thoughts on Writing Exercise (4Q341)," *QC* 13/2 (2006) 149–50.

[21] Ibid. 150–51.

[22] In fact, 1QS gives the impression with its rigorous multi-year entrance procedure that members were probably tested regularly, not just annually, regarding their knowledge of the sacred traditions and were also observed to see how they behaved with others.

[23] Yardeni, "A New Dead Sea Scroll in Stone? Bible-like Prophecy was Mounted in a Wall 2,000 Years Ago," *BAR* 34/1 (2004) 60–61. Callaway, "A Dead Sea Scroll in Stone or Simply a Prophetic Text on Stone from the First Century BCE?" *PJBR* 7/1 (2008) 5–13.

[24] Hendel, https://www.bib-arch.org/scholars-study/messiah-son-of-joseph.asp (*BAR*, January/February 35/1 (2009), per email communication with the author on January 17, 2011.

[25] Davies, *The Complete World of the Dead Sea Scrolls*, 76–77.

[26] Tov and White, "Reworked Pentateuch," in H. W. Attridge et al., *Qumran Cave 4. VIII. Parabiblical Text, Part 1*, *DJD* 13, 187–351. Callaway, "Limitations in Reconstructing Dead Sea Scrolls Manuscripts," *QC* 16/1–2 (2008) 43–44.

[27] Cross, "The Development of the Jewish Scripts," in *The Bible and the Ancient Near East: Essays in Honor of William Foxwell Albright*, ed. G.E. Wright, 133–202.

[28] Parsons, "Palaeography," in *Qumran Cave 4*, *DJD* 9, 7–13.

[29] Yardeni, "Palaeography," in *Qumran Cave 4*, *DJD* 18, 4Q266 (26–30), 4Q268 (116–18), and 4Q271 (170–72).

[30] Yardeni, "A Draft of a Deed?" *IEJ* (1997) 233–34.

[31] VanderKam and Flint, *The Meaning of the Dead Sea Scrolls*, 22–27. Tov, "Some Thoughts on the Diffusion of Biblical Manuscripts in Antiquity," in *The Dead Sea Scrolls. Transmission of Traditions and Production of Texts*, (eds.) Sarianna Metso, Hindy Najman, and Eileen Schuller, 153, 155, 169–72. Davies, *The Complete World of the Dead Sea Scrolls*, 70–72.

[32] Callaway, "A Second Look at Ostracon 1," 153–55.

[33] VanderKam and Flint, *The Meaning of the Dead Sea Scrolls*, 27–32. For a critique of how palaeographers sought out physicists to prove their case, see Callaway, "Methodology, the Scrolls and Origins," in *Methods of Investigation of the Dead Sea Scrolls and the Khirbet Qumran Site*, 413–14.

[34] VanderKam and Flint, *The Meaning of the Dead Sea Scrolls*, 55–59.

[35] Ibid., 70–72.

[36] Ibid., 74.

[37] Ibid., 76–83.

CHAPTER FIVE: THE BIBLE AND THE DEAD SEA SCROLLS

[1] For the number of Qumran manuscripts for each biblical work, see Abegg et al., *The Dead Sea Bible*, the introductions to each book. This can be compared with the statistics presented in Davies, *The Complete World of the Dead Sea Scrolls*, 165; and VanderKam, *The Dead Sea Scrolls Today*, 48–49.

[2] Abegg et al., *The Dead Sea Bible*, 196–97 (*Jubilees*), 480–81 (*Enoch*), psalms (539–40, 570–73, 576–77, 582–83, 588–89.

[3] The section on readings from the Qumran biblical manuscripts is indebted to Abegg et al., *The Dead Sea Bible*. These reading can be verified easily in Ulrich, *The Biblical Qumran Scrolls*. Of course, one should also refer to the editions of biblical manuscripts in the series Discoveries in the Judaean Desert (vols. 9, 12, 14, 16, 17, 15, 32, 8, 16, 39, 8, 6).

[4] Skehan, "The Qumran Manuscripts and Textual Criticism," in *Qumran and the History of the Biblical Text*, 213–14.

[5] VanderKam and Flint, *The Meaning of the Dead Sea Scrolls*, 113–14.

[6] Ulrich, *The Qumran Text of Samuel and Josephus*; Tov, *Textual Criticism and the Hebrew Bible*, 342–44.

[7] Tov, *Textual Criticism and the Hebrew Bible*, 114–17.

[8] Milik, "Prière de Nabonide et autres écrits d'un cycle de Daniel," *RB* 63 (1956) 407–11. Newsom, "Why Nabonidus? Excavating Traditions from Qumran, The Hebrew Bible, and Neo-Babylonian Sources," in *The Dead Sea Scrolls. Transmission of Traditions and Production of Texts*, 56–79.

[9] Sanders, *The Psalms Scroll of Cave 11*; Flint, *The Dead Sea Psalms Scrolls and the Book of Psalms*.

[10] Charlesworth, "Announcing a Dead Sea Fragment of Nehemiah," http://www.ijco.org?categoryId=28681, 2008.

CHAPTER SIX: THE PSEUDEPIGRAPHA, THE APOCRYPHA, AND THE SCROLLS

[1] A mere glance at the "Table of Contents" in Vermes, *The Complete Dead Sea Scrolls in English*, x–xi shows the size of the category pseudepigrapha. Vermes translates portions of three dozen such pseudepigraphic works. Had these works survived intact, this collection would have constituted an even larger percentage of the entire inventory. Had cave 4 never been discovered, many of these titles would now be absent from our inventory and our broader picture of the Scrolls.

[2] Milik, *The Books of Enoch*, 4.

[3] Ibid.

[4] Boccacini, *Beyond the Essene Hypothesis*, 119–62.

[5] Milik, *The Books of Enoch*, 298–300.

[6] VanderKam and Milik, "4QJubilees," *in Qumran Cave 4. VII: Parabiblical Texts*, Part 1, 11–22. VanderKam, "Moses Trumping Moses," in *The Dead Sea Scrolls. Transmission of Traditions and Production of Texts*, 225–44. Najman, *Seconding Sinai*, 41–69.

[7] Avigad and Yadin, *A Genesis Apocryphon*, 1–5.

[8] Brooke, "Commentaries on Genesis and Malachi," in *Parabiblical Texts, Part 3, DJD* 22, 185–212; Bernstein, "From Rewritten Bible to Biblical Commentary," *JJS* 45 (1994) 1–27.

[9] Davies, et al., *The Complete World of the Dead Sea Scrolls*, 128; VanderKam, *The Dead Sea Scrolls Today*, 60–61.

[10] Tov and White, "Reworked Pentateuch," in *Qumran Cave 4. VIII. Parabiblical Texts*, Part 1, 187–351. Segal, "4QReworked Pentateuch or 4QPentateuch," in *The Dead Sea Scrolls: Fifty Years After Their Discovery*, 391–99.

[11] Callaway, "Limitations in Reconstructing Dead Sea Scrolls Manuscripts," *QC* 16/1–2 (2008) 43–44.

[12] Ploeg and van de Woude, *Le Targum de Job de la grotte XI de Qumrân*.

[13] Yadin, *The Temple Scroll*, I, 1–8.

[14] Ibid., 38–88. Then "The Festivals" (89–142), "Offerings and Holy Gifts" (143–76), "The Temple and Its Courts" (177–276), "The Temple City and the Laws of Uncleanness and Purity" (277–342), "The Statutes of the King" (344–63), "Miscellaneous Laws" (363–85). Stegemann, "The Composition of the Temple Scroll and its Status at Qumran," in *Temple Scroll Studies*, 123–48. Callaway, "Extending Divine Revelation: Micro-Compositional Strategies in the Temple Scroll," in *Temple Scroll Studies*, 149–62 (and literature mentioned there). Wise, *A Critical Study of the Temple Scroll from Cave 11*, 35–234. Paganini, *Nicht darst du zu diesen Wörtern etwas hinzufügen*, 241–62.

[15] Callaway, "The Temple Scroll and Precedent Law," *QC* 15/1–2 (2007) 25–33.

[16] Paganini, *Nicht darfst du zu diesen Wörtern etwas hinzufügen*. The entire book is devoted to describing the systematization of Deuteronomy in 11QT^a. According to Paganini, the writers of 11QT^a wanted to present the ideal picture of a future society (268).

[17] Wacholder, *The Dawn of Qumran*, 135–40.

[18] Chiyutin, *The New Jerusalem Scroll from Qumran*; Licht, "The Ideal Town Plan from Qumran: The Description of the New Jerusalem," *IEJ* 29 (1979) 47–59; VanderKam and Flint, *The Meaning of the Dead Sea Scrolls*, 369–76; García-Martínez, "New Jerusalem," *Encyclopedia of the Dead Sea Scrolls*, 2, 606–10.

[19] Newsom, "The 'Psalms of Joshua' from Qumran Cave 4," *JJS* 39 (1988) 56–73.

[20] Ibid. Callaway, *The History of the Qumran Community*, 237–38 note 10.

[21] Sanders, *The Psalms Scroll from Cave 11*. For an explanation of the peculiarities of 11QPsa, see Abegg, et al., *The Dead Sea Bible*, 505–11.

[22] Abegg, et al., *The Dead Sea Bible*, 506.

[23] Schuller, "380. 4QNon-Canonical Psalms A," 80 (Obadiah), "381. 4QNon-Canonical Psalms B," 111 (man of God), 119 (king of Judah), and 124 (Manasseh, king of Judah).

[24] Newsom, "Why Nabonidus?" in *The Dead Sea Scrolls. Transmission of Traditions and Production of Texts*, 58–72.

[25] See Chapter 8.

[26] Identifications of Jonathan (see Chapter 3 notes 2 and 5).

[27] Sukenik, *The Dead Sea Scrolls of the Hebrew University* (in Hebrew); Holm-Nielsen, *Hodayot, Psalms from Qumran*; Kittel, *The Hymns of Qumran*.

[28] Harrington, "Wisdom Texts," *Encyclopedia of the Dead Sea Scrolls*, 976–80. Collins, *Jewish Wisdom in the Hellenistic Age*. Goff, "Recent Trends in the Study of Early Jewish Wisdom Literature," 377–416. Schiffman, "Halakhic Elements in the Sapiential Texts from Qumran," in *Sapiential Perspectives*, 89–100. Several volumes in DJD are devoted to wisdom: *Qumran Cave 4 XV Sapiential Texts, Part 1*, edited by Elgvin et al.; *Qumran Cave 4 Sapiential Texts, Part 2*, edited by Strugnell et al; *Qumran Grotte 4 III (4Q482–4Q520)*, edited by Baillet, several manuscripts; and *Qumran Cave 4. XXVI Cryptic Texts*, edited by Pfann et al, several manuscripts.

[29] Abegg, et al., *The Dead Sea Scrolls Bible*, 636–46.

[30] Ibid., 576.

[31] Abegg, et al., *The Dead Sea Scrolls Bible*, 629.

[32] O'Callaghan, "Papiros neotestamentarios en la cueva 7 de Qumran?" *Bib* 53 (1972) 91–100.

CHAPTER SEVEN: THE COMMUNITY SCROLLS

[1] Charlotte Hempel, *The Damascus Texts*; Baumgarten, Chazon, and Pinnick, *The Damascus Document: A Centennial of Discovery.*

[2] Milik, *Ten Years*, 151–52.

[3] Davies, *The Damascus Document.* For a brief summarize of this still very relevant work, see Callaway, *The History of the Qumran Community*, 93–100.

[4] Metso, *The Serek Texts.* Metso, *The Texual Development of the Community Rule.*

[5] Ibid. Schiffman, *The Eschatological Community of the Dead Sea Scrolls: A Study of the Rule of the Congregation.*

[6] Barthélemy and Milik, *Qumran Cave I*, 118–29. Brooke and Robinson, "A Further Fragment of 1QSb: The Schøyen Collection MS 1909," *JJS* 46 (1995) 120–33.

[7] Jean Duhaime, *The War Texts.* Davies, *1QM, The War Scroll from Qumran.* Yadin, *The War of the Sons of Light against the Sons of Darkness.*

[8] Holm-Nielsen, *Hodayot Psalms from Qumran.*

[9] Wise, *The First Messiah*, is a fairly recent attempt to identify the Teacher of Righteousness with a messianic personality named Judah. The Teacher is mentioned in CD 1:1, 9–10, 6:11, 20:1, 14, 28, 32; 1QpHab 1:2, 2:1–3, 5:10–11, 7:1–5, 8:1–3, 9:8–10, 11:3–8; 4QpPs37 3:15, 4:5–11, 25; 4QPs 127 l. 5.

[10] Callaway, *The History of the Qumran Community*, 190–97, offers a critique of using the hymns of the Teacher to reconstruct history. See also Davies, *The Complete World of the Dead Sea Scrolls*, 95, especially the box entitled "History or Hagiography?"

[11] Brooke, *Exegesis at Qumran*, 80–278; Campbell, *The Exegetical Texts*, 33–44.

[12] Brooke, "Testimonia," in *Anchor Bible Dictionary*, 6, 391–92; Cross, *The Ancient Library*, 147–55; Campbell, *The Exegetical Texts*, 88–99.

[13] See Chapter 6 note 19.

[14] Kobelski, *Melchizedek and Melchiresaʿ.* Jonge and van der Woude, "11QMelchizedek and the New Testament," *NTS* 12 (1966) 301–26; Campbell, *The Exegetical Texts*, 56–66.

[15] Callaway, *The History of the Qumran Community.* Besides examining the archaeology, palaeography, and the Essenes, Callaway scrutinized CD, the *pesharim*, 4Q175 (*Testimonia*), and 1QH to describe the theological language of these so-called historical writings. He doubted that one should continue to try to reconstruct historical episodes based on the evidence available at that time. Cave 4 manuscripts were found that mentioned several names that can be connected to the public history of the 1st century BCE (see Chapter 3 notes 2–10). See also Lim, *The Pesharim.*

[16] Schiffman, "4QOrdinancesa, b," *Rule of the Community and Related Documents*, I (ed.) J. H. Charlesworth, 145–57.

[17] VanderKam, *Calendars in the Dead Sea Scrolls*; Callaway, "The 364-Day Calendar Traditions at Qumran," *Mogilany 1989*, I, 19–29; Ben-Dov, *Head of All Years: Astronomy and Calendars at Qumran in their Ancient Context* (Studies in the Desert of Judaea 78).

[18] Greenfield and Sokoloff, "An Astrological Text from Qumran (4Q318) and Reflections on Some Zodiacal Names," *RQ*, 507–25; Wise, *Thunder in Gemini*, 186–221. Popović, *Reading the Human Body: Physiognomics and Astrology in the Dead Sea Scrolls and Hellenistic-Early Roman Period Judaism* (Studies in the Desert of Judaea 67).

[19] Popović, "The Emergence of Aramaic and Hebrew Scholarly Texts," in *The Dead Sea Scrolls. Transmission of Traditions and Production of Texts* (Studies in the Desert of Judaea 92), 96–97.

[20] Qimron and Strugnell, *Qumran Cave 4. V. Miqsat Ma'ase Ha-Torah, DJD* 10, 44–63 (the composite text). Kampen and Bernstein, eds., *Reading 4QMMT: New Perspectives on Qumran Law and History.*

[21] Ibid., 123–74.

[22] Strugnell, "The Angelic Liturgy at Qumran—4QSerek Šîrôt 'Olat Haššabbat," *VTSup* 7 (1959) 318–45.

[23] Newsom, *The Songs of the Sabbath Sacrifice.*

[24] Idem., "'He Has Established for Himself Priests'," in *Archaeology and History in the Dead Sea Scrolls*, 102–13.

[25] Schiffman, *Reclaiming the Dead Sea Scrolls*, 353–62.

[26] Vaux and Milik, *I. Archéologie, II. Tefillin, Mezuzot et Targums (4Q128–4Q157).*

CHAPTER EIGHT: THE SCROLLS AND JEWISH HISTORY

[1] Eshel , Eshel, and Yardeni, "4Q448, 4QApocryphal Psalm and Prayer," in *Qumran Cave 4. VI: Poetical and Liturgical Texts, Part 1, DJD* 11, 421.

[2] Stegemann, The *Library of Qumran*, 104.

[3] Vermes, *The Complete Dead Sea Scrolls in English*, 331.

[4] Chapter 3 notes 2–10. Abegg provides an inventory of personal names in the Scrolls in *An Introduction to the Discoveries in the Judaean Desert Series*, 229–84.

[5] VanderKam and Flint, *The Meaning of the Dead Sea Scrolls*, 291.

[6] For the earlier identification, see Strugnell, "The Historical Background to 4Q468 [= 4Q Historical B],"*RQ* 73 (1999)137–38; Schwartz, "4Q468g: Ptollas?"308–309. For the later one, see Broshi, "Potlaas and the Archelean Massacre [4Q468 = 4Q Historical B]," *JJS* 49 (1998) 341–35.

[7] Vermes, *The Complete Dead Sea Scrolls in English*, 237–38.

[8] See Chapter 4 note 6.

[9] Walters, *The Copper Scroll: Overview, Text, and Translation*; Lefkovits. The *Copper Scroll (3Q15): A Reevaluation*; Goranson, "Sectarianism, Geography and the Copper Scrolls," *JJS* 43 (1992) 282–87; Goranson, "Further Reflections on the Copper Scroll," in *Copper Scroll Studies* (eds.) George J. Brooke and Philip R. Davies, 226–32; Shanks, *The Copper Scroll and the Search for the Temple Treasure*; Muchowski, "The Origin of 3Q15: Forty Years of Discussion," in *Copper Scroll Studies*, 257–70.

[10] Wise, "David Wilmot and the Copper Scroll," in *Copper Scroll Studies*, 291–310.

[11] Stegemann, *The Library of Qumran*, 74.

[12] McCarter, "The Mysterious Copper Scroll: Clues to Hidden Temple Treasures?" *BR* 8 (1992) 34–41, 63–64.

[13] Pixner, "Unraveling the Copper Scroll Code," *RQ* 11 (1983) 323–65.

[14] Cotton and Yardeni, *Aramaic, Hebrew, and Greek Documentary Texts from Nahal Hever and Other Sites.*

[15] Callaway, *The History of the Qumran Community*. See Chapter 7 note 15.

[16] Brooke, *The Dead Sea Scrolls and the New Testament*; Lim, *Holy Scripture in the Qumran Community and the Pauline Letters*; Fitzmyer, "The Qumran Scrolls and the New Testament after Forty Years," *RQ* 13 (1988) 609–20. Fitzmyer, "Paul and the Dead Sea Scrolls," in *The Dead Sea Scrolls after Fifty Years*, 2, 599–621. Eisenman, *Maccabees, Zadokites, Christians and Qumran: A New Hypothesis of Qumran Origins*. Eisenman, *James the Just in the Habakkuk Pesher*. Eisenman, *James the Brother of Jesus: The Key to Unlocking the Secrets of Early Christianity and the Dead Sea Scrolls.*

[17] Davies, *The Complete World of the Dead Sea Scrolls*, 54–63. Callaway, *The History of the Qumran Community*, 63–85 (an analysis of the Essene identification).

[18] Boccaccini, *Beyond the Essene Hypothesis.*

[19] Hamel, *The Book: A History of the Bible*, 327–29.

CHAPTER NINE: EPILOGUE

[1] Kenyon quoted in Driver, *The Judaean Scrolls*, 15.

Bibliography

Abegg, Martin. "Concordance of Proper Nouns in Non-Biblical Texts from Qumran." In *The Texts from the Judaean Desert: Indices and an Introduction to the Discoveries in the Judaean Desert Series*, edited by Emanuel Tov et al., 219–35. DJD 39. Oxford: Clarendon, 2002.

Abegg, Martin Jr., et al. *The Dead Sea Scrolls Bible*. San Francisco: HarperCollins, 1999.

Adler, Yonatan. "Identifying Sectarian Characteristics in the Phylacteries from Qumran." *RQ* 89 (2007) 79–92.

Allegro, John. *The Treasure of the Copper Scroll: The Opening and Decipherment of the Most Mysterious of the Dead Sea Scrolls, a Unique Inventory of Buried Treasure.* Garden City, NY: Anchor, 1960.

———. *The Dead Sea Scrolls and the Christian Myth*. Buffalo: Prometheus, 1984.

Atkinson, Kenneth. "Representations of History in 4Q331 (4QPapHistorical Text C), 4Q332 (4QHistorical Text D), 4Q333 (4QHistorical Text E), and 4Q468 E (4Q Historical Text F): An Annalistic Calendar Documenting Portentous Events?" *DSD* 14 (2007) 125–51.

Avigad Nahman, and Yigael Yadin. *A Genesis Apocryphon*. Translated by Sulamith Schwartz Nardi. Jerusalem: Magness, 1956.

Baillet, Maurice. *Qumran Grotte 4 III (4Q482–4Q520)*. DJD 7. Clarendon: Oxford, 1982.

Baumgarten, Joseph M. et al., editors. *The Damascus Document: A Centennial of Discovery: Proceedings of the Third International Symposium of the Orion Center for the Study of the Dead Sea Scrolls and Associated Literature*. Studies on the Texts of the Desert of Judah 34. Leiden: Brill, 2000.

Bearman, Gregory et al. "Imaging the Scrolls: Photographic and Direct Digital Acquisition." In *The Dead Sea Scrolls after Fifty Years: A Comprehensive Assessment,* edited by Peter W. Flint and James C. VanderKam, 472–95. Leiden: Brill, 1998.

Benoit, Pierre et al., editors. *Les grottes de Murabba'at, II, Part 1*. DJD 2. Oxford: Clarendon, 1961.

Bernstein, Moshe. "From Re-Written Bible to Biblical Commentary." *JJS* (1994) 1–27.

Black, Matthew. *The Book of Enoch or 1 Enoch*. Studia in Veteris Testamenti Pseudepigrapha 7. Leiden: Brill, 1985.

Boccaccini, Gabriele. *Beyond the Essene Hypothesis: The Parting of the Ways between Qumran and Enochic Judaism*. Grand Rapids: Eerdmans, 1998.

—————. *Enoch and the Mosaic Torah: the Evidence of Jubilees.* Grand Rapids: Eerdmans, 2009.

Brooke, George J. *Exegesis at Qumran, 4QFlorilegium in its Jewish Context.* JSOTSup 29. Sheffield: JSOT Press, 1985.

—————. "Testimonia." In *Anchor Bible Dictionary,* 6:391–92. New York: Doubleday, 1992.

—————. *The Dead Sea Scrolls and the New Testament.* Minneapolis: Fortress, 2005.

Brooke, George J., and James M. Robinson. "A Further Fragment of 1QSb: The Schøyen Collection MS 1909." *JJS* 46 (1995) 120–33.

Broshi, Magen. "The Archaeology of Qumran—A Reconsideration." In *The Dead Sea Scrolls: Forty Years of Research,* edited by Devorah Dimant, 103–15. Studies on the Texts of the Desert of Judah 10. Leiden: Brill, 1992.

—————. "Potlaas and the Archelaus Massacre (4Q468g = 4Q Historical Text B)." *JJS* 49 (1998) 341–55.

Burrows, Millar, editor. *The Dead Sea Scrolls of St. Mark's Monastery,* vol. 2, fasc. 2: *The Manual of Discipline.* New Haven: Yale University Press, 1951.

Callaway, Phillip R. *The History of the Qumran Community. An Investigation.* Journal for the Study of the Pseudepigrapha 3. Sheffield: Sheffield Academic, 1988.

—————. "Extending Divine Revelation: Micro-Compositional Strategies in the Temple Scroll." In *Temple Scroll Studies,* edited by George J. Brooke, 148–62. Journal for the Study of the Pseudepigrapha Supplement Series 7. Sheffield: Sheffield Academic, 1989.

—————. "The 364-Day Calendar Traditions at Qumran." In *Mogilany 1989,* 19–29. Cracow: Enigma, 1993.

—————. "A Second Look at Ostracon No. 1 from Khirbet Qumran." *QC* 7/3 (1997) 145–70.

—————. "Future Prospects of Scrolls and Khirbet Qumran Research: A Prophecy of Concrete Realism." *QC* 8/1–2 (August 1998) 35–36.

—————. "What Have 'En Gedi and Jericho to Do with Qumran?" *QC* 8/3 (November 1999) 169–70.

—————. "Some Thoughts on Writing Exercise (4Q341)." *QC* 13/2 (2006) 149–50.

—————. "A Dead Sea Scroll in Stone or Simply a Prophetic Text on Stone from the First Century BCE?" *PJBR* 7/1 (September 2008) 5–13.

—————. "Limitations in Reconstructing Dead Sea Scrolls Manuscripts." *QC* 16/1–2 (July 2008) 37–48.

Campbell, Jonathan. *The Exegetical Texts.* Companion to the Qumran Scrolls 4. London: T& T Clark, 2004.

Charles, R. H. *The Apocrypha and Pseudepigrapha of the Old Testament.* 2 vols. Oxford: Clarendon, 1913.

Charlesworth, James H. *The Discovery of a Dead Sea Scroll (4QTherapeia): Its Importance in the History of Medicine and Jesus Research.* Lubbock: Texas Tech Univeristy, 1985.

—————. *The Dead Sea Scrolls. Rule of the Community and Related Documents.* Louisville: Westminster John Knox, 1996.

—————. "Announcing a Dead Sea Fragment of Nehemiah." Online: http://www.ijco.org?categoryId=28681, 2008.

Chyutin, Michael. *The New Jerusalem Scroll from Qumran: A Comprehensive Reconstruction.* Journal for the Study of the Pseudepigrapha Supplements 25. Sheffield: Sheffield Academic, 1997.

Clermont-Ganneau, C. "Kumran," in *Archaeological Researches in Palestine during the Years 1873–1874,* II, 14–16. London: Palestinian Exploration Fund, 1896.

Coggins, R. J. *Samaritans and Jews.* Atlanta: Scholars, 1975.

Crawford, Sidnie White. *The Temple Scroll and Related Texts*. Companion to the Qumran Scrolls 2. Sheffield: Sheffield Academic, 2000.

Cross, Frank M. "The Development of the Jewish Scripts." In *The Bible and the Ancient Near East: Essays in Honor of William Foxwell Albright*, edited by G. Ernest Wright, 170–264. Garden City, NY: Doubleday, 1961.

Cross, Frank M. Jr., and Esther Eshel. "Ostraca from Khirbet Qumran." *IEJ* 47 (1997) 17–28.

Cross, Frank M. Jr., and Shemaryahu Talmon, editors. *Qumran and the History of the Biblical Text*. Cambridge: Harvard University Press, 1975.

Dalman, Gustav. "Jahresbericht." *Palestina-Jahrbuch* 10 (1914) 9–12.

———. "Jahresbericht." *Palestina-Jahrbuch* 16 (1920) 40–41.

Davies, Philip R. *1QM, The War Scroll from Qumran. Its Structure and History*. Biblica et orientalia 32. Rome: Biblical Institute Press, 1977.

———. *Qumran*. Cities of the Biblical World. Guillford, UK: Lutherworth, 1982.

———. *The Damascus Covenant: An Interpretation of the 'Damascus Document*. JSOT-Sup 25. Sheffield: JSOT Press, 1983.

———. "How Not to Do Archaeology: The Story of Qumran." *BA* (1988) 203–7.

Davies, Philip R. et al. *The Complete World of the Dead Sea Scrolls*. London: Thames & Hudson, 2002.

Drawnel, Henryk. *An Aramaiac Wisdom Text from Qumran: A New Interpretation of the Levi Document*. Leiden: Brill, 2004.

Driver, G. R. *The Judaean Scrolls: The Problem and the Solution*. Oxford: Blackwell, 1965.

Donceel-Voûte, Pauline. "'Coenaculum'— La sale a l'étage du locus 30 a Khirbet Qumrân sur la mer norte." *Banquets d'Orient* (Res Orientales) 4 (1993) 61–84.

Donceel, Robert, and Pauline Donceel-Voûte. "The Archaeology of Khirbet Qumran." In *Methods of Investigation of the Dead Sea Scrolls and the Khirbet Qumran Site: Present Realities and Future Prospects*, edited by Michael O. Wise et al., 1–38. Annals of the New York Academy of Sciences 722. New York: New York Academy of Sciences, 1994.

Elgvin, Torleif. *Qumran Cave 4 XV Sapiential Texts, Part 1*. DJD 20. Clarendon: Oxford, 1997.

———. "How to Reconstruct a Fragmented Scroll: The Puzzle of 4Q422." In *Northern Lights on the Dead Sea Scrolls: Proceedings of the Nordic Qumran Network*, edited by Anders Klostergaard Petersen, 223–36. Leiden, Boston: Brill, 2006.

Fields, Weston W. *The Dead Sea Scrolls: A Full History*. Leiden: Brill, 2009.

Fitzmyer, Joseph A. "The Qumran Scrolls and the New Testament after Forty Years." *RQ* 13 (1988) 609–20.

Fitzmyer, Joseph. "Paul and the Dead Sea Scroll." In *The Dead Sea Scrolls after Fifty Years: A Comprehensive Assessment*, edited by Peter W. Flint and J. VanderKam, 2:599–621. 2 vols. Leiden: Brill, 1998–1999.

Flint, Peter W. *The Dead Sea Psalms Scrolls and the Books of Psalms*. STDJ 17. Leiden: Brill, 1997.

———. *The Bible at Qumran: Text, Shape, and Interpretation*. Grand Rapids: Eerdmans, 2001.

———. "Five Surprises in the Qumran Psalms Scrolls." In *Flores Florentino: Dead Sea Scrolls and Other Early Jewish Studies in Honour of Florentino García Martínez*, edited by A. Hilhorst, 183–96. Journal for the Study of the Judaism Supplements 122. Leiden: Brill, 2007.

Freedman, David Noel, and K. A. Matthews. *The Paleo-Hebrew Leviticus Scroll (11Qpaleo-Lev)*. Philadelphia: American Schools of Oriental Research, 1985.

Golb, Norman. *Who Wrote the Dead Sea Scrolls? The Search for the Secret of Qumran.* New York: Scribner, 1995.

Goransen, Stephan. "Sectarianism, Geography and the Copper Scroll." *JJS* 43 (1992) 282–87.

———. "Further Reflections of the Copper Scroll." In *Copper Scroll Studies*, edited by George J. Brooke and Philip R. Davies, 226–32. Journal for the Study of the Pseudepigrapha Supplement Series 40. Sheffield: Sheffield Academic, 2002.

Grabbe, Lester L. *Judaism from Cyrus to Hadrian.* 2 vols. Minneapolis: Fortress, 1992.

Greenfield, Jonas C., and Michael Sokoloff. "An Astrological Text from Qumran (4Q318) and Reflections on Some Zodiacal Names." *RQ* (1995) 507–25.

Harrington, Daniel J. *The Wisdom Texts from Qumran.* Literature of the Dead Sea Scrolls. London: Routledge, 1996.

Hempel, Charlotte. *The Damascus Texts.* Companion to the Qumran Scrolls 1. Sheffield: Sheffield Academic, 2000.

———. "The Place of the Book of Jubilees at Qumran and Beyond." In *The Dead Sea Scrolls in Their Historical Context*, edited by Tim H. Lim et al. Edinburgh: T. & T. Clark, 2000.

Hendel, R. https://www.bib-arch.org/scholars-study/messiah-son-of-joseph.asp, 2009.

Hirschfeld, Y. "The Architectural Context of Qumran." In *The Dead Sea Scrolls: Fifty Years After Their Discovery: Proceedings of the Jerusalem Congress, July 20–25, 1997*, edited by Lawrence H. Schiffman, 673–83. Jerusalem: Israel Exploration Society, 2000.

———. *Qumran in Context. Reassessing the Evidence.* Peabody, MA: Hendrickson.

Holm-Nielsen, Sven. *Hodayot: Psalms from Qumran.* Aarhus: Universitetsforlaget, 1961.

Horbury, William. "The Proper Name in 4Q468a: Peitholaus?" *JJS* 50 (1999) 310–11.

Horgan, Maurya P. *Pesharim: Qumran Interpretations of Biblical Books.* CBQ Monograph Series 8. Washington, DC: Catholic Biblical Association of America, 1979.

Humbert, J.-B., editor. *Fouilles de Khirbet Qumrân et de Aïn Feshka.* Göttingen: Vandenhoeck & Ruprecht, 1994.

Kampen, John, and Moshe J. Bernstein, editors. *Reading 4QMMT: New Perspectives on Qumran Law and History.* SBL Symposium Series 2. Atlanta: Scholars, 1996.

Karveit, Magnar. *The Origin of the Samaritans.* VTSup 128. Leiden: Brill, 2009.

Kiraz, George A. *Anton Kiraz's Dead Sea Scrolls Archive.* Piscataway, NJ: Gorgias, 2005.

Kittel, Bonnie. *The Hymns of Qumran: Translation and Commentary.* SBL Dissertation Series 50. Chico, CA: Scholars, 1981.

Kobelski, Paul J. *Melchizedek and Melchireša'.* Catholic Biblical Quarterly Monograph Series 10. Washington, DC: Catholic Biblical Association of America, 1981.

Lim, Timothy H. *Holy Scripture in the Qumran Commentaries and Pauline Letters.* Oxford: Clarendon, 1997.

———. *Pesharim.* Companion to the Qumran Scrolls 3. Sheffield: Sheffield Academic, 2002.

Magness, Jodi. "The Chronology of the Settlement at Qumran in the Herodian Period." *DSD* 2 (1995) 58–65.

———. *The Archaeology of Qumran and the Dead Sea Scrolls.* Studies in the Dead Sea Scrolls and Related Literature. Grand Rapids: Eerdmans, 2002.

Masterman, E. G. W. "Observations on the Dead Sea Levels." *Palestine Exploration Fund Quarterly Statement* (1902, 1902–1903, 1917).

———. "Notes on Some Ruins and a Rock-cut Aqueduct in the Wady Kumran." *Palestine Exploration Fund Quarterly Statement* (1903) 267.

Metso, Sarianna. *The Textual Development of the Qumran Community Rule.* STDJ 21. Leiden: Brill, 1997.

———. *The Serekh Texts*. Library of Second Temple Studies 62. London: T. & T. Clark, 2007.

Milik, J. T. *The Books of Enoch*. Oxford: Clarendon, 1976.

———. "Prière de Nabonide et autres écrits d'un cycle de Daniel." *RB* 63 (1956) 407–11.

Mor, Menahem. *Samaritans: Past and Present: Current Studies*. Berlin: de Gruyter, 2010.

Muchowski, Piotr. "The Origin of 3Q15: Forty Years of Discussion." In *Copper Scroll Studies*, edited by George J. Brooke and Philip R. Davies, 257–70. Journal for the Study of the Pseudepigrapha Supplements 40. Sheffield: Sheffield Academic Press, 2002.

Najman, Hindy. *Seconding Sinai: The Development of Mosaic Discourse in Second Temple Judaism*. Journal for the Study of Judaism Supplements 77. Leiden: Brill, 2003.

Nakman, D. "The Contents and Order of the Biblical Sections in the Tefillin from Qumran, and Rabbinic Halakah: Similarity, Difference, and Some Historical Conclusions." *Cathedra* 112 (2004) 19–44 [Hebrew].

Nam, Roger S. "How to Rewrite Torah: The Case for Proto-Sectarian Ideology in the Reworked Pentateuch (4QRP)." *RQ* 90 (2007) 153–65.

Naveh, J. "A Medical Document or a Writing Exercise? The So-Called 4QTherapeia." *IEJ* (1986) 52–55, pl. II.

———. "341. 4QExercitium Calami C." In *Qumran 4. XXVI. Cryptic Texts*, edited by Stephen Pfann et al., 291–93. DJD 36. Oxford: Clarendon, 2000.

Newsom, Carol A. *The Songs of the Sabbath Sacrifice: A Critical Edition*. Harvard Semitic Studies 27. Atlanta: Scholars, 1985.

———. "The 'Psalms of Joshua' from Qumran Cave 4." *JJS* 39 (1988) 56–73.

———. "'He Has Established for Himself Priests': Human and Angelic Priesthood in the Qumran Sabbath Shirot." In *Archaeology and History in the Dead Sea Scrolls*, edited by Lawrence H. Schiffman, 101–20. Journal for the Study of the Pseudepigrapha Supplement Series 8. Sheffield: JSOT Press, 1990.

———. "Why Nabonidus? Excavating Traditions from Qumran, the Hebrew Bible, and Neo-Babylonian Sources." In *The Dead Scrolls: Transmission of Traditions and Production of Texts*, edited by Sarianna Metso et al., 56–79. Leiden: Brill, 2010.

Nickelsburg, George W. E. *Jewish Literature between the Bible and the Mishnah: A Historical and Literary Introduction*. 2nd ed. Minneapolis: Fortress, 2005.

Nitzan, Bilhah. *Qumran Prayer and Religious Poetry*. Studies on the Texts of the Desert of Judah 12. Leiden: Brill, 1994.

O'Callaghan, José. "New Testament Papyri in Qumran Cave 7?" *JBLSup* 91 (1972) 1–14.

———. "Papiros neotestamentarios en la cueva 7 de Qumrán?" *Bib* 53 (1972) 91–100.

Parry, Donald W., et al. "New Technological Advances: DNA, Electronic Databases, Imaging Radar." In *The Dead Sea Scrolls after Fifty Years: A Comprehensive Assessment*, edited by Peter W. Flint and James C. VanderKam, 496–515. 2 vols., Leiden: Brill, 1998–99.

Parsons, P. J. "Palaeography." In *Qumran Cave 4. IV: Paleo-Hebrew and Greek Biblical Manuscripts*, edited by Patrick W. Skehan et al., 7–13. DJD 9. Oxford: Clarendon, 1992.

Patrich, J. "Khirbet Qumran in Light of New Archaeological Exploration in the Qumran Caves." In *Methods of Investigation of the Dead Sea Scrolls and the Khirbet Qumran Sites: Present Realities and Future Prospects*, edited by Michael O. Wise, et al., 73–95. Annals of the New York Academy of Sciences 722. New York: New York Academy of Sciences, 1994.

Pfann, Stephen et al. *Qumran Cave 4. XXVI: Cryptic Texts*. DJD 36. Clarendon: Oxford, 2000.

Ploeg, J. P. M. van der, and A. S. van der Woude. *Le Targum de Job de la grotte XI de Qumrân*. Leiden: Brill, 1971.

Pummer, Reinhard. *The Samaritans and Flavius Josephus*. Tübingen: Mohr/Siebeck, 2009.

Reich, R. "Miqwaòt at Khirbet Qumran." In *The Dead Sea Scrolls: Fifty Years after Their Discovery: Proceedings of the Jerusalem Congress, July 20–25, 1997*, edited by Lawrence H. Schiffman, et al. 728–31. Jerusalem: Israel Exploration Society, 2000.

Rivkin, E. *The Hidden Revolution: The Pharisees' Search for the Kingdom Within*. Nashville: Abingdon, 1978.

Qimron, Elisha, and John Strugnell. *Qumran Cave 4. V: Miqsat Maàse Ha-Torah*. DJD 10. Oxford: Clarendon, 1994.

Rost, Leonhard. *Judaism Outside the Hebrew Canon*. Nashville: Abingdon, 1971.

Saldarini, Anthony J. *Pharisees, Scribes and Sadducees in Palestinian Society: A Sociological Approach*. Wilmington, DE: Glazier, 1988.

Sanders, James A. *The Psalms Scroll of Cave 11 (11QPsa)*. DJD 4. Oxford: Clarendon, 1965.

Saulcy, F. de. *Narrative of a Journey Round the Dead Sea and in the Bible Lands, in 1850 and 1851. Including an Account of the Discovery of the Sites of Sodom and Gomorrah*. Philadelphia: Parry & M'Millan, 1854, I.

Schiffman, Lawrence H. *The Eschatological Community of the Dead Sea Scrolls: A Study of the Rule of the Congregation*. SBL Monograph Series 38. Atlanta: Scholars, 1989.

———. "Ordinances." In *Rule of the Community and Related Documents*, edited by James H. Charlesworth, 145–57. Louisville: Westminster John Knox, 1994.

———. *Reclaiming the Dead Sea Scrolls: The History of Judaism, the Background of Christianity, the Lost Library of Qumran*. Philadelphia: Jewish Publication Society, 1994.

———. *The Courtyards of the House of the Lord: Studies in the Temple Scroll*, edited by Florentino García-Martínez. Studies on the Texts of the Desert of Judah 75. Leiden: Brill, 2008.

Schiffman, Lawrence H., and James C. VanderKam, editors. *The Encyclopedia of the Dead Sea Scrolls*. New York: Oxford University Press, 2000.

Schofield, Alison. *From Qumran to the Yahad: A New Paradigm of Textual Development for the Community Rule*. Leiden: Brill, 2003.

Schuller, Eileen. *Non-Canonical Psalms from Qumran: A Pseudepigraphic Collection*. Atlanta: Scholars, 1986.

———. "380. 4QNon-Canonical Psalms A," and "381. 4QNon-Canonical Psalms B." In *Qumran Cave 4 VI, Poetical and Liturgical Texts, Part 1*, edited by Eshel et al, 80–124. DJD 11. Oxford: Clarendon, 1998.

Schulz, Brian. "The Qumran Cemetery: 150 Years of Research." *DSD* 13 (2006) 194–228.

Schwartz, D. R. "4Q468g: Ptollas?" *JJS* 58 (1999) 308–9.

Shanks, Hershel, editor. *Understanding the Dead Sea Scrolls: A Reader from the Biblical Archaeology Review*. New York: Vintage, 1993.

———. *The Copper Scroll and the Search for the Temple Treasure*. Washington, DC: Biblical Archaeology Society, 2007.

Skehan, Patrick W. "The Qumran Manuscripts and Textual Criticism." In *Qumran and the History of the Biblical Text*, edited by Frank Moore Cross and Shemaryahu Talmon. Cambridge: Harvard University Press, 1975.

Smith, Mark S. "What Is a Scriptural Text in the Second Temple Period? Texts between Their Biblical Past, Their Inner-Biblical Interpretation, Their Reception in Second Temple Literature, and Their Textual Witnesses." In *The Dead Sea Scrolls at 60: Scholarly Contributions of New York University Faculty and Alumni*, edited by Lawrence H. Schiffman and Shani Tzoref, 271–98. STDJ 89. Leiden: Brill, 2010.

Stegemann, Hartmut. "Methods for the Reconstruction of Scrolls from Scattered Fragments." In *Archaeology and History in the Dead Sea Scrolls: The New York University Conference in Memory of Yigael Yadin*, edited by Lawrence H. Schiffman, 189–220. Journal for the Studies of the Pseudepigrapha Supplement 8. Sheffield: JSOT Press, 1990.

———. "How to Connect Dead Sea Scrolls Fragments." In *Understanding the Dead Sea Scrolls: A Reader from the Biblical Archaeology Review*, edited by Hershel Shanks, 246–55. New York: Vintage, 1993.

———. *The Library of Qumran. On the Essenes, Qumran, John the Baptist and Jesus.* Grand Rapids, Leiden: Eerdmans, 1998.

———. "Towards Physical Reconstruction of the Qumran Damascus Document Scrolls." In *The Damascus Document: A Centennial of Discovery: Proceedings of the Third International Symposium of the Orion Center for the Study of the Dead Sea Scrolls and Associated Literature*, edited by J. Baumgarten, et al., 177–200. STDJ 34. Leiden: Brill, 2000.

Stemberger, G. *Jewish Contemporaries of Jesus: Pharisees, Sadducees, Essenes.* Minneapolis: Fortress, 1995.

Steudel, Annette. "Assembling and Reconstructing Manuscripts." In *The Dead Sea Scrolls after Fifty Years: A Comprehensive Assessment*, edited by Peter W. Flint and James C. VanderKam, 1:516–34. Leiden: Brill, 1998–99.

Strugnell, John. "The Historical Background to 4Q468g [= 4Q Historical B]." *RQ* 73 (1999) 137–38.

———. *Qumran Cave 4 Sapiential Texts, Part 2.* DJD 34. Clarendon: Oxford, 1999.

Stuckenbruck, Loren. *The Book of Giants from Qumran. Texts, Translations, and Commentary.* Texte und Studien zum antiken Judentum 63. Tübingen: Mohr/Siebeck, 1997.

Sukenik, Eleazar. *The Collection of the Hidden Scrolls in the Possession of the Hebrew University.* Edited by Nahman Avigad. Jerusalem: Bialik Institute, 1954.

Swanson, Dwight D. *The Temple Scroll and the Bible: The Methodology of 11QT.* STDJ 14. Leiden: Brill, 1995.

Thordson, Thord. *The Samaritans and Qumran.* London: Minerva, 2000.

Tov, Emanuel. *Textual Criticism of the Hebrew Bible.* 2nd ed. Minneapolis: Fortress, 2001.

———. "The Biblical Texts from the Judaean Desert—An Overview and Analysis of the Published Texts." In *The Bible as Book: The Hebrew Bible and the Judaean Desert Discoveries* edited by Edward D. Herbert and Emanuel Tov, 139–66. London: British Library, 2002.

———. "Some Thoughts about the Diffusion of Biblical Manuscripts in Antiquity." In *The Dead Sea Scrolls: Transmission of Traditions and Production of Texts*, edited by Sarianna Metso, et al., 151–72. Leiden: Brill, 2010.

Tov, Emanuel, and Sidnie A. White. "Reworked Pentateuch." In *Qumran Cave 4. VIII. Parabiblical Text, Part 1*, edited by Harold W. Attridge et al., 187–351. DJD 13. Oxford: Clarendon, 1994.

Ulrich, Eugene, editor. The *Dead Sea Scrolls and the Origins of the Bible.* Studies in the Dead Sea Scrolls and Related Literature. Leiden: Brill, 1999.

———. *The Biblical Qumran Scrolls: Transcriptions and Textual Variants.* VTSup 134. Leiden: Brill, 2010.

Trever, John C. *The Untold Story of Qumran.* Westwood, NJ: Revell, 1965.

VanderKam, James C. *Enoch and the Growth of an Apocalyptic Tradition.* Catholic Biblical Quarterly Monograph Series 16. Washington, DC: Catholic Biblical Association of America, 1984.

———. *Calendars in the Dead Sea Scrolls.* London, New York: Routledge, 1998.

———. "Revealed Literature in the Second Temple Period." In *Revelation to Canon: Studies in the Hebrew Bible and the Second Temple Literature*, 1–30. Supplements to the Journal for the Study of Judaism 62. Leiden: Brill, 2000.

———. "Moses Trumping Moses." In *The Dead Sea Scrolls: A Transmission of Traditions and Production of Texts*, edited by Sarianna Metso et al., 225–44. Leiden: Brill, 2010.

———. *The Dead Scrolls Today*. 2nd ed. Grand Rapids: Eerdmans, 2010.

VanderKam, James C., and Peter W. Flint. *The Meaning of the Dead Sea Scrolls*. San Francisco: HarperCollins, 2002.

VanderKam, James C., and J. T. Milik. "4QJubilees." In *Qumran Cave 4. VII: Parabiblical Texts, Part 1*, edited by Harold Attridge et al, 11–12. DJD 13. Oxford: Clarendon, 1994.

VanderKam, James C. et al. *The Dead Sea Scrolls after Fifty Years: A Comprehensive Assessment*. 2 vols. Leiden: Brill, 1998–99.

Vaux, Roland de. *Archaeology and the Dead Sea Scrolls*. London: Oxford University Press, 1973.

Vermes, Geza. *The Complete Dead Sea Scrolls in English*. New York: Penguin, 1997.

Wacholder, Ben Zion. *The Dawn of Qumran*. Cincinnati: Hebrew Union College, 1983.

———. *The New Damascus Document*. Leiden: Brill, 2007.

Weissenberg, Hanne von. *4QMMT: Reevaluating the Text, the Function, and the Meaning of the Epilogue*. Studies in the Desert of Judaea 82. Leiden: Brill, 2009.

Wise, Michael Owen. *A Critical Study of the Temple Scroll from Qumran Cave 11*. Chicago: University of Chicago, 1990.

———. *Thunder in Gemini. And Other Essays on the History, Language, and Literature of Second Temple Palestine*. Sheffield: Journal for the Study of the Old Testament Press, 1994.

———. "David Wilmot and the Copper Scroll." In *Copper Scroll Studies*, edited by George J. Brooke and Philip R. Davies, 209–10. Sheffield: Sheffield Academic, 2002.

Wolters, Al. *The Copper Scroll: Overview, Text and Translation*. Qumran Literature 1. Sheffield: Sheffield Academic, 1996.

Yadin, Yigael. *The War of the Sons of Light against the Sons of Darkness*. Oxford: Clarendon, 1962.

———. *The Temple Scroll*. Jerusalem: Israel Exploration Society, 1983.

Yardeni, Ada. "Palaeography." In *Qumrân Cave 4. XIII. The Damascus Document (4Q266–273)*. DJD 18, edited by Joseph M. Baumgarten, 26–30, 116–18, 170–72. Oxford: Clarendon, 1996.

———. "A Draft of a Deed on an Ostracon from Khirbet Qumran." *IEJ* 47 (1997) 233–37.

———. "A New Dead Sea Scroll in Stone? Bible-like Prophecy was Mounted in a Wall 2,000 Years Ago." *BAR* 34/1 (2008) 60–61.

Zahn, Molly M. "New Voices, Ancient Words: The *Temple Scroll's* Reuse of the Bible." In *Temple and Worship in Biblical Israel*, edited by John Day, 435–58. Library of Hebrew Bible/Old Testament Studies 422. London: T. & T. Clark, 2005.

———. "The Problem of Characterizing the 4Q Reworked Pentateuch Manuscripts: Bible, Rewritten Bible, or None of the Above." *DSD* 15 (2008) 315–39.

Zias, Joseph. "The Cemeteries of Qumran and Celibacy: Confusion Laid to Rest?" *DSD* 7 (2000) 220–53.

Ancient Document Index

THE COMMUNITY SCROLLS

Rabbinic Writings

CODE OF MAIMONIDES